The Politica
Human Rigl

The language of human rights is the most prominent 'people-centred' language of global justice today. This book looks at how human rights are constructed at local, national, international and transnational levels and considers common-alities and differences around the world. Through discussions of key debates in the interdisciplinary study of human rights, the book develops its themes by considering examples of human rights advocacy in international organisa-tions, national states and local grassroots movements. Case studies relating to specific organisations and institutions illustrate how human rights are being used to address structural injustices: imperialist geo-politics, authoritarian-ism and corruption, inequalities created by 'freeing' markets, dangers faced by transnational migrants as a result of the securitisation of borders, and violence against women.

Kate Nash is a professor in the Department of Sociology at Goldsmiths, University of London.

Thank you so much with, Kate x

Key Topics in Sociology

Consulting Editor **John Scott**, Plymouth University

This series of textbooks surveys key topics in the study of sociology. Books cover the main theoretical and empirical aspects of each topic in a clear, concise but sophisticated style, and relate the topic to wider sociological debates. Titles are useful to undergraduates studying a first course on the topic, as well as graduates approaching the subject for the first time. Designed for ease of use, instructors may teach from individual books, or select a collection from the series for a broader sociology course.

Published Titles
GEMMA EDWARDS, *Social Movements and Protest*

Forthcoming Titles
SUKI ALI, *The Sociology of Race and Ethnicity*

The Political Sociology of Human Rights

Kate Nash

CAMBRIDGE
UNIVERSITY PRESS

CAMBRIDGE
UNIVERSITY PRESS

University Printing House, Cambridge CB2 8BS, United Kingdom

Cambridge University Press is part of the University of Cambridge.

It furthers the University's mission by disseminating knowledge in the pursuit of education, learning and research at the highest international levels of excellence.

www.cambridge.org
Information on this title: www.cambridge.org/nash

First published 2015

Printed in the United Kingdom by Clays, St Ives plc

A catalogue record for this publication is available from the British Library

Library of Congress Cataloguing in Publication data
Nash, Kate, 1958–
The political sociology of human rights / Kate Nash.
  pages   cm. – (Key topics in sociology)
Includes bibliographical references and index.
ISBN 978-0-521-19749-6 (hardback) – ISBN 978-0-521-14847-4 (pbk)
1. Human rights–Social aspects.   2. Political sociology.   I. Title.
JC571.N285 2015
306.2–dc23
2015005648

ISBN 978-0-521-19749-6 Hardback
ISBN 978-0-521-14847-4 Paperback

Equality, in contrast to all that is involved in mere existence, is not given to us, but is the result of human organization insofar as it is guided by the principle of justice. We are not born equal; we become equal as members of a group on the strength of our decision to guarantee ourselves mutually equal rights.

(Arendt 1979: 301)

Contents

Preface and acknowledgements

This book has been more challenging to write than I expected. The first big challenge was how to avoid Eurocentrism. By Eurocentrism I mean the assumption that what happens in what I call the 'Northwest' – in the European settler states of the United States, Western Europe and Australasia – is the norm, and that other parts of the world will or should follow their example. Eurocentrism is quite evident in some human rights advocacy. However, critics of human rights who see governments and corporations from the Northwest as facilitating or legitimating 'Western neo-liberal imperialism' do not necessarily escape it either: when their analyses are limited to discourses that originate and circulate in the United States, for example, they seem to assume that it is only what happens there that is really important. In this book I have tried to develop theory and methodology to understand how contexts, actors and claims for human rights *differ* around the world as well as what they share in common. The task is complicated because one of the most important contexts for the realisations of respect for human rights is the dominance of the owners of financial and industrial capital, state officials, and also international non-governmental organisations that are based in the Northwest. To get a good understanding of the range of possibilities represented by human rights today we must take seriously both the variety of local constructions of human rights people are creating to deal with specific injustices and also the effects of global geo-politics on what they are able to achieve using a language of human rights.

This brings me to the second challenge of studying human rights. I develop a version of sociology that enables us to study structures as well as meanings; what is 'social' as well as what is 'cultural' about constructions of human rights. Broadly speaking sociologists and anthropologists have tended to focus on the small-scale and local: on meanings that are created and sustained in communities and movements. Most international relations (IR) scholars and political scientists studying human rights focus instead on large-scale structures, networks and international organisations. In this book I argue that we must do both. Studying structures (of capitalism, post-colonialism, gender) and organisations (corporations, non-governmental organisations, inter-governmental organisations, and above all states – which are not all the same) is crucial to understanding both the possibilities *and* the limitations of human rights today. Sociology is a relatively open discipline: there is very little disciplining out of fundamental questions in social theory. We must keep the big picture in sight: the whole range of conditions that must be transformed if respect for human rights – civil, political, social and cultural – is to be realised. At the same time we can be inspired to try not to lose sight of the smallest details: how what seems possible may be shifted as a result of framing injustices as matters of human rights. Of course, this makes for a huge task. As far as human rights are concerned it is one which sociologists are only just beginning to address.

You, the reader of the book, will judge how successful I have been in meeting these challenges – and of course I hope you find the efforts I have made worthwhile! Regardless of the outcome, however, I am very grateful for help and encouragement from a number of people to write this book. I want to thank especially the people who read particular chapters and who gave me their invaluable advice on the basis of expertise in particular areas: Alice Bloch, Kirsten Campbell, David Hansen-Miller, Monika Krause, Fran Tonkiss, Neil Washbourne. Thank you also to Patrick Legalès who disagreed so strongly with my approach to the state when I presented a paper on it at Sciences Po at the beginning of the project that, no doubt inadvertently, he led me to think about it again. For emotional and intellectual support and interest in the project, thank you to Jeff Alexander, Lilie Chouliaraki, Nick Couldry, Marie Dembour, Monica Greco, Clare Hemmings, Caroline Knowles, Daniel Levy, Giovanna Procacci, Roberta Sassatelli, Alan Scott, Damien Short, George Steinmetz, Paul Stenner and Bryan Turner.

1 The social construction of human rights

> Where, after all, do universal human rights begin? In small places, close to home – so close and so small that they cannot be seen on any maps of the world.
>
> (Eleanor Roosevelt, United Nations, New York, 1958)

> The contemporary production of human rights is exuberant … [H]uman rights enunciations proliferate … [N]ot merely do they reach out to 'discrete' and 'insular' minorities, they also extend to wholly new, hitherto unthought of justice constituencies.
>
> (Baxi 2008: 46–7)

In 1972 Amnesty International organised a worldwide campaign to end torture. The organisation published reports on how torture remained a widespread practice in many states, and gathered one million signatures from eighty-five countries on a petition to present at the UN. Politicians, diplomats and military leaders denied that torture was going on in their states. However, the UN Convention Against Torture became international law in 1987, committing states that had signed and ratified it to outlawing torture for ever (Clark 2001; Kelly 2013).

In 2007, after decades of campaigning by grassroots organisations, supported by the Sub-Commission on the Prevention of Discrimination and the Protection of Minorities and a Working Group on Indigenous Populations set up inside the UN, the Declaration of the Rights of Indigenous Peoples was finally signed and ratified by most countries in the world (with the notable exceptions of the United States, Canada and Australia). It is unclear as yet what difference international recognition of the Rights of Indigenous Peoples will make to people's lives (Morgan 2011). Nevertheless, the transnational grassroots organisation

Via Campesina is following the lead of indigenous peoples' movements in proposing a declaration of the rights of peasants to protect rural ways of life (see pp. 106–10).

In 2003 a campaign was organised by Amnesty International and Human Rights Watch to put pressure on an Islamic court in Nigeria that was hearing the appeal of a woman named Amina Lawal. She had been convicted for adultery, solely on the word of the alleged father of the child she had conceived, and she faced death by stoning as punishment. Her suffering gained a good deal of media publicity especially in North America and Europe. But a small local organisation called Baobab asked for people outside Nigeria to stop sending protest letters because they misrepresented the facts of the case and angered local politicians, religious leaders and judges. The transnational campaign was undermining Baobab's authority. The court reversed Lawal's conviction (Tripp 2006: 298–9).

In 2014, as I write, there are people who have crossed European borders without authorisation who are being detained in inadequate, prison-like facilities. They cannot be immediately returned to the countries of which they are citizens because ongoing human rights violations would make it too dangerous for them to live there. Their imprisonment would seem to be a clear violation of human rights that are supposed to protect individuals against arbitrary detention (Article 5 of the European Convention on Human Rights, Article 9 of the International Convention on Civil and Political Rights). Nevertheless, what is self-evidently a violation of human rights has been legal since the European Court of Human Rights decided in 2008 (*Saadi* v. *UK*) that states can detain 'asylum-seekers' for up to eighteen months without guaranteed legal representation and with only a very tenuous right to appeal (Webber 2012: 136).

These stories, complex as they are, do no more than hint at the immense diversity and scope of human rights today. Human rights demands are supported by a range of different actors: grassroots movements as well as huge international non-governmental organisations (INGOs); politicians, lawyers and judges in national states; experts and bureaucrats in inter-governmental organisations (IGOs). These actors are often at odds with each other in defining and defending particular justifications of what human rights are and should be. Human rights mobilise millions of supporters across borders, inspiring passion and hope. And they operate at and between all the different scales involved in globalisation: local, national, international, transnational. These scales are not 'nested', rising in a hierarchy from 'local' to a more inclusive and progressive 'global'. The scales of human rights have different significance for different actors. For some the corridors of the UN are 'local'; for some the 'national' is represented in a capital city that is several days' journey away; for some 'international' is a source of hope; for others, of fear. The stories also give some indication of the complexities of trying to achieve human rights in different contexts. Whilst in the Amina Lawal case transnational support for upholding her human rights appears to have been a liability, it was essential to winning international recognition of human rights to end torture and to respect for indigenous peoples' rights. At the same time, these examples also lead us to question the value of international human rights law as such. Is torture ended? Are indigenous peoples living in peace on their ancestral lands? The European system of human rights, for example, is highly developed, but it apparently allows violations of the right to freedom from arbitrary detention – a right that is generally fundamental at the UN.

What are human rights?

To study human rights we must try to take account of all these complexities. There is no doubt that this is very difficult, and much of the literature on human rights is polarised in ways that over-simplify. Much has been written, generally by political theorists, that is vehemently critical of human rights. Critics argue that human rights are depoliticising, individualising: they are enabling the world to be made secure for neo-liberal global elites rather than ending the suffering of ordinary people.[1] But human rights are not only used in justifications of military adventures on the part of the US-led 'coalition of the willing', and nor does using the language of human rights necessarily involve submission to neo-liberalism. Human rights *also* represent a language within which a variety of claims for justice are articulated *against* imperialism and neo-liberalism. In this respect human rights seem to offer a language to enable the taming of globalisation, to make the world more people-centred and peaceful, enhancing rather than restricting freedom, equality and trans-border solidarity.[2] But then it would equally be a mistake to focus *only* on *these* possibilities. The tendency (which no doubt comes to us as a legacy of the Enlightenment) to treat human rights as future-oriented, as if they are tending, eventually but inevitably, towards a progressive end is just as inadequate as over-generalising critique. We need a research programme that is able to address *both* the progressive *and* the problematic dimensions of human rights.

Similarly over-simplified are analyses that oppose good uses of human rights 'from below' (claimed by popular movements, in civil society), from bad uses of human rights 'from above' (made by international elites, in formal organisations).[3] 'Bottom up' and 'top down' can be useful as a rough and ready way of distinguishing where human rights claims are coming from, and defining human rights at the grassroots level is crucial to realising rights (as we shall see in this book). But there is no sense in claiming a right unless there is a corresponding duty to uphold that right. Claiming a right almost invariably involves altering what *elites* do – as well as, very often, re-ordering 'common sense' in everyday life. It is, therefore, impossible in practice to separate out 'pure' ethical uses of human rights from the power plays and structured inequalities that exist at every scale at which those claims are addressed.

Finally, if over-simplification is a risk in studying human rights, so too is analysis that is too complex and too vague with respect to the significance of particular actors, organisations and structures. It is IR scholars who have developed the term 'global governance'. Thomas Weiss defines it very generally as 'the sum of the informal and formal values, norms, procedures and institutions that help all actors – states, IGOs, civil society, transnational corporations (TNCs), and individuals – to identify, understand, and address trans-boundary problems' (Weiss 2013: 2). From a more Foucauldian perspective, Janet Halley argues that 'global governance' enables analyses of power as fragmented and dispersed, alerts us to the way in which uses of human rights continually call the distinction between politics and law into question, and calls attention to how human rights demands address both state and non-state forms of authority (Halley 2006: 341). These are valuable insights. But what Foucauldian approaches to 'global governance' tend to neglect is the wide range of human rights claims, and the detail of the *variable* outcomes for those who claim them. Human rights claims do not only involve expert forms of knowledge and the unfolding of ever-wider and ever-tighter rational-legal administration. Although realising ideals of human rights does generally mean greater (or at least different) regulation of how (at least some) people act, peoples' thinking and behaviour is *always* regulated by norms – informally through social interaction if not through law. In practice, although uses of human rights may, on occasion, be undemocratic or unjust, they do not always and necessarily work to close down freedom and the possibility of more radical alternatives.

Human rights are moral claims to justice. They are not the same as legal rights. This is easily overlooked because it is so often codifications in international law that frame how human rights are understood. Human rights are almost always associated with law, at least symbolically. As we see from the stories with which I opened this chapter, however, law can be an *obstacle* to achieving human rights. To claim a right is to make a moral claim: when a person has rights they should be treated more fairly, more kindly, with more respect. It is the universality of rights – the moral conviction that just because we are human beings you and I have certain rights – that enables them to be claimed in such a wide range of ways by different actors, and in different parts of the world. It is because there is an irreducibly moral component of human rights that they can be claimed where *no* legal rights are codified – even if changes in the law are almost invariably called for as part of human rights advocacy (Sen 2007).

Being open-minded about the possibilities of human rights need not, however, mean being blindly or stupidly idealistic. It *is* possible to work against the moralising tendency within which some studies of human rights are framed – the tendency to see them as *inherently* valuable because they are beyond politics (Ignatieff 2003). Human rights are irreducibly moral, but they are also irreducibly *political*. What is politics? We can distinguish between 'politics' and 'the political' – or, as Monika Krause suggests, between politics with a small 'p' and politics with a capital 'P' (Krause 2014: 77). 'Politics' with a capital 'P' is the lobbying, debating, party politics and policy-making that takes place in and around official government organisations situated in the capitals of the world: the politics of legislatures, bureaucrats, administrators and diplomats. It is concerned above all with the *regulation* of what people do by law and public policy and it always involves negotiation, strategy and compromise. In contrast, politics with a small 'p' concerns much more fundamental questions about the very constitution of 'the social': who and what 'we' are as a society; what is known and how; what is valued; who is to be included or excluded from consideration. Human rights are political in both senses. Human rights claims are made in 'Politics': they are claims for justice that aim to rearrange what is already accepted and normal through organisations that formally regulate how we live. But human rights claims also engage 'politics', disrupting and re-ordering taken-for-granted common sense, transforming what is accepted as normal, what counts as fair and good. In fact, studying human rights makes it clear that, at least in this case, there is no absolute separation between politics and Politics: lobbying, debating in governments and bureaucracies, and making public policy also involve the 'big questions' about who 'we' are and what we understand to be the boundaries and the ultimate values of our society.

In this book, then, I develop the political sociology of human rights to analyse the range of actors involved in making human rights claims, the types of action in which they are engaged, and the organisations through which claims are addressed. I introduce a framework for studying human rights as they are embedded in structures that give us some idea of the *difficulties* of successfully making claims for human rights, as well as the promise they seem to hold for a fairer and more peaceful world. This enables us to avoid pre-judging human rights as *either* the tools of the powerful *or* of the powerless; or as *necessarily* creating new forms of power and inequality that are as just as bad as those that already existed. As *ideas* human rights are indeterminate. Human rights claims are made in ways that are quite contradictory. One group's rights may clash with those of another group – and groups themselves are fluid and only contingently unified in alliances and in relation to 'outsiders' or enemies. And human rights are always open to being re-articulated in different ways. It is only in *practice*, in the ways in which they are put to use, that human rights take on definite, relatively fixed, forms. It is the inherently indeterminate and contestable nature of human rights that makes them so interesting and so challenging to study.

Human rights are socially constructed

Given their complexity, it is not surprising that human rights are of interest to people working in different academic disciplines. In the social sciences, each discipline, with its own history, concepts, debates and methodologies, brings distinctive tools to the study of human rights. Despite the differences, however, there is consensus on one point amongst those who study them: human rights are socially constructed.

In IR, 'social constructivism' is opposed to 'realism', the dominant perspective in the discipline. For realists, states only comply with international norms where it is in their rational self-interest to do so – to enhance their security or wealth – or where they are forced to comply by stronger states. Social constructivists in IR have shown how the processes by which human rights are constructed involve *persuasion*, and not just reason or force. In IR, 'social constructivists' have been especially important in bringing the work of NGOs into focus. Under the right conditions, they argue, persuasion by NGOs can shame elites into working to end torture and murder in which they are involved – either by giving orders or by their active participation. Once valuing human rights becomes part of the *identity* of elites, they will work actively to *prevent* human rights abuses.[4] According to social constructivists in IR, respect for human rights can become routinised as normal in ways that constrain and guide behaviour, putting an end to abuses even in the worst cases.

There is crossover of social constructivist theories from IR to international legal studies.[5] In international legal studies it is common to make a distinction between 'soft' and 'hard' law. 'Hard' or 'black letter' law involves specific and precise rules, and their interpretation and implementation is delegated to a court. 'Soft' law is non-binding: although it may on occasion be referred to in courts (on its way to becoming 'hard' law), it involves norms, accepted ways of doing things that have an influence on behaviour but that are not (yet) considered as law (Abbot and Snidal 2001). For social constructivists in legal studies, 'soft' and 'hard law' is not different in kind, but only in degree. Both are developed and maintained by becoming norms of accepted behaviour. Harold Koh – an international lawyer who was an advisor to the Clinton administration – suggests that even 'soft' law can become effective where norms are debated, interpreted and eventually *internalised*: not violating human rights can become as taken for granted as observing the law that requires us to do up our seat belts when we get into a car. In his words, when it works, observing the law becomes an 'internalized normative form of behavior': part of a person's dispositions, their identity (Koh 1999). For international legal scholars, then, as for 'social constructivists' in IR, norms influence behaviour *even when they are not backed by force.* Members of elites can be persuaded to observe human rights because they like to think of themselves as decent people. We may doubt that law ever works so well: don't people disregard it if they think they can get away with it? And we may be sceptical about Koh's confidence in the progress of human rights law in particular. Indeed, Koh himself admits that the *failures* of international human rights law are far more spectacular than its successes. But for him what is important is that international law *can* be effective *because* it is socially constructed: human rights circulate in international and domestic legal systems in ways that can come to be taken-for-granted as 'how things are' because law itself is only successful when it is part of routinised social practices.

The study of human rights is now quite well established in anthropology. This is quite a turnaround. In 1999 the American Anthropological Association confirmed its *suspicion* of human rights, declaring that '[it] founds its approach on anthropological principles of respect for concrete human differences, both collective and individual, rather than the abstract legal uniformity of Western tradition'. The focus of anthropologists was on the diversity of cultures. Since then, both 'culture' and 'human rights' have come to be understood as pluralist and dynamic, opening up a rich field of study.[6] For anthropologists today, human rights are not timeless, grounded in self-evident reason, nor bounded by 'culture', inherently 'Western'. Sally Engle Merry's concept of 'vernacularization', developed through her fieldwork on women's organisations resisting domestic violence, is an influential example of how anthropologists study human rights as constructed. Merry shows how human rights can be adapted to specific, local demands for justice, and at the same time – where they refer to international law that specifies rights as individual freedoms and to bodily integrity and equality – they can retain their critical force within local communities. Human rights can be local, specific *and* global, universal. They can be constructed so that they are valued in very different local contexts, whilst they enable criticisms of *other* local understandings that sanction and support inequality and violence (Merry 2006; see pp. 125–31).

It is often noted that the discipline of sociology came late to the study of human rights. Interestingly, the debate over social construction between Bryan Turner and Malcolm Waters in the journal *Sociology*

in the mid-1990s is very commonly referred to as the beginning of
the study of human rights in contemporary sociology.[7] Turner argued
that human rights need to be grounded, they must be treated as *more
than* social constructions otherwise sociologists will continue to study
them only as instruments of power, as positive law, or as particular to
Western culture. For Turner, understanding human rights as socially
constructed is one of the reasons they have been *neglected* in classical sociology (Turner 1993). Turner argues that as embodied creatures,
we are inherently fragile and we need each other, but the institutions
we create to reduce our vulnerability and attain security are always
flawed. We should therefore understand rights as necessary: they are
what people call on to protect them from institutions and from each
other. In response to Turner, Waters argues that human rights cannot
be seen as universal because they vary so much at different times and
places. Human rights can only, therefore, be studied as social constructions (Waters 1996). Turner is correct that it is the rights of vulnerable
people – the marginalised and impoverished – that are most likely to be
abused. But in general it is Waters' argument that has won favour with
contemporary sociologists (even if Waters actually smuggles in a real-
ist notion of 'interests' that is not much remarked on today). We tend
to be in agreement with our colleagues in other disciplines that human
rights are socially constructed. Sociologists today, however, are at the
same time willing to understand human rights as having effects *as if
they were moral universals*; as if we must respect rights because it is
the right thing to do – at least in some cases. The explosion of human
rights talk since the end of the Cold War suggests that people do not
need human rights to be grounded in something that is 'extra-social' in
order to experience their appeal. And as sociologists we can study how
human rights are socially constructed without reducing them to instruments of power or the determinants of sectional interests.

Social constructions of human rights:
the constraints of structures

All these variants of social constructionism share a key insight. To
show that something is 'socially constructed' is to show that it is not
inevitable or natural *but that it has effects that make it seem as if it
is.* What is common to the study of human rights across disciplines

is the understanding that human rights do not rest on firm foundations, on God-given reason, 'Western' culture or human nature. What human rights are at any given time and place is contingent, historical – but they can be established to regulate what we understand and what we do.

If it is clear what 'construction' brings to the study of human rights, what is not so clear is what '*social*' adds to 'construction'. How are constructions '*social*'? And does the fact that we talk about '*social* construction' mean that sociologists have a special contribution to make to the study of human rights?

Sociologists are now beginning to study human rights – though to date we have not made as much impact as those working in IR, international legal studies and anthropology. It seems to me that because 'social' is our business, sociology does have a special contribution to make to understanding human rights. It is true that use of 'social' is everywhere in the social (!) sciences, to the point of becoming almost meaningless. As William Sewell notes, it is practically impossible for sociologists to answer the question 'What is "the social"?' without tautology; without using 'social' in the answer (Sewell 2005: 319). But what 'the social' conveys in all versions of 'social construction' is the idea of *stability* (Latour 2005: 1). Everything may be constructed, but only *some* constructions become established, enduring across time and space. Constructions become 'social' when they become taken-for-granted context, the 'built environment' in Sewell's apt phrase, into which we are all born and in which we live (Sewell 2005: 362). It is one of the main tasks of sociologists to bring into view the unremarked background, the enduring 'social' of the 'social construction' of human rights, *as well as* the foreground, the possibilities of exciting new ways of doing human rights that we read and hear about now almost on a daily basis.

'Structure' is another necessary (and over-used) concept in the social sciences. It is a way of differentiating 'the social'. Constructions are frames (or 'meanings'): ways of categorising reality through which people learn to understand events, situations, processes, persons in certain ways.[8] Structures are sequences of frames that shape how we think and what we do through *repetition*. Sociologists talk about structures of capitalism, gender and sexuality, colonialism, racism – when we analyse regular patterns in the frames that guide action. But as these examples suggest, structures are more than *just ideas*: they organise resources, moral and material. In terms of moral resources, authority – the ability to persuade people to think and act in certain ways – is what is most important to the realisation of human rights. Authority is supported by professional training and credentials and the articulation of principles that should be respected. In some cases, when people are 'in authority' as well as 'an authority', it may be backed by force: the organisation of military and police. Material resources include those we humans must have to meet our basic needs, like food and shelter. They also include raw materials and ownership of machinery, buildings and land that are sources of inequalities in wealth. As humans we are *ourselves* material. We are not just creatures of ideas and words; we are embodied, sensory beings, feeling emotions and pain as well as thinking, planning and dreaming. Things as well as more abstract ideals like 'freedom', 'equality' and 'dignity' are organised by the frames through which we make sense of our world.

It is *critics* who most commonly introduce the concept of 'structures' into discussions of human rights. It is on the grounds that human rights are 'idealist', that they do not address how 'reality' is structured to perpetuate inequalities that human rights are criticised by Marxists, feminists and post-colonial critics. Are not structures of capitalism, imperialism, sexism, racism too deeply rooted, too systematic, too complex, to be undone by constructions of human rights?[9]

In part the answer to this question depends on how human rights are defined. As the stories with which I opened this chapter suggest, Upendra Baxi's description of human rights as 'carnivalistic' is a good one because of the variety of claims for human rights that are now being made around the world (Baxi 2008: 46).[10] The Universal Declaration of Human Rights itself is extensive, including social, economic and cultural rights to the redistribution of resources as well as civil rights to protection from state violence. Today it is supplemented by a range of conventions and declarations that are more detailed and specific, as well as definitions on the part of NGOs and social movements that have not (yet) been included in the UN regime of human rights. In many cases human rights demands do aim to transform structures of wealth distribution, and of respect for people who are marginalised and mistreated. As we will see in the following chapters, they include indigenous people, small farmers, women and migrants.

The response to the question of whether human rights can alter structures also depends in part on social theory: on how we conceptualise and study the structures that underpin injustices. The sociological perspective I am developing here takes the approach of sociologists of practice.[11] Rather than thinking of structures as necessarily reinforcing each other, systematically tending towards total domination and ideological closure, I take it that structures are inherently open to change. Structures are sequences of frames that are repeated in ways that constrain thought and action. They are maintained over long distances in impersonal mediated sequences that make them *difficult* to change even where there is the political will to do so. And political will is often lacking. Since structures organise access to and control over moral and material resources, it is in the interests of those who gain advantages from the way things are that they should be maintained. Interests themselves are socially constructed. But this does not make them any less deeply felt or less strenuously defended. Nevertheless, because structures are reproduced by active interpretations in specific contexts, they are open both to gradual alteration in everyday life and to radical transformation by collective action. Because they are maintained by the 'social construction of reality' structures are always, in principle, open to being *reconstructed*.

Finally, a response to the question of whether human rights can really alter social structures depends on empirical study. It may be *theoretically* possible to transform social structures through constructions of human rights, but is it actually happening in reality? The complexity of social life makes it impossible to give a definitive answer to this question. This does not, however, make it irrelevant or unnecessary. It is precisely the value of sociology to enable us to pose such far-reaching questions, and to prompt thinking about the conceptual frameworks, arguments and evidence through which they are addressed.

Constructions: cultural politics

Making constructions 'stick', getting them accepted and making them effective, is a matter of 'cultural politics'. 'Culture' is a way of naming the complexity of flows of meanings we experience all the time in everyday life: sometimes taken for granted as 'reality'; at other times confusing and uncertain, often with more than one possibility of interpretation.[12] The cultural politics of human rights involves challenging and remaking common-sense understandings: of what people assume to be true, useful and valuable; how we feel about contradictory facts and competing values; and how we act as a result.

The cultural politics of human rights involves the contestation and reframing of some people who are seen as 'other', the widening of the frame to include people who do not count as fully 'human'. Today this *rarely* means actually challenging what it is to be human as such: it is not usual today to categorise people we do not know well (as Christians tended to categorise non-Christians in the nineteenth century, for example) as simply not human at all. Nevertheless, it does mean challenging representations of people that allow them to be treated as less than 'one of us': as exceptionally brutal and dangerous, as less susceptible to persuasion, or as unable to adapt to what is reasonably demanded of them in our modernising, globalising age. As 'less-than-human', where we assess 'human' as 'like us', those who are different may legitimately be treated in ways that we would otherwise consider cruel, violent, or destructive of homes and livelihoods. Who counts as 'human'? It is one of the aims of the cultural politics of human rights to open up this question in particular cases, and to widen the frame of reference to include those who are currently ignored or marginalised.

The cultural politics of human rights also involves framing situations and events as 'human rights wrongs'. Who has rights, and to what, that really make a difference to how they are treated, what they are due, the conditions in which they live? Other people are often seen as obstacles or as instruments by people with plans and power. When treating people fairly and well is inconvenient, it is through the reframing of that difficulty as a matter of right and wrong that the cultural politics of human rights can shape and alter thought and action. People who are 'in the way' or who resist being the instruments of other peoples' purposes should not be murdered, tortured, imprisoned, raped, pushed out of their homes.

The cultural politics of human rights is a kind of 'politics' with a small 'p'. It involves the big picture: who is included and who is excluded as 'one of us'; how can actions that are violent, cruel, and that deprive people of what is necessary for them to live with dignity be stopped? The media is especially important to the cultural politics of human rights. Challenging and remaking common sense is rarely, if ever, achieved only by rational argument. The transformation of what is already accepted as normal is far more likely to emerge as a result of striking images, shocking facts that disturb what was previously 'known', new stories about what seemed familiar. In advanced capitalist societies, as well as the influence of people around us, the media play an important role in the disruption and recreation of taken-for-granted common sense concerning what is true, useful and valuable.

The cultural politics of human rights is also relevant in the formal settings of states and IGOs where Politics with a capital 'P' goes on, in the policy-making of legislatures, bureaucrats, administrators and diplomats. Definitions of 'otherness' matter when people are vulnerable to mistreatment by state officials: to imprisonment, torture, summary execution, deprivation of shelter, food, the necessities of life. In the committee rooms and corridors of the UN and in national states, it is not just the details of policy that are at stake in defining rights. The cultural politics of human rights involves challenges to assumptions about the priority of 'national interests' where security, foreign policy and economic growth are concerned. What are citizens due? Do citizens always have priority over non-citizens? What difference does it make to take human rights into account in bureaucracies, governments and courts of national states? These are questions that are raised in the cultural politics of human rights *inside* the formal settings of Politics, as well as *outside*, in the media and in everyday life.

Duty-bearers, responsibility and authority

As well as meanings and structures, organisations have a crucial role to play in realising human rights in practice. Human rights advocates invariably engage with 'duty-bearers', people who work in organisations that are recognised as having *responsibilities* to realise human rights. Authority is needed to successfully frame suffering as a human rights issue. Authority is itself a social construction – it does not exist without a degree of consent from other actors. Authority does not result automatically in obedience; it is not the same as force. It works only through persuasion. Who is able to claim authority to define human rights and how is a matter of cultural politics. Nevertheless, as Michael Barnett and Martha Finnemore emphasise in their study of IGOs, what it is to be '*an* authority' – a person who should be respected because of their training, knowledge and principles – very often overlaps with what it is to be '*in* authority' – to be a person who should be respected because of their official position. A professional who is an expert, a bureaucrat or a lawyer at the UN, someone who holds the office of an elected politician or a judge appointed in a national or international court, a fieldworker who reports on human rights abuses for an INGO – all these people may be both 'an authority' and 'in authority'.[13]

Authority is not always respected. In fact, it is often criticised as 'false'. Because human rights are often represented as transcending politics, the authority to define human rights is challenged when it is argued that an organisation or a person is acting out of an interest in their own status or wealth, or because they are promoting a particular perspective or ideology. In addition, there is a variety of types of authority. Not only can human rights be claimed in ways that are quite contradictory, but types of authority that frame human rights themselves vary. In fact, different kinds of authority may co-exist even within the same organisation. As a result, what counts as authority – what kind of argument *should be* persuasive – is often itself in question.

'Moral authority' is one important way of justifying human rights claims. It rests on the construction of the duty-bearer as above politics and personal interests, as concerned only with impartial justice, with getting better treatment for people who are currently being treated unfairly. Moral authority is achieved when a duty-bearer is seen as above politics: they have no particular stake in the outcome of their actions except to see that justice is being done. Moral authority is especially important in NGOs and IGOs. In contrast, there is a type of authority that we might call 'popular' ('of the people'), which is based on the view that advocates of a particular construction of human rights are *themselves* suffering the indignities, cruelties and insecurity of injustice. 'Popular authority' rests not on *transcending* politics, but on representing the voice of the people. It is especially important to the leaders of grassroots organisations, but also to state officials in international settings. A third type of authority is constructed by 'experts'. 'Expert' authority is also represented as above self-interest, because it rests on the rigorous training of the professional, the neutral methodology of science, and the impartial knowledge of complex affairs to which specialists have access. Legal expertise is especially important in framing human rights – though knowledge of development economics, country-specific knowledge, sociological knowledge about how social change is achieved can all be relevant. Legal expertise is linked to a fourth type, rational-legal authority, which is founded on procedures, on adherence to the letter of the law and the administration of knowledge that is only possible where bureaucracy is highly developed. Rational-legal authority is claimed on the basis that an organisation is run by people who are neutral and impartial, in service only to the values that have been decided on elsewhere. Very often when we are studying human rights, the values in question have already been established in international law. Finally, there is 'delegated authority'. This is authority that is 'lent' to organisations. It is very important as the basis of authority of IGOs, which largely depends on the moral resources of legitimacy as well as the material resources they are lent by states.

'Duty-bearers' are not passive recipients and intermediaries of human rights claims. Co-operating and competing within and across organisational boundaries, 'duty-bearers' act in a human rights field in which what is shared is the value of being able to define what it is that human rights really mean. Successfully claiming authority enables actors to shape what is important for human rights advocates and claimants, as well as what counts as the 'facts of the matter' concerning 'human rights wrongs' and how to put a stop to them.

Towards a political sociology of human rights

Sociology has a special contribution to make to the study of human rights. In the following pages I will develop the sociological perspective I have outlined in this chapter to study human rights as *constructions* that are created through the cultural politics of 'human' and 'rights', and how they impact on the *social*, the enduring structures that create and sustain the suffering and injustices addressed by human rights advocates.

In Chapters 2, 3 and 4 we look at duty-bearers in different types of organisations. The main theme in this part of the book is the difficulty of claiming human rights through organisations structured around elite forms of authority. We begin in Chapter 2 by discussing forms of organising through which human rights demands are made. Differences in the variety of organisations are ignored when they are all described as 'a human rights movement' or 'the NGO sector'. Grassroots organisations and INGOs are very different in terms of the types of authority those who work in them can plausibly claim. Looking at a successful campaign for human rights, the Treatment Action Campaign based in South Africa, we consider the importance of cultural politics in the settings of peoples' everyday lives, as well as in the formal settings of IGOs, TNCs and states.

In Chapter 3, we look at the most important organisations for realising human rights in practice: states. States have received remarkably little attention in social constructionist studies of human rights in any discipline – especially when we consider that it is people employed in official positions in states who are the principal duty-bearers to which human rights claims are addressed. In part this neglect is no doubt due to the difficulties of conceptualising states from a social constructionist perspective. In this chapter we consider how states are guarantors and at the same time violators of human rights in international human rights law. When state officials sign and ratify international human rights treaties, it is assumed that they are embedded in a type of state that is 'juridical', with capacities and procedures to realise in practice what officials promise on paper. From a sociological perspective, however, what is far more important is the way states are situated in very different structures: in large part as a result of histories of colonialism. To ignore differences between states is to limit our understanding of what is necessary if human rights are to be claimed successfully. It is clear that if human rights are to be realised, states will have to be significantly restructured in projects with aims that go far beyond the legal and bureaucratic reforms commonly envisaged by experts at the UN.

In Chapter 4 we look at the UN, the principal organisation to which human rights claims are addressed at the international level. It is not that the UN is the only IGO concerned with human rights, or even the most effective.[14] But it was in the UN that human rights were first constructed as global, and it continues to be the only organisation within which authority to set standards and to monitor adherence to human rights norms for the whole world is claimed. The moral, expert and rational-legal authority of professionals at the UN is, however, in chronic tension with the delegated authority on which it was founded by the 'Great Powers' at the end of the Second World War. Without a transformation of UN structures it is hard to see how the conditions for genuinely universal human rights might be established in practice.

Building on our understanding of the difficulties of claiming human rights through the elite authority of 'duty-bearers' developed in the first part of the book, in Chapters 5, 6 and 7 we turn our attention to themes of human rights campaigns that specifically address structures of injustice. In Chapter 5 we consider campaigns that address gross inequalities, insecurities and situations of absolute poverty produced by structures of globalising capitalism. We look at a range of duty-bearers addressed in these campaigns: from experts employed in IGOs to managers of transnational corporations and state officials. We assess the possibilities and limitations of 'human rights' as a frame through which the injustices of contemporary capitalism are being challenged. In Chapter 6 we look at violence against women. Constructing violence against women as a 'human rights wrong' challenges structures of sex, gender and sexuality that normalise women's subordination, especially in the family. Campaigns that frame violence against women as a 'human rights wrong' are notable because they cannot succeed solely by addressing duty-bearers in organisations. Constructions of human rights must also impact on everyday understandings of what women are worth and what they are due if they are to alter the structures in which many forms of violence against women are seen as justified. In Chapter 7, we consider structures of nationality and citizenship that support abuse suffered by migrants who cross borders to escape hopelessness and violence in their own countries. Very serious violations of human rights are tolerated because of the acceptance of the 'rightness' of securing borders and prioritising citizens – even though discriminating against non-citizens goes against the letter and the spirit of international human rights law. Here too, then, remaking constructions of everyday common sense is as important as advocacy for human rights in forms of elite authority.

In conclusion, in Chapter 8 we turn to the question of how successful human rights advocacy has been, and how likely it is that contemporary forms of activism will be successful in the future. We look first at work that has been done on the effectiveness of international human rights law by quantitative analysts in political science, IR and international legal studies. This represents the most focused and coherent attempt in the social sciences to answer the question. Although statistics appear to represent objective, unbiased certainty we look at the very shaky foundations on which these analyses are based. Given these differences I argue that the sociological contribution to understanding human rights is not best understood as a definitive answer to the question 'do they work?'. It lies rather in showing the range and the complexities of cultural politics of human rights in which advocates are engaged, and the paradoxes that are intrinsic to framing 'human rights wrongs' as such. The value of sociology lies in mapping the paradoxes of the global human rights field, to avoid over-simplifying the study of what is today – for better or for worse – the most significant 'people-centred' language of global politics.

2

(A) human rights movement(s) and other organisations

> Open your newspaper – any day of the week – and you will find a report from somewhere in the world of someone being imprisoned, tortured or executed because his [sic] opinions or religion are unacceptable to his government. The newspaper reader feels a sickening sense of impotence. Yet if these feelings of disgust all over the world could be united into common action, something effective could be done.
>
> (Peter Benenson, founder of Amnesty, 1961)

If the cultural politics of human rights is to bring about any real change in practices of injustice and suffering, they must be organised. In many respects the ideal form of organisation to achieve the enjoyment of human rights is a global social movement or movements.[1] Social movements are distinctive forms of organisation for social change that are understood to be flexible, popular and innovative, engaging people in their everyday life decisions as well as trying to change elite power structures.[2] Social movements are made up of loosely connected networks of individuals, groups and what are often called non-governmental organisations (NGOs). 'NGO' is a useful category insofar as it puts together organisations that are independent of governments and that pursue 'not-for-profit' aims. NGOs are a 'third sector' in relation to governments and corporations.[3] The category is misleading, however, if it leads us to neglect the enormous differences between organisations that are included within it. In general NGOs have a similar structure to corporations and to political parties: they are bureaucratic and hierarchical, and they employ professionals and experts. They can be very large, like Amnesty and Human Rights Watch, called international NGOs (INGOs) because they have branches in more than one state. NGOs can also be very small: some human rights NGOs consist of no more than a couple of people with some form of relevant expertise, a computer and an office.[4] Social movements invariably contain NGOs, but they always also contain grassroots organisations (GROs). In general GROs are different from NGOs in that they are less formally organised, less bureaucratic and they do not employ professionals. GROs can be support and self-help groups, they may involve members of communities who are directly affected by certain issues, and sometimes they include people who have chosen to live and work in solidarity with people suffering 'human rights wrongs'.[5]

INGOs, NGOs and GROs are all involved in the cultural politics of human rights, but in different ways. GROs are crucial to making the issues visible that really concern people directly suffering human rights abuses; NGOs may then take up those issues, putting their own spin on what is important in the process. GROs and NGOs try to change common sense, especially through the media. But NGOs also engage strategically with states and IGOs, providing expert knowledge to influence the frames through which professionals understand the world and lobbying to influence and alter law-making and public policy. As we shall see, it is especially through IGOs that INGOs are important to altering elite actions that lead to violations of human rights. In contrast, GROs are associated more with disruptive action, civil disobedience on the streets, and with more creative approaches to the cultural politics of human rights. Because they are attractive as genuinely representing 'the people' they are often taken up by intellectuals and artists who publish and broadcast in mainstream and alternative media, and produce novels, music, painting, theatre and film that explore ways of thinking against the grain of taken-for-granted 'common sense'.

A global human rights movement?

In the fourth edition of their authoritative textbook on international human rights, Alston and Goodman state: 'In today's world, human rights is characteristically imagined as a movement involving international law and institutions, as well as a movement involving the spread of liberal constitutions among states' (Alston and Goodman 2013: 59). Similarly, Aryeh Neier, former Executive Director of Human Rights Watch, says: 'The international human rights movement is made

up of men and women … who are united by their commitment to promote human rights for all, everywhere'. He goes on to list civil liberties
as 'the fundamental rights to which they are committed' (Neier 2012: 2).

What do these writers mean by 'movement'? They do not discuss it.
They use 'movement' more to claim popular authority for INGOs than
as an analytic term to raise questions and encourage research on the
organisational forms through which human rights may successfully be
claimed. 'Human rights movement' suggests that INGOs are channelling popular demands for human rights 'from below'. This may be especially relevant given that the largest and most influential human rights
organisations like Amnesty and Human Rights Watch are based in the
Northwest (Amnesty in London, Human Rights Watch in New York)
while the injustices they address generally take place elsewhere.[6]

It is on the basis that 'the human rights movement' *only* involves
elite groups that INGO claims to popular authority have been challenged. The legal scholar David Kennedy is an especially eloquent and
influential critic of human rights. He argues that 'the human rights
movement' is caught in a series of traps that limit political imagination and action through an overestimation of the value and power of
international law. The human rights movement puts too much faith in
lawyers and procedures rather than challenging grossly unequal relations of power and voice through struggles to articulate more utopian
visions. It moves power upward, to professionals working at the international level, disempowering ordinary people at the local and national
level (Kennedy 2002).

Transnational advocacy networks: naming and shaming elites

From an analytic point of view, the most influential research on the
organisational form of human rights claims comes from 'social constructivist' IR scholars. It is perhaps this work that has helped generate
the idea that there is a 'human rights movement'. Transnational advocacy
networks do resemble social movements in some ways. Most obviously,
like social movements, they are networks rather than a single organisation. According to Margaret Keck and Kathryn Sikkink, who developed the concept, a transnational advocacy network 'includes those
relevant actors working internationally on an issue, who are bound
together by shared values, a common discourse, and dense exchanges

of information and services' (Keck and Sikkink 1998: 3). Transnational advocacy networks link at least some – usually not all – the following major actors: (1) international and domestic NGOs; (2) local social movements; (3) philanthropic foundations; (4) the media; (5) churches, trade unions, consumer organisations and intellectuals; (6) parts of regional and international IGOs; (7) parts of the executive and/or parliamentary branches of government (Keck and Sikkink 1998: 9). When they are effective, transnational advocacy networks achieve a 'boomerang effect'. In the first place, where possible (and in extremely repressive states, it may not be possible) NGOs and local movements make human rights claims that put pressure on their home states. At the same time or instead of mobilising openly against their own states they make links to international partners – including INGOs, donors, other states and IGOs – to put pressure on the state from the outside. Where successful, external actors facilitate the demands of domestic NGOs, which put effective pressure on the state from the inside (Keck and Sikkink 1998: 12–13).

Keck and Sikkink's analysis of 'transnational advocacy networks' is based on campaigns for human rights in Latin America from the 1970s onwards (Sikkink 2011). An excellent example of the 'boomerang effect' is the campaign to find out what happened to the 'disappeared' in Argentina that followed the military coup of 1976, and to stop the kidnapping, torture and murder that was still going on years afterwards. Inside Argentina, the Madres de la Plaza de Mayo, who protested the loss of their children weekly in Buenos Aires, and an NGO that was set up explicitly to deal with these issues, the Center for Legal and Social Studies, worked with Amnesty International to publicise torture, murders and 'disappearances' that the Argentinian government at first denied. At the international level, Amnesty worked with sympathetic states, foundations and churches in the Northwest to support protestors against human rights violations inside Argentina, and to put pressure on Argentinian leaders to acknowledge the murders and torture for which it was responsible. A special committee, the Working Group on Enforced or Involuntary Disappearances, was set up at the UN. The US government, headed by President Jimmy Carter, was crucial to the campaign, cutting military aid and assistance to Argentina because the government refused to acknowledge what it had done. Eventually, in 1978, the Argentinian government, trying to restore its international image and to regain US aid, invited the Inter-American Commission on Human Rights to visit the country. From that point onwards the human rights situation improved – though work to find out what really happened to each of the 'disappeared' still continues today, and physical attacks by the government on its enemies did not end until after democracy was restored in 1985 (Keck and Sikkink 1998: 103–110; Sikkink 2011).

The international campaign against disappearances in Argentina shows how strategic framing by an INGO can be successful. Framing 'disappearances' in Argentina and elsewhere in Latin America in the 1970s involved creating *new* interpretations of international human rights law whilst building on what was already, at least nominally, accepted. It seems that 'disappearances' were a tactic that was used by the Argentinian dictators at this time precisely to avoid *imprisoning* and then executing their political enemies. They avoided locking up 'prisoners of conscience' and executions, which would attract Amnesty campaigns and bad publicity – which is apparently what happened in Chile following General Pinochet's military coup in 1973. Instead in Argentina the government had its political enemies secretly kidnapped and murdered. Amnesty worked with legal experts at the UN to have 'disappearances' recognised as a serious violation of human rights, similar to, and often including, torture, murder and arbitrary detention (Keck and Sikkink 1998: 103–4; Clark 2001).

Although 'disappearances' meant new *interpretations* of international human rights law, they were framed as wrongs according to human rights norms *that were already agreed*. Framing 'disappearances' in human rights terms resonated with Argentinian elites. This may seem strange: how can state officials be committed to principles which they are at the same time violating on a routine basis? As Sophie Cardenas points out, there is a strong tradition of commitment to human rights in Latin America that is often overlooked. Historically, the American Declaration of Human Rights was actually drawn up *before* the Universal Declaration of Human Rights (UDHR), and Latin Americans made important contributions to the conditions and the text of the UDHR (Cardenas 2010). Commitment to human rights *principles* remained strong in Latin America, even as gross violations of human rights were carried out by military dictatorships in practice.

To what extent are transnational advocacy networks elitist? They are certainly aimed at changing elite behaviour. According to Keck and Sikkink, transnational advocacy networks are effective when they are able to *shame* political elites into changing how they construct their state's interests, and – eventually – the policies and practices that lead to human rights abuses. They are able to do so where elites are not opposed to human rights in *principle*. In Argentina this was the case; it is why state officials initially denied that violations had happened at all: they covered up what they had done because they were ashamed of their actions. According to Keck and Sikkink's analysis, even where violating human rights has become routine, elites can nevertheless be shamed into stopping arbitrary imprisonment, torture and murder because they do not want to see themselves, and they certainly do not want others to see them, as responsible for such practices (Keck and Sikkink 1998: 29).

In fact, relatively little is known about connections between INGOs, NGOs and GROs in transnational advocacy networks. We know that at least in some cases transnational advocacy networks link INGOs and officials acting for IGOs with people who are directly suffering as a result of human rights violations. This was the case in the campaign for the human rights of the Argentinian 'disappeared', which directly involved their families and friends. But the focus of IR analyses is on the *transformation of international elites*. 'Social constructivists' in IR have not raised questions about how definitions of human rights at the grassroots might differ from those of elites. Nor have they considered how claims for human rights might alter structures and organisations beyond achieving respect for civil rights not to be physically harmed by officials representing the state (see Risse *et al.* 1999: 2–3).

IR analysts of transnational advocacy networks have not concerned themselves with differences between organisations. It is clear from the example we have looked at here that Amnesty International played a crucial role in negotiating how 'disappearances' were to be understood as violating basic human rights, and in persuading international elites to take the suffering of families and friends of the 'disappeared' seriously. Human rights INGOs are now enormous organisations, with huge budgets, employing professionals and experts. In the analysis of transnational advocacy networks, however, they are treated simply as one kind of organisation amongst others, as nodes in networks that are presumed to be much the same as NGOs and local social movements. This is clearly misleading. Before we turn to further discussion of human rights and social movements, therefore, we will look at INGOs in a bit more detail.

International non-governmental organisations

The largest and most influential human rights INGOs are based in, and receive funding and support from, the Northwest. Amnesty International is by far the most important; it was the first, and it is still the largest. In 2012 Amnesty had an estimated budget of £200 million (Stroup 2012: 145). In 2010, although it had offices in eighty countries, 84 per cent of staff and 87 per cent of members and supporters in Amnesty came from the 'Global North' (including Japan) (Hopgood 2011). Amnesty gets its funding exclusively from membership (except the US office, which does accept donations from foundations) and individual bequests. Human Rights Watch is smaller, and it was always more professional and centralised than Amnesty. It relies on philanthropic foundations, primarily now the George Soros Foundation, as well as on corporate sponsorship and fund-raising from individuals (Stroup 2012: 145–8).[7]

In addition, since the 1990s, large development INGOs, including Oxfam, CARE, Save the Children and Action Aid, have begun to combine humanitarian relief, development work and rights-based advocacy. Unlike Amnesty or Human Rights Watch, these organisations are funded by governments as well as through private donations. To get an idea of the scale of their operations we can note that CARE received over $700 million dollars from the US government in 2009 – and smaller sums from other governments in Europe (Stroup 2012: 81).

When Amnesty was originally set up in in 1961 the organisation claimed moral authority. The largely volunteer membership worked to 'shine a light in the darkness'. Amnesty was founded originally to free political activists imprisoned for their beliefs (prisoners of conscience) and its work was rigorously neutral. Members of Amnesty wrote letters to prisoners in 'Threes' to avoid Cold War politics – to one person imprisoned in a communist state, another under a right-wing dictatorship, and to a third in a non-aligned state. And until the 1990s Amnesty did not allow its members to report or campaign on violations in their own countries in order to avoid political bias. In other words, in its early days Amnesty was self-consciously *apolitical*, working only on injustices that were seen as self-evidently *morally* wrong, that must be condemned by anyone with a conscience, regardless of their political beliefs (Hopgood 2006).

In addition to moral authority, all human rights and humanitarian organisations construct themselves as having *expert* authority.

The reports produced by Amnesty and Human Rights Watch are very well known and respected outside the organisations. INGOs have greater capacities to collect information 'on the ground' on human rights abuses than governments, using a range of informants, amateur and professional, and their reports are widely read and used by journalists, politicians, lawyers and diplomats. Reports published by human rights INGOs have been criticised by social theorists for their tone. They are 'objective' in style, concentrating on putting forward facts of human rights abuses, most commonly with reference to international human rights law. The style of these reports is to 'let the facts speak for themselves'. Though direct testimonials from eyewitnesses or victims of human rights abuses are invariably included, critics argue that they are still too dry, lacking in the ability to move people to action to end human rights abuses. INGO reports are also criticised as problematic because they do not represent the structural conditions of systematic violations (Dudai 2009; Moon 2012). On the other hand, INGOs have won a good deal of credibility for their expert authority using this 'objective' style of report on human rights. According to Theo van Boven, a director of the UN Centre for Human Rights in the 1970s, '85 percent of our information came from NGOs', and INGO reports are still crucial to UN monitoring of human rights (Keck and Sikkink 1998: 96).

Although the expert authority of Amnesty and Human Rights Watch has been consolidated since Amnesty was set up in the 1960s, in other respects the work human rights INGOs do now is very different; it is far more complex and diverse. As the numbers and types of organisations that work on human rights have expanded and become more professional, it becomes obvious that INGOs do not rely *solely* on moral and expert authority for their effectiveness.

INGOs are involved in politics: in the framing of facts and values that constitute 'common sense'. This has become more evident as they work on a far greater range of human rights issues than Amnesty did in the beginning, focusing less on individuals and more on themes and on regions. And although the work they do is still primarily in the area of civil rights, both Amnesty and Human Rights Watch are now involved in confronting abuses of human rights by corporations, in claims for economic, social and cultural rights, and in the human rights of women, sexual minorities and refugees.[8] Human Rights Watch is also – unlike Amnesty – involved in monitoring human rights violations in armed conflicts, including the abuses of non-government actors. The range of rights for which INGOs stand makes it impossible for them to avoid becoming entangled in fundamental questions over how people should live: over the respective value of state intervention and markets with respect to social and economic rights; what is acceptable and permissible in intimate relationships and the role of women in society with regard to women's and LGBT rights; whose culture and ways of life should be valued and defended where there is conflict between indigenous and rural groups and state-sponsored development projects.

INGOs are also engaged in Politics. Human rights INGOs are *opposed* to states in that they are on the side of those whose human rights are being violated. But they also work *with* governments to restructure states that have been involved in human rights violations. Collaboration with the US government has been especially important to INGO influence. Human Rights Watch was set up as Helsinki Watch in 1978 to monitor civil rights violations against political dissidents in the Soviet bloc. Making use of the power of the US government was an explicit part of its strategy from the beginning (Neier 2012). In contrast, Amnesty has tried to keep its distance from collaboration with the United States, and it has been much more overtly opposed to US policies (Stroup 2012: 197–8). Nevertheless, Amnesty has also collaborated closely with US state officials, as well as with European governments, as we saw from the example of the campaign in Argentina in which it was involved in the 1970s.

Engaging in Politics makes it difficult for INGOs to claim moral authority. An example of the complications and compromises that result from collaboration with states that has proved especially difficult for both Human Rights Watch and Amnesty is their relationship with the United States during the 'Global War on Terror'. Human rights INGOs have found themselves in the difficult situation of trying to oppose violations of human rights by states that are enemies of the United States, at the same time opposing US violations of human rights, *and* justifications of military intervention by US elites in the name of ending human rights violations. In 2003 Human Rights Watch was heavily criticised for not opposing the invasion of Iraq, which the Bush administration was partly justifying as humanitarian, a response to human rights violations committed by the Saddam regime. Human Rights Watch appeared to give credibility to these claims because it published reports on the gross violations of human rights for which Saddam Hussein had been responsible a decade earlier in the run up to the invasion. They included the summary execution and disappearances of tens of thousands of Kurdish villagers, young men, women, children and elderly people. In 2004 Kenneth Roth, director of Human Rights Watch, tried to distance his organisation from the Bush administration, arguing very clearly that the invasion of Iraq was definitely *not* a 'humanitarian intervention' – but by then the damage to the organisation's reputation had been done (Roth 2005; Stroup 2012: 195–201). From its beginning Amnesty has had a policy of neutrality with regard to armed conflict. For this reason the organisation did not take a position on the invasion of Afghanistan in 2001, even though US officials justified it on the grounds of human rights abuses to which women especially were being subjected by the Taliban. Employees of Amnesty were not permitted to use the Amnesty logo in demonstrations against it. Later Amnesty did reinterpret its policy to oppose the invasion of Iraq on the grounds that war should only be used as a last resort (Hopgood 2006: 198–200). In 2012, however, Amnesty USA was campaigning for a law to be passed in the UN Congress to ensure that the Department of Defense reported regularly on its efforts to ensure the protection of women's rights in Afghanistan as UN-led security forces were preparing to formally withdraw from the country in 2014 (Amnesty International USA 2013). INGOs find it difficult to distance themselves from US interests, to gain moral authority as neutral and above politics, because 'naming and shaming' depends in large part on persuading US elites to put pressure on the elites of other states. This is of course especially controversial where military intervention is involved – a topic we explore further in Chapter 4.

As well as becoming implicated in 'Politics', human rights INGOs also have economic interests. They must 'do well to do good'. They must cultivate sources of funding in order be able to do their work. As we have already noted, human rights INGOs vary in how they are funded. Amnesty is funded exclusively by its members – except Amnesty USA, which, like Human Rights Watch, accepts money from foundations too. Many of the humanitarian organisations, like CARE and Oxfam, receive a significant portion of their funding from governments. But insofar as human rights INGOs are based in the Northwest and gain most of their funding and public support in these countries, economic considerations put similar constraints on all of them with regard to how they select the campaigns on which they work.

In a very interesting study of the work of INGOs, Clifford Bob argues that INGOs are not *only* concerned with justice when they choose which campaigns they will take up of the many that they could in principle support. The selection of campaigns is also intended to enhance the brand name and the success of the INGO itself. Bob argues that 'marketing rebellion' is especially problematic when it affects *how human rights are claimed*. He argues that how 'causes' are chosen and packaged may distort or leave out aspects of people's experience that they find vital, but which are simply too complex or too controversial for mainstream audiences in Northwestern states. In fact, in some cases, Bob suggests, the way INGO support is offered may even make people's situation worse. The main example Bob gives to support his argument is that of the Movement for the Survival of the Ogoni People. This was a movement that was established and led by the articulate and charismatic journalist and TV presenter, Ken Saro-Wiwa. INGOs, including Amnesty, were at first reluctant to take up the cause of the Ogoni people, which was presented in the same terms in which it was debated in Nigeria, as a movement for regional autonomy. It was only after Saro-Wiwa decided to risk escalating nonviolent confrontation with the Nigerian state that the media, INGOs and Northwestern states become involved. Saro-Wiwa's strategy for gaining international attention was successful in large part because the conflict involved Shell, a brand name that drew the attention of Northwestern audiences to learn more about human rights violations of the Nigerian state from which the corporation was clearly benefitting. Saro-Wiwa paid for the success of his strategy with his life when he was summarily hanged along with nine other members of the movement after a hasty military tribunal in 1995. What is more, Bob argues that violent repression of the movement by the Nigerian state increased *at the same time* as support in Northwest states for their environmental and human rights. According to Bob, Saro-Wiwa's campaign did change how people think about links between environmental and human rights issues. But Bob argues that it is doubtful that it led to any long-term gains for the Ogoni people, in part because their demands for regional autonomy were too complex to find adequate representation in transnational campaigns (Bob 2005).

INGOs are still able to persuade many that they have moral and expert authority: they are still trusted and respected.[9] And they still attract idealistic supporters. It may be distasteful to think of INGO images as 'brand names' rather than in the more noble and disinterested terms of 'reputation', but however we think about them it is clear that INGOs can never be governed solely by concerns of the market and competition. Indeed, concern for their market share in terms of donations and funding is one of the considerations that makes INGOs careful to protect their reputations/ brands. This is nowhere more evident than in the care that is taken to make sure that research reports into human rights violations are accurate and reliable. Indeed, it is an indication of their continuing moral authority that even people who are suspicious and critical of INGOs make use of reports by Amnesty and Human Rights Watch.[10]

Moreover, it is also important to note that those who oppose INGOs on the grounds that they are not simply concerned with ideals are also engaging in 'politics', and very often in 'Politics' too. In 2012 the Russian government passed a law requiring NGOs that receive foreign funding and are engaged in political activities to name themselves as 'foreign agents'. In making this law, the Russian government drew on xenophobia and nationalism to demonise and restrict the activities of organisations it feared as critical of the government (see Human Rights Watch 2013a). A similar law has existed in India since the 1975 Emergency, requiring all organisations seeking foreign funding to apply for permission from the Union Home Ministry. According to Ravi Nair, it has resulted in self-censorship on the part of organisations, which avoid working on rights that implicate the government for fear of being refused permission to apply for funding from abroad (Nair 2013).

Their moral and expert authority may be in reasonably good shape, then, but the leaders of INGOs are still concerned about 'pollution' – about appearing to compromise too much in order to succeed politically. They have to negotiate how their moral commitments are inevitably tangled up with money and power, and how they *appear* to other actors in the human rights field (Krause 2014: chapter 4). It is surely in part such concerns that lead to INGO claims in terms of *popular* authority: the suggestion that they are channelling demands for human rights from below. In this respect, however, INGOs are in real difficulties. INGOs demand accountability of elites for human rights violations, but as they are currently set up they are accountable only to funders and to their members (where they have them). Humanitarian organisations have developed ways of monitoring and evaluating projects (see Jordan and van Tuijl 2006). But they fall far short of enabling people to represent their needs to INGOs. Primarily accountable to governments, foundations and members in the Northwest, popular authority is clearly a problem where INGOs are engaged in controversial and complex campaigns in countries of which few of their supporters have had any direct experience.

Both Amnesty and Human Rights Watch are restructuring to try to put down roots in the Global South. Amnesty is currently in the process of setting up 'hubs' in African, Asian and Latin American cities as part of a strategy called 'moving closer to the ground'. Amnesty has tried before to establish offices outside the Northwest without much success. The aim now is to build up regional centres that will co-ordinate research and campaigning, that will be able to respond more quickly to violations, and that will be able to claim popular authority because they have more grassroots support in states that are being targeted. In addition, with growing prosperity in Latin America and Asia, and the decline of Northwestern economies, they are seen as potentially offering new sources of funding (Hopgood 2011). Human Rights Watch is also trying to build up its international capacities in research and campaigning by establishing offices in the Global South (Stroup 2012: 143–4).

It remains to be seen how successful these efforts will be. Will 'moving closer to the ground' increase Amnesty's authority in the Global South? Will globalising enable Human Rights Watch to put pressure on elites involved in human rights violations through governments there rather than relying so heavily on the United States? Or given their histories, and their close association with support and funding in the Northwest, will it prove too difficult for human rights INGOs to establish themselves elsewhere? If so, does this mean that they will not have the remarkable influence in international affairs they have managed to achieve in recent decades? Will we see the rise of other, Southern-based INGOs that will take their place?

Grassroots movements for human rights

Alternatively, there is quite a different way in which social movements are thought of as contributing to claims for human rights. Post-colonial social theorists suggest that there are *many* movements addressing grievances 'from below' rather than a single 'human rights movement' led by INGOs. These movements claim popular authority because they are made up of people who live at the very edges of global markets that threaten their ways of life. They are movements of indigenous people, landless peasants and urban squatters that have been especially prominent in Latin America, and who have also been involved in particular campaigns in Asia and Africa.

Emancipatory movements

The most interesting theorist of grassroots movements for human rights
is Boaventura De Sousa Santos. For Santos, it is only grassroots social
movements that represent real possibilities of transformation using
human rights. In his view this is because they have quite a different
relationship to *law* than INGOs and transnational advocacy networks,
and therefore to states and to 'Politics' (Santos 2002a, 2002b).

Santos works in the tradition of legal pluralism. Broadly speaking,
'legal pluralism' simply means that there is 'a multiplicity of legal orders'
within a single social field or political unit (Tamanaha 2008: 375). Legal
pluralism has become topical in relation to globalisation, where it is
thought of as *transnational*. Transnational legal pluralism includes
the range of forms of legal regulation emerging at different scales,
from local, informal mechanisms of dispute resolution at the local
level, through national and international law. But legal pluralism has
long been understood as important within post-colonial societies in
the Global South. It is a product of the way Europeans governed colonies through existing forms of authority, including so-called 'native
courts' that enforced customary or religious laws. In many places the
result was a dual legal system: legal norms were applied to economic
and government affairs through state courts, while officially recognised customary and religious courts and authorities dealt with family
and 'local' matters. Legal pluralism continued following decolonisation, so that it is a feature of many countries today. A recent report for
the International Council on Human Rights Policy gives the following
example: '[I]f a member of a peasant community in the Department of
Ayacucho, Peru, is involved in a dispute, she can resort to the authorities of her own peasant *comunidad*, to the local Justice of the Peace, to
an NGO-based Rural Centre for the Administration of Justice, or to the
state courts' (International Council on Human Rights Policy 2009: 2).[11]

For Santos, legal pluralism opens up the possibility of progressive forms
of law developed by marginalised and oppressed peoples. He sees national
state law (which is what is ordinarily thought of as law in Northwestern
societies) as problematic because it turns law into a science that is inaccessible to the majority of the people. It intimidates people, suppresses dissent,
and helps elites to maintain their power. According to Santos, engaging in
Politics is counter-productive because people will never be able to defend
ways of life they value through state law. Emancipatory law, on the other

hand, does not separate state and society. It emerges from the lived experience of marginalised, oppressed and impoverished people. Emancipatory law must be developed by communities according to their own norms of justice. But to be emancipatory, local law must be political. It must be developed in ways that enable people to determine the conditions of their own lives, resisting multinational corporations, capitalist commodification and the domination of elites, as well as dealing with power relations based on inequalities of wealth and status within communities (Santos 2002a).[12]

According to Santos, where they contribute to emancipatory law international human rights can be progressive. Human rights may encourage progressive interpretations of existing traditions, where they are 'translated' into local cultures and become relevant to legal practice. Santos gives the example of women's status in sharia law (Santos 2002b: 50–2). But it works the other way too. Local understandings usefully contribute to the development of progressive, multicultural human rights as a result of cross-cultural dialogue between oppressed peoples (Santos 2002b). In both respects, Santos sees creative uses of international human rights as having a progressive part to play as long as they are developed 'from below', by grassroots social movements.[13]

The social movement that comes closest to Santos' understanding of the potential of human rights is the Zapatistas. The Zapatistas came to international prominence in 1994 with an armed insurrection against the Mexican government. At that time they made demands on the Mexican state, including for self-rule for the Chiapas region where they are based. But the Zapatistas quickly developed quite differently, creating autonomous forms of participatory governance in which they gave rights to *themselves*, rather than conceiving of rights as being granted by states or international agencies (Speed 2008). For Santos, at this time the Zapatistas were exemplary because their conception of rights was radically inclusive of all forms of inequality (social and economic as well as civil and political); and because they tried to take all forms of oppression into account (of workers but also of women, lesbians and gay men, and indigenous peoples).[14] In addition, unlike previous revolutionary movements, they did not seek to 'take power' (through the state) but aimed rather to create a fundamentally new world beginning from 'where we are' by contesting relations of power in everyday practices (Santos 2002a: 459–65). The Zapatistas are exemplary of Santos' ideas about emancipatory human rights. They developed local forms of governance outside

state-centred law, close to lived experience and progressive in relation to diverse forms of inequality and domination.

The Zapatistas are clearly an extraordinary movement. They have
captured the imagination of people all over the world. The Zapatistas
are autonomous of INGOs as well as of the Mexican state – and at
the same time they have become famous worldwide through their
creative use of spectacle and poetry. Subcomandante Marcos has
become a radical icon, a postmodern Che Guevara of our times.
'Revolutionary tourism' to the remote parts of Mexico in which the
Zapatistas are based was already well established by 1995, and celeb-
rities and activists flocked to the region. The Internet has proved
especially important to mobilising support for the Zapatistas, inspiring intellectuals and activists like 'Ya Basta!' in Italy, and the 'hori-
zontals' who became Occupy Wall Street in the United States (Castells
1997: 79–83).

But the fact that the Zapatistas are so extraordinary might give
us pause. Are they actually unique, quite exceptional in their use of
human rights? Unlike most organisations involved in claiming human
rights they avoid formal politics altogether. It is telling in this respect
that Santos – with Cesar Rodríguez-Garavito, the director of the Latin
American Human Rights Centre based in Colombia – has compiled an
edited collection of case studies concerning emancipatory law in which
there is no case of autonomous organising for human rights that is
anything like the Zapatistas (Santos and Rodríguez-Garavito 2005). It
is surely far more common for movements to engage in Politics as well
as politics?

Using law, not depending on it

An example of a grassroots movement that engages in the cultural politics
of human rights both inside and outside formal governmental organisations is the Treatment Action Campaign in South Africa. The Treatment
Action Campaign is an NGO and a nation-wide movement for people with
HIV/AIDS who could not get treatment in the 1990s and who were often
shunned by their families and communities because of their illness. The
Treatment Action Campaign has engaged Politics, making use of state and
international human rights law and INGOs to engage elites in the South
African state and transnational corporations. At the same time, it has also
engaged in politics at the grassroots: transforming how people value the

lives of HIV/AIDs sufferers, and empowering people to see themselves as having a 'right to rights'.

The Treatment Action Campaign is largely made up of young, urban South Africans who are themselves HIV-positive. The NGO also formed alliances with the Congress of South African Trade Unions and the South African Council of Churches, which helped put pressure on the state at local, national and international levels. Activists used many of the techniques of protest that had been learned in the anti-apartheid movement, including civil disobedience. Demonstrations kept the issue in the media as activists staged illegal sit-ins at which they were arrested. The Treatment Action Campaign also successfully took the South African government to court on a couple of occasions. It was able to do so because the South African constitution requires the government to respect social and economic rights. The South African Constitutional Court may require that the state take reasonable steps to realise social and eocnomic rights 'progressively' and 'within available resources'. In the case of AIDS medication, the Court found that the government was not reasonable in withholding affordable drugs to prevent and treat HIV/AIDS. President Thabo Mbeki had resisted buying and administering the necessary drugs on the grounds that AIDS was caused by poverty, not HIV infection, and that 'Western' medicine was not the best treatment for illness in Africa. But the Court's judgement did not immediately lead to government action. At this point, the Treatment Action Campaign made links with INGOs, including Oxfam, to put pressure on transnational pharmaceutical companies to allow drugs to be distributed more cheaply. And later, when the government was still reluctant to abide by Court rulings, it called for international demonstrations against the South African government, which took place across Europe and the United States and Asia (Forbath *et al.* 2011; see also Friedman and Mottiar 2005; Heywood 2009).

The Treatment Action Campaign was successful in its aims: the price of drugs for HIV/AIDS was reduced, and the South African government committed resources to a national programme of treatment. As a result, Mark Heywood, who was one of the leaders of the campaign, estimates that at least 350,000 people are alive who would have died (Heywood 2008). In addition, however, the Treatment Action Campaign may have been successful in that it is empowering ordinary people to claim social and economic rights for themselves.

Lucie White and Jeremy Perelman, the editors of a collection on human rights activism, *Stones of Hope*, stress that what is most significant about grassroots mobilisations in general, including the Treatment Action Campaign, is the way campaigns *use* but do not *depend* on, human rights law. As well as legal strategies, they involve people mobilising where they find themselves to make human-rights claims on their own behalf. As a result, these campaigns are empowering. They enable people not only to learn that they have rights, and what those rights are; they also learn and develop tactics that will serve them well in actually getting and defending what they need (White and Perelman 2011). Through these mobilisations people develop a sense of their 'right to rights' that they had not previously experienced. According to William Forbath and his colleagues who studied the Treatment Action Campaign, this may be what was most important about it: it not only empowered poor South Africans to demand the treatment they needed; at the same time they also gained detailed knowledge of how to claim social rights from the government more generally (Forbath *et al.* 2011).

Certainly the accounts of these campaigns demonstrate that human rights do not necessarily *dis*empower the poor. A prominent criticism of human rights campaigns is that they invest the law with too much power. Making human-rights claims using law can represent a huge obstacle for poor people. It requires legal expertise – whether to take a case to court, or to lobby governments or IGOs. 'Translators' are invariably necessary to mediate between legal definitions and local understandings of human rights in order to develop effective campaigns for justice (Merry 2006: 193–4). There is a danger then that people lose control of the issues that concern them: lawyers become the only ones who can direct campaigns because they are confident in a language that is inaccessible to anyone else.

One aspect of the Treatment Action Campaign that has been neglected in this respect is *how* the language of human rights united and inspired people to action. How did lawyers 'translate' human rights law into frames that were relevant to and that resonated with ordinary people's concerns? According to Forbath *et al.* human rights education in the South African townships involved:

> [A]n untidy, uneven, many-layered process of new rights-bearing identities in the making. Religious structures of thought and feeling and customary local knowledge, witchcraft, and spirit worlds merge and

jostle with medico-scientific 'enlightenment' and liberal and social rights consciousness.

(Forbath et al. 2011: 81)

People in South Africa make use of 'folk medicine' as well as Western medicine (Decoteau 2013). An important dimension of the Treatment Action Campaign was a 'treatment literacy programme'. It was designed to help people with the complicated routines of drug taking that treating HIV/AIDs involves: knowing when to take drugs regularly throughout the day and when it is necessary to alert medical staff to changing symptoms which require different drugs. In accounts of the Treatment Action Campaign, however, we learn neither about how local medical knowledges were negotiated in relation to the treatment literacy programme, nor how they were combined with human-rights claims in the Treatment Action Campaign. Grassroots mobilisations are inherently difficult to study, and what we have are accounts from those involved in *leading* the campaigns, not ethnographic research on how the meanings of human rights were contested and negotiated in order to create new possibilities. It seems likely, as Forbath *et al.* seem to suggest, that human rights would not always be understood in the same way, that there would be different interpretations, even within the same group. What is the effect on peoples' identities, their understanding of who they are in relationship to others, of grafting an understanding of oneself as a claimant of human rights on to local understandings of who 'I' am and who 'we' are?[15]

What *can* be learned from the Treatment Action Campaign is the way in which the NGO put pressure on international elites. Friedman and Mottiar, who have made an in-depth study of Treatment Action Campaign's organisation and strategies, argue that the leadership of the movement took care that the international links they made with INGOs like Oxfam to put pressure on the South African state did *not* influence their campaign (Friedman and Mottiar 2005). This was surely relatively easy for Treatment Action Campaign organisers. It is clear from the range of organisations that funded the campaign, including INGOs, foundations, governments, the EU and the UN as well as individuals, that they had no difficulty in attracting international attention.[16] Clearly, the organisers of the Treatment Action Campaign were not in the same position as the ill-fated movement of the Ogoni people led by Ken Saro-Wiwa. They were much more able to deal with INGOs on their own terms.

If the Zapatista movement is emancipatory by Santos' standards, what about the Treatment Action Campaign? In many ways they are not really comparable. The Zapatista movement is revolutionary: it aims to fundamentally restructure society 'from the bottom up' by people taking control of the social and economic conditions of their own lives. In contrast, the aims of the Treatment Action Campaign were far more limited: the objective is to change how people are positioned in relation to markets (in this case, the market in drugs), and to claim rights from the state of which they are citizens. Nevertheless, the accounts we have of the Treatment Action Campaign suggest that this type of campaign has been empowering for people who have been able to bring about changes in economic and political structures; and who have gained a sense of themselves as having a 'right to rights'. In this respect, the Treatment Action Campaign has been emancipatory: it has enabled people to take a greater degree of control over the conditions of their own lives not by disengaging from transnational markets, INGOs and national states but by engaging with elites to transform how they are structured. At the very least, unless the accounts we have – limited though they surely are – are wildly optimistic, what we know about the Treatment Action Campaign suggests that campaigns for human rights that address international and national elites and that link grassroots networks and INGOs are not necessarily *dis*empowering for the poorest and most disenfranchised, even when they do call on the authority of lawyers and other professionals.

Claiming rights effectively

In his book on human rights and poor people in Africa, Harri Englund recounts a very moving story that shows how people can be cheated out of what they are due *even* when they already clearly have legal rights. The story is of a man called Chikondi who worked for a wealthy hardware merchant in Malawi. He was regularly sent away on long-distance trips for several weeks at a time as a 'lorry boy', guarding the lorry and its goods, sleeping sometimes in the lorry and sometimes alongside it on the ground, even when it was raining. He was never told when he would have to leave, so he had no time to prepare. He did not even have time to tell his wife and family he was leaving, nor to gather clothes and food for the journey. Things came to a head one day when his employer accused Chikondi of conspiring with others to steal from his shop – though he was miles away at the time – and then refused to pay him the month's salary he was owed. The suspected thieves were not only dismissed; they were also beaten up by the employer's sons. Englund recounts how Chikondi then tried to get help from the Centre for Human Rights and Rehabilitation, an NGO specialising in legal advice, to force his employer to pay him for the work he had done. There is a legal minimum wage in Malawi, but Chikondi was not asking for that – his employer had only ever agreed to pay him below the minimum wage, with vague promises that he would increase it later. He was also due a daily allowance for living and working away from home, which his employer had never told him about. The man who dealt with his case at the Centre did not tell Chikondi about his legal rights to the minimum wage and to a daily allowance. Eventually Chikondi managed to get just a fraction of what he was due from the employer (Englund 2006).

The point of Englund's story is not just that Chikondi was cheated out of what he was legally owed by his employer, and also then by the man working for the Centre for Human Rights and Rehabilitation. It is also that the way in which Chikondi was treated was systematically *dehumanising*. His employer showed no respect for Chikondi's well-being or his dignity as a person. He treated him as nothing but a nuisance when he was not making use of him. But Chikondi was also treated as a problem when he tried to claim just some of what he was legally due. Effectively the officer at the Centre identified with the employer, 'as two gentlemen clearly above the client, whose fate they had the power to decide' (Englund 2006: 162). It was not so much that Chikondi was intimidated by the status and wealth of those he had to deal with, or even the very real threat of violence he faced in pursuing his claim. It was more that as members of the local elite the men who should have dealt with him according to his rights were so sure that he was beneath their consideration: very far from a human being with entitlements to be treated with dignity and fairness.

There is no doubt that elites cause suffering when they abuse human rights. But 'elite' is better seen as naming a *relationship* to relatively less powerful people, rather than a fixed structural position or an identity. In the case Englund recounts, it was an official of an NGO, the Centre for Human Rights and Rehabilitation, as well as a wealthy employer, who treated a poor man as less than human. It was *local* elites that caused the problems for Chikondi. For the Treatment Action Campaign the problem was the national government headed by President Mbeki

that refused to acknowledge the real needs of the very large numbers of people in South Africa who have HIV/AIDS as well as large
pharmaceutical companies that could clearly cut the prices and still
make a profit (as they eventually did). The targets of the campaigns
for the Argentinian 'disappeared' were national military and political
elites who tortured and killed their enemies. And, by extension, the
campaigns also targeted people with international influence in wealthy
and powerful states who turned a blind eye to the torture and murder
that was going on there, treating the Argentinian military dictatorship
as the leaders of a sovereign state like any other.

Grassroots campaigns are necessary to frame 'human rights wrongs'
effectively. Without collective mobilisation, people will generally find
themselves at a disadvantage faced with those who have more information, higher status, more education, more money – however small those
differences may be in the greater scheme of things. Individuals like
Chikondi cannot be expected to alter definitions of what is right and
wrong on their own, however hard they may try. Clearly, as Englund
shows so well, in many cases they cannot even count on people working for human rights NGOs to help them. People have to develop understanding of their 'right to rights' as well as to learn how to claim them.

It is also clear, however, that to be effective, human rights claims
must generally travel beyond the localities in which grassroots movements are formed. If local elites can be a problem, so too can national
and international elites. Transnational advocacy networks also, therefore, have an important role to play in creating the conditions for the
realisation of human rights in practice. In this respect, although we
have been discussing the *difficulties* of linking INGOs, NGOs and GROs
in this chapter, the authority of INGOs and the pressure they can bring
to bear on states and IGOs is an important aspect of the cultural politics
of human rights. Emancipation, achieving a greater degree of control
over the conditions of our lives, is achieved by remaking structures,
making markets and states more people-centred. The important question is surely, then, how grassroots movements *connect to* INGOs in
transnational advocacy networks. How can INGOs *collaborate* with
grassroots movements to advance human rights claims in ways that
actually meet people's needs? And under what conditions can grassroots movements collaborate with INGOs to mediate claims to elites
without losing control of their own aims?

3 States of human rights

> The States Parties to the present Covenant,
> Considering that ... recognition of the inherent dignity and
> of the equal and inalienable rights of all members of the
> human family is the foundation of freedom, justice and
> peace in the world,
> Recognizing that these rights derive from the inherent dig-
> nity of the human person ...
> Considering the obligation of States under the Charter of
> the United Nations to promote universal respect for, and
> observance of, human rights and freedoms ...
> Agree upon the following articles ....
>
> (Preamble to the International Convention on
> Civil and Political Rights)

States are the most important organisations for the enjoyment of human rights. Officials acting in the name of states assemble structures and concentrate resources in ways that make them exceptionally *dangerous* – well equipped to benefit from torture, rape and murder, and from turning funds that are ostensibly collected for public benefit through taxes and international aid to their own purposes. At the same time states are crucial to the *realisation* of human rights in practice: they enable officials to exercise authority nationally and internationally that can make a positive impact on how people live within their territories and in other states too. States are at the same time the violators *and* the guarantors of human rights.

It may seem odd to think of states as the *guarantors* of human rights. Where states have been considered from a social constructionist perspective in studies of human rights, they tend to be seen as obstacles to the realisation of human rights in practice. State sovereignty, the principle that there should be no outside interference in the affairs of states or in what goes on inside their territories, is seen as a problem for the realisation of human rights: it must be contradicted or transformed so that everyone, no matter where they are born or where they are living, can enjoy rights (see Levy and Sznaider 2006). But states are not just violators of human rights. International law does support state sovereignty (though precisely what this means is now changing, as we shall see in Chapter 4). But international law also makes states responsible for guaranteeing human rights. There is a paradox at the heart of international human rights law that we will be exploring in the following chapters: states are supposed to ensure the human rights of individuals within their territories *against their own violations*.[1] It is in the name of states, and only states, that international human rights law is made. It is only officials representing states who sign and ratify treaties and conventions, and who agree that compliance with human rights should be monitored by the UN and judged in national and international courts. It is also through states that resources are organised to set up inter-governmental organisations IGOs, international courts and commissions. In addition states today are overwhelmingly constitutional states: the rights of individuals and groups – including both citizens and non-citizens – inside virtually all state territories are guaranteed, in principle, to at least the standards of international law. In fact, many national constitutions today go beyond international human rights standards. In Latin America constitutions that were made after military dictatorships are explicitly multicultural, specifying that the customs of indigenous peoples should be treated with respect (Go 2003; Cardenas 2010). And in South Africa the post-apartheid constitution provides for people to claim social and economic rights in the Supreme Court (Gauri and Brinks 2008).

   Of course, signing and ratifying international treaties and conventions, even creating national constitutions, do not turn violating states into human rights guarantors. Far more important than international law to whether states are violators or guarantors of human rights is the form they take, and the political strategies through which they are reproduced, challenged or transformed.

What are states?

In the language of international human rights documents – as in the preamble to the International Convention on Civil and Political Rights extracted above – 'State Parties' 'consider', 'recognise' and 'realise' their human rights obligations. In such texts states are treated as if they were people: individuals with awareness, feelings and agency. Treating states as unified actors is common too in IR, political science and political sociology.

It is notoriously difficult to study states from a social constructivist perspective (see Abrams 2006). Given that in reality there is no clear-cut distinction between 'state' and 'civil society', how can we study something that is so sprawling and heterogeneous *without* reifying 'the state'? What is most tempting from a social constructionist perspective is to treat 'the state' as no more than a construction of language, an illusion that traps us into thinking 'it' exists.[2] This approach does not, however, help us to understand what it is that is so *exceptional* about states – how they concentrate and control resources, material and moral. Nor does it help us to understand the specificity of actions authorised and carried out 'in the name of the state'.

What makes states distinctive as organisations? Charles Tilly's definition is often cited as covering much of what we intuitively understand as relevant and specific about states. According to Tilly a state is:

> An organization which controls the population occupying a definite
> territory … insofar as 1) it is differentiated from other organizations
> operating in the same territory; 2) it is autonomous; 3) it is centralized;
> and 4) its divisions are formally coordinated with one another.
>
> (Tilly quoted in Poggi 1990: 19)

States distinguish themselves and they are distinguished from other organisations in the same territory: we have only to think of how government buildings are marked out with national flags and special names: 'State Department', 'Department of Defence', 'Department of Social Security', and so on. States are centralised: their offices are invariably to be found in the capital cities of the countries in which they have jurisdiction. And states are formally co-ordinated: all officials who are employed in states are in hierarchies of bureaucracy and management, answerable to higher officials within the same department; the highest officials within each department are in turn answerable to a still higher rank of officials brought together across departments, and so on. Eventually ultimate responsibility lies with the head of state (most commonly a president, sometimes a monarch).

The question of state 'autonomy' is, however, far more complex than Tilly's definition suggests. States are only ever *relatively* autonomous. The effectiveness of those who carry out actions 'in the name of the state' depend on the organisation of moral and material resources that officials never fully control. States are never unified, nor 'complete'. Except perhaps in conditions of extreme authoritarianism, and despite their hierarchical, bureaucratic form, there is inevitably political conflict *within* states and *across state boundaries*. There is competition over resources between politicians, bureaucrats and experts within states, and between these officials and managers of corporations, organised workers, members of dissenting political parties, social movements. There is also competition for resources between state officials and the officials of other states, and with experts, diplomats and bureaucrats in IGOs.[3] State officials try to influence how resources are collected and concentrated 'in the name of the state' and how they are used; and they try to block the ambitions and projects of others with designs on the same resources. Ultimately these are cultural political struggles over the form of the state itself.

One type of resource on which states depend is economic. The relative autonomy of states from the owners and managers of capitalist production is the focus of the extensive Marxist literature on the state.[4] Irrespective of politicians' ideological preferences, or their personal ambitions, states depend on the collection and distribution of money. Through law and regulation – sometimes involving force – money is made and collected by officials acting 'in the name of the state' as taxation, and then distributed according to political programmes and projects decided on by state officials. As a result, the leaders of businesses that promise to contribute to national economic growth will generally be listened to very carefully. But this does not mean that shareholders and the managers of corporations control states. The dependence of states on capital investment for economic growth is not one-way. Even transnational corporations (TNCs) must go through states to be able to achieve their aims: states provide (or do not provide) many of the conditions that make business profitable, including infrastructure, relative peace and security, monetary stability, guarantees for legal contracts. And corporations must adapt to conditions set by state officials: they must observe laws and pay taxes, or avoid them by complex accounting that appears legally valid, or threaten and bribe officials. This gives state officials a degree of bargaining power even in globalising markets.

In addition, state officials have other sources of income besides taxation. They may negotiate loans from other states and international banks, and they may have access to international aid. In some states, sources of income from other states and IGOs are very significant, and this gives lenders and donors bargaining power. Again, however, even the officials of small states are not completely controlled by politicians, experts and bureaucrats in wealthy states, IGOs and international banks. The fact that in recent times the officials of some states have withdrawn from these sources of income (defaulting on loans, refusing to agree to what they see as unfair terms of international trade) is an indication that states have relative autonomy even in these situations. We discuss international regulation and banking, TNCs, and national economic policies with respect to demands for social, economic and cultural rights in Chapter 5.

State officials also depend on military resources that they do not fully control. The history of state formation is in large part the history of successful armed gangs that have consolidated their ability to continue warring by extracting money and labour from settled populations. As Tilly puts it, the history of state formation is the history of organised crime (Tilly 1985; see also Giddens 1985). However, no state has ever had an army and military that fully monopolised the means of violence within its territory. Forms of violence that support or threaten the projects of state officials vary a good deal in different states. There are organised and violent criminals in all countries; armed militias more or less control parts of some state territories; and some areas are more vulnerable than others to bombing and invasion by the armies of other states. How state officials create and make use of military resources to realise their projects, how they respond to armies and armed militias that appear to threaten their position, and how their decisions are encouraged or constrained by other actors nationally and internationally: these are all crucial to how states guarantee or violate human rights.

In addition to material resources, state officials also rely on *moral* resources to carry out their projects. They rely – to a greater extent in different cases – on authority to act 'in the name of the state'. State officials mobilise a mixture of types of authority both nationally and internationally to justify laws, public policies and foreign policy. As we shall see, the mix and the balance of claims to authority is quite different in different types of state. In each case, however, the authority that is claimed is open to challenge on precisely the grounds on which projects are justified. Professionals employed in non-governmental organisations (NGOs), IGOs and other states, sometimes in association with people involved in grassroots movements, challenge state officials' claims to rational-legal authority on the grounds that the law has not been observed, that the content of national law is not compatible with international human rights law, or that proper procedures have not been followed. They challenge expert authority as mistaken and ill founded, or as biased and self-interested. They challenge popular authority on the grounds that the government has betrayed its promises to the people, or that it is not acting in the national interests. To varying degrees in different states, officials are responsive to these challenges. Officials are likely to be especially responsive where challenges are backed up by the possibility that they may lose their positions – whether through elections, prosecution, revolution or military coup.

The actions of state officials are only ever *relatively* autonomous, then, with respect to the structures of material and moral resources on which they depend. The control states exercise over populations within their territories varies in different cases and at different times. 'Actually existing' states are the product of previous political struggles over resources. State formation privileges the strategies of certain individuals and groups to pursue projects that they see as in their interests or as of value. This aspect of states is sometimes called 'path-dependence': what seems reasonable to solve problems that arise today is constrained by decisions that were taken in the past. In some states 'path dependence' is more hospitable to respecting human rights than in others. There are no states, however, that respect human rights completely. In every state, the structures through which resources are collected and used in political projects must be transformed if human rights are to be realised in practice.

Differences of 'stateness' and states

How resources are collected, concentrated and used in different states varies enormously. States have been formed through different histories, and state officials reproduce and sometimes alter the structures they inherit to pursue their own projects. To make states into guarantors rather than violators of human rights in practice, then, different strategies are needed in different states. In the rest of this chapter I will outline brief sketches of different types of states in order to emphasise these differences. I draw on concrete examples, but the aim is not to build an exhaustive typology of states. It is rather to make general points about the differences between states by emphasising particular aspects of some. All states have characteristics of more than one of the types outlined here. These sketches are intended as sensitising devices, to open up questions for analysis concerning what is needed to realise human rights beyond the making of international human rights law.

Juridical state

I begin with the juridical state because it is presupposed in international human rights law. When a politician ratifies a human rights treaty or convention (at least as far as it is assumed to be made in sincerity), what is presupposed is that he or she is embedded in structures that will ensure that what has been agreed will be respected in the future. All states are assumed to be juridical states in international human rights law.

In fact, however, the juridical state is only ever approximated: it does not really exist. In ideal terms, the juridical state is characterised by the legal organisation and constraint of officials who act 'in the name of the state'. International human rights law and constitutions determine the 'checks and balances' of state power and limit its reach in relation to those under its jurisdiction, citizens and non-citizens. This requires further conditions. First, that public policies are codified as legal directives and subject to review by judges and courts. Second, that law is created by proper procedures. In addition to extending the functions of law, juridical states are marked by the growth of bureaucracy. Even if they are not eliminated completely in practice, any actions based on personal interest, sentiment or belief can be seen as corrupt when they are carried out by individuals who occupy official positions in the state. Rational-legal authority that comes from strictly following procedures 'according to the book' is what justifies actions by officials of the juridical state. State officials are expected to deal with the resources for which they are responsible *only* according to the instructions of their superiors in the bureaucratic hierarchy, and to use their skills and knowledge *only* in the public interest, by fulfilling the criteria of their appointments strictly according to the letter.

Sociologists see Northwestern states as quite closely resembling the juridical (sometimes called 'constitutional') type as a result of the long history of their development. In fact, the very idea of the juridical state is based on a rather idealised history of Northwestern states.[5] It follows, then, that Northwestern states should be best placed to ensure respect for human rights in practice. Let us look a little more closely at this assumption.

Let us first consider how the juridical state is structured in relation to civil rights *inside* national territory. In the Northwest these are often supposed to be the most fundamental human rights. It is fundamental to the juridical state and to respect for civil rights in practice that the actions of officials must stay within the law. But what if the *content* of the law does not respect civil rights? A very mundane and routine difficulty of ensuring civil rights in Northwestern states is what David Kennedy calls 'background laws' that enable state actors *legally* to violate human rights (Kennedy 2002). Summary executions by the police, torture at the hands of police and military officers, kidnap and murder by prison guards – these are all violations of human rights that are very clear, even if identifying and punishing those responsible may not be easy or politically expedient for governments. Similarly, so too are violations of political rights: election fraud, the corruption of elected politicians, misuse of party political funds and so on. What are far less obvious, but equally important, are laws that enable the police to break up or harass peaceful protestors on the grounds that they are violating obscure bye-laws: 'obstructing the highway', 'causing a public nuisance', 'disturbing the peace'. The legal powers enjoyed by police forces to prevent peaceful political protest in Northwestern states are extensive, and they can easily be used in ways that violate the spirit of human rights, to intimidate and contain the organised expression of dissent.

A far more dramatic difficulty for civil rights in Northwestern states is that all states allow themselves the *legal* possibility of making exceptions when faced with dangers to national security. They all have *built-in* exceptions to observing civil rights when faced with security risks. Infringements on civil rights in Northwestern states within national territories have been very well-documented in recent years, with laws in the United States and Europe enabling racial profiling, detention without charge, and extensive surveillance over citizens and non-citizens. It is important to be clear: exceptions are not *outside the law* in these states. Security laws adopted in national emergencies are subject to legal review, and they very often have limitations put on them, such as 'sunset clauses', intended to constrain the period in which they are active (Alston and Goodman 2013: 394–7). However, it is in the climate created by security fears that the US and European governments have been involved in collecting and analysing the email exchanges of every single person to which their programmes have access. It is only due to the whistle-blower Edward Snowden that we even know this is going on. Although there has been widespread outrage about the surveillance activities of the United States and its European allies as contravening fundamental rights to privacy, the initial response on the part of governments was that the surveillance was not against the law (though, as a result of intense legal and political pressure, President Obama subsequently stated publicly that the programme will be ended) (*New York Times* 2013; *Guardian* 2014). Finally, it is in the context of 'national emergencies' and the securitisation of borders that the civil rights of unauthorised migrants into Northwestern states are violated when they are incarcerated in prison-like facilities without due process of law. Supported by the popular media, what are generally considered fundamental human rights to freedom from arbitrary detention and to a fair trial are routinely violated for non-citizens in Northwestern states (as we shall see in more detail in Chapter 7).

In terms of social and economic rights, the juridical state is not necessarily a minimal state. In Scandinavia and Western Europe the welfare state was formed in the twentieth century, redistributing wealth through taxation in the form of public provision of education, housing and health-care as well as through direct transfers to families and to those unable to work in the labour market (Marshall 1987; Esping-Andersen 1990). In large part the formation of the welfare state represented a shift in the authority claimed by state officials as a result of democratisation: 'popular authority' became more important with the rise of social democratic parties. However, welfare states were also possible because of the relationship between rational-legal bureaucracy and economic resources that had already been established: taxes are set, collected and administered bureaucratically, and the routinised means by which they are collected and administered is necessary for bureaucracies to function as such. But whilst an approximation of the juridical state may be *necessary* to the administration of social and economic rights, it is not *sufficient* to ensure that they are universally enjoyed. A good deal has been written on how social and economic rights are being eroded in Europe with the extension and deepening of neo-liberal public policies and growing inequalities.[6] Neo-liberal public policies clearly show that the enjoyment of social and economic rights depends on structures that go far beyond the ideal of the juridical state and the rule of law. It depends on how governments deal with global capitalist elites in national economic policies, how TNCs are treated, and how markets, including financial markets, are created and regulated nationally and internationally (as we shall see in Chapter 5). The growth of public–private partnerships to deliver services that are the responsibility of states, the promotion of markets in health-care, education and housing and cuts to welfare budgets to reduce public spending are undermining social and economic rights. This is the case even when elites observe law and regulation – though we also know that neo-liberalism offers numerous opportunities for corporations to illegally (as well as legally) avoid paying taxes, and for investors to lend money regardless of regulations designed to protect borrowers, to make use of differences between national legal regimes and so on. In addition, as Foucauldians have persuasively argued, social and economic rights also depend on how professional and technical knowledge is incorporated into policy-making and the administration of what are necessarily limited resources. Where expert authority is successfully claimed to allocate resources and fix identities from within the bureaucratic structures of the state, the effect can be less equalising and liberating, more limiting and deadening of alternative ways of life.[7]

Ensuring human rights does not depend on the rule of law alone. Limiting the actions of state officials by the rule of law is important, but so too is the content of that law. In the case of civil rights, 'cause lawyers' are vital to ensuring that state officials do not just stick to the letter of the law of human rights but also abide by its spirit. 'Cause lawyers' are employed in NGOs and across different branches of the state (Scheingold 2004). Whistle-blowers who have access to inside information, and journalists willing and able to put pressure on governments through the media are also necessary if states are to observe civil and political rights in practice to which they are committed in principle. In the case of social and economic rights, in addition to lawyers and experts, popular movements, social democratic parties and trades unions have been necessary in the past, and will continue to be necessary in the future. These are rights that are won by political organising and lobbying inside and outside government. It is only once they are established in legislation and policy that social and economic rights become relevant in law.

Finally, law is limited as a means of ensuring human rights where states are involved in violations *outside* their territories, but for different reasons. Where violations are committed as a part of foreign policy, they are often *permitted* in national law as the prerogative of the executive, the defender of state security. At any rate it is rare that they are considered by constitutional courts within states.[8] To some extent this is now changing with the development of international human rights and humanitarian law. Even heads of state can now be prosecuted for torture, disappearances, summary executions and war crimes in international courts where domestic courts do not deal with them (see pp. 77–8). On the other hand, the administration of law in international courts is extremely uneven. We have only to consider, for example, that since the International Criminal Court was established in 2002, it is *only* African leaders who have been prosecuted there. There is clearly no question of prosecuting either George Bush or Tony Blair for the part they played in the illegal invasion of Iraq. The application of national law is, of course, uneven too. But if law is supposed to be routine and predictable, to provide a framework within which actions are clearly legal or illegal, international law is *so* uneven that it is doubtful whether it can be considered law at all. When the administration of human rights in international courts is so uneven, it looks more like another way of doing geo-politics than law administered by rational-legal institutions.

Post-colonial states

Up until decolonisation in the second half of the twentieth century, European states – although they were already being talked about and analysed as juridical states – were *formally* imperial states, ruling directly over the peoples of other countries. During the revolutionary periods of the great declarations of human rights in the eighteenth century, state officials had no interest in extending citizenship rights to the subjects of empires, nor to slaves. Across the world structures of empire governed from London, Paris, Berlin and Brussels were extended throughout the nineteenth century. Post-colonial states have their origins in this period as structures of rule were grafted onto existing arrangements within colonised territories, dividing up continents and populations quite arbitrarily and often relying pragmatically on existing forms of rule, so entrenching ethnic divisions within territories. There was little concern to develop the intensity and uniformity of rule of states in the Northwest, and as subject peoples were not citizens there was no possibility at all of democratising the state. There was also little attempt to develop the industrial capacities of these societies. On the contrary, the development of cash crops for export and the exploitation of mineral resources were undertaken only to benefit metropolitan owners and local elites who assisted with colonial rule. As Hansen and Stepputat put it, 'The emphasis was rarely on forging consent and the creation of a nation-people, and almost exclusively on securing subjection, order, and obedience through performance of paramount sovereign power and suppression of competing authorities' (Hansen and Stepputat 2005: 4).

The historical formation of states that were imported into colonial societies means that they are structured quite differently from juridical states. In the first place, rational-legal authority has been much more tenuous as a means of gaining consent to administer public policies. According to Partha Chatterjee, post-colonial states were grafted on to 'cellular societies': extended networks of reciprocal obligations based on 'moral communities' of kinship, caste or religion (Chatterjee 2004). Consequently, in states of this type, to varying degrees, it is expected that the resources to which officials have access are to be shared with those who have claims on them as part of the extended network to which they belong. Although decolonisation was generally linked – to a greater or lesser degree in different states – with national movements for liberation and democratisation, 'popular authority' in post-colonial states is often associated with direct rewards to supporters, kin and neighbours of politicians, bureaucrats and judges. 'Micro-strategies' necessary for survival as well as for enriching oneself (what appear as corruption and clientelism where they are considered in terms of rational-legal authority) are built into the very structures of the post-colonial state. The everyday acceptance of 'micro-strategies' that reinforce cellular structures makes claiming rights difficult, even when they exist in law and public policy.

Second, as they are built on historical structures in which consent to rule was far less important than force, and often set in contexts in which national identity is especially hard to achieve because of politicised ethnic differences, states that approximate this type tend to be authoritarian. This is true of India, for example, which is Chatterjee's focus. In India the Indian Armed Forces (Special Powers) Act has legally permitted the police and military to use a range of methods, including lethal force, against gatherings of more than five people in 'disturbed areas' like Kashmir since 1958. According to Balakrishnan Rajagopal, so-called emergency legislation of this type comes directly from anti-colonial wars euphemistically called 'emergencies' in the British Empire (Rajagopal 2003: 176–82). Authoritarianism has also been marked in Latin American states, where claims to 'popular authority' have often been made by military officers claiming that their particular skills in the use of force are needed to keep order and ensure progress. The role of the military in Latin America has declined since the end of the Cold War and the discrediting of the Chilean and Argentinian dictatorships, and constitutions have been rewritten to consolidate human rights oriented democracies. According to the constitutional lawyer Roberto Gargarella, however, what has been left largely untouched is the scope of presidential power that was established in the nineteenth century. Gargarella argues that this explains how it is that constitutions that now include expanded sets of rights, including social, economic and cultural rights, are relatively ineffective in curbing the violent treatment of political protests when people mobilise to secure those rights in practice (Gargarella 2013; see also Mendez *et al.* 1999).

In India and Latin America, grassroots movements and NGOs are trying to create mechanisms to bring state officials to account for violations of human rights. They involve strategies that are quite different from those employed in Northwestern states. In juridical-type states what is most important is to change the content of the law and public policy, to expose how it contravenes human rights in spirit. In post-colonial-type states, it is not only the *content* of the law that is at issue; it is also how law and public policy are *administered.*

Can the structures of the post-colonial state be transformed through the cultural politics of human rights? Chatterjee himself is sceptical about this possibility in India: he argues that so many of the poorest people are only able to gain any kind of stability and well-being through 'fixers' – well-connected, influential people linked to political parties who co-ordinate with state officials – that a strict line between legality and illegality would actually work to the detriment of those most vulnerable to violence and exploitation (Chatterjee 2004). In contrast Jean Dreze and Armartya Sen argue that transformation of the administrative structures of the Indian state is not only possible, it is happening. Dreze and Sen see the Right to Information Act 2005, which allows ordinary people to have access to government records, combined with media 'naming and shaming' of corrupt officials, as an important advance in reforming state administration. They also see the decentralisation of decision-making in the Panchayats, or village councils, as enabling people to bring local public officials to account where provision of services is inadequate (Dreze and Sen 2013: 99–102). In addition, grassroots movements have been involved in carrying out 'social audits', surveys of villages and poor urban areas to ensure that people know what they are due from the state, holding people's courts to make local officials accountable, large-scale marches and demonstrations (Jenkins and Goetz 1999; Madhok and Rai 2012). Like Chatterjee, Dreze and Sen are concerned with the everyday norms and expectations in which state officials and ordinary people operate in the Indian state. They argue that it is necessary to alter how administrators themselves see corruption, as well as how ordinary members of public approach administrators. Dreze and Sen look forward to the day when 'one day, a bureaucrat who asks for a bribe will ... be ridiculed, admonished or reported, because it just will not be "the done thing" by then, as it is today' (Dreze and Sen 2013: 102).

Predatory states

The predatory state is associated with gross violations of human rights, including genocide, murder, disappearance, rape and enslavement, as well as mass migrations, loss of livelihood, and consequent malnutrition and starvation. In this type of state, officials control resources 'in the name of the state' to further their own status and to amass wealth for themselves and their supporters by means of violence and criminal activity. Internally, they operate through force, achieving domination by inspiring fear rather than by winning consent to rule. Internationally, however, they make use of rational-legal and popular authority to secure official positions that enable them to access material resources.

   The Democratic Republic of Congo (DRC) has been, and probably still resembles the predatory type of state. When the country was called Zaire, General Mobutu, supported by the United States and European allies, systematically stripped the country of wealth from natural resources, putting millions of dollars into foreign bank accounts, and encouraging violent confrontations between different sectors of the military and police which he organised along ethnic lines. Mobutu's regime was finally ended in 1997 when it became clear that there was no central control over provincial governments, which were themselves involved in systematic pillaging, and it was overturned by forces from neighbouring territories in the Great Lakes region of Africa led by Laurent Kabila. The coup was uncontested by representatives of the United States and European states that, with the end of the Cold War, no longer saw a strategic interest in the region. Predatory states invariably involve bloody conflict, and in the DRC and neighbouring states fighting is still going on today. The African wars have been described as the most devastating since the Second World War, with gross violations of human rights and estimates of over five million civilian deaths as a result (Castells 1998; Reyntjens 2009).

Political sociologists have put forward a variety of explanations for the structures of predatory state formation. Jean-Francois Bayart understands predatory states as the product of elite strategies which have historically relied on what he calls 'extraversion', profiting from dependence on external sources of wealth to secure power (Bayart 2009; see also Mbembe 2001). Bayart argues that 'extraversion' is historically continuous as 'normal politics' in sub-Saharan Africa. Bertrand Badie, on the other hand, links 'extraversion' to decolonisation, arguing that as colonial powers withdrew, leaving behind states that lacked the capacity or the means to raise taxes from largely agricultural societies, ruling elites turned to international aid and business contacts to strengthen their official position. What Badie calls 'imported states' relied less on an established tax base, generating wealth within their territories, than on the wealth they could attract from international agencies, other states, and sometimes investment in large-scale projects (Badie 2000). In contrast, Lothar Brock and his colleagues argue that local autonomy can be the principal aim of those who capture official positions in states that are predatory, rather than power and wealth being ends in themselves. They analyse Afghanistan and Haiti as sharing the characteristics of predatory states (Brock *et al.* 2012; see also Castells 1998).[9]

Predatory-type states depend on structures that are maintained by armed force, looting and violence, rather than by winning consent to rule. Ruling elites control access to wealth to pay their political and military allies and they use violence to prevent rival 'warlords' from seizing the state. Internally, to reward their allies and to stir up violence against their enemies, they make use of ethnic, religious and political divisions. It is largely to external actors that they claim rational-legal and popular authority. 'Sovereignty', international recognition of state independence, enables governments to get control of international aid and loans, and to establish business contracts for their own purposes. They present what Bayart calls a 'virtual state' to the world – with evidence of rational-legal procedures for ensuring governmental accountability and democratic participation to bolster claims to popular authority. At the same time, Bayart argues, the 'real state' is at work behind the scenes to maintain the wealth of the ruling elite (Bayart 2009).

What are the possibilities of realising human rights in practice in predatory-type states? The DRC has signed and ratified all the major international human rights treaties and conventions, including the International Covenant on Civil and Political Rights (ICCPR) and the International Covenant on Economic, Social and Cultural Rights (ICESCR). But what does this mean where the very form of the state involves people being systematically deprived of their homes, livelihoods and, frequently, their lives? Clearly more is required than reform of the content of law and public policies (as in the juridical-type state) or the transformation of administration (as in the post-colonial-type state).

When a state is structured in ways that systematically violate human rights, citizens of a state are not in a position to influence how officials make use of resources. Today responses to human rights violations often involve *supplementing* states with resources that are organised internationally. In predatory-type states ruling elites concentrate their efforts on particular regions within their territories, effectively leaving much of the country stateless. They maintain control over the offices of state in the capital, in order to be officially recognised by international agencies. They also try to retain control over the regions where valuable resources (precious minerals or crops) are to be found. The conflict they incite to divide and rule further undermines possibilities of maintaining state control outside the areas in which they have an interest, as violence breeds violence. Supplementing a predatory-type state, then, effectively amounts to replacing it in at least parts of its territory: UN peacekeeping forces and humanitarian NGOs take over the roles and services that are normally understood to be the prerogative, and the duty, of a sovereign state.

A range of international solutions to human rights violations that supplement the state have been developed in the case of the DRC. First, since 1999 there have been various UN peacekeeping operations in the DRC which have aimed to protect civilians and ensure civil rights (Brock *et al.* 2012: 123). Since March 2013, UN peacekeeping forces have been deployed to stabilise the region and build up the capacities of the police and military. The mandate for these troops replaces the previous mission, authorised in 2010, to protect the human rights of civilians (especially women, children and 'vulnerable people') in the Eastern area (of a country which is in total the size of Western Europe). Troops were mandated to 'use all means necessary' to demobilise and disarm rebel forces and militias, some of which originated in neighbouring states (especially Rwanda, Uganda and Burundi) and over which no government has complete control. They were also there to curb the excesses of the Congolese Army itself, which has been accused of looting and rape (UN 2013). The area is not stable, and there does not seem to be an end in sight to UN peacekeeping operations in and around the DRC. Second, humanitarian NGOs have been providing food and shelter to some of the millions of people who have had to flee their homes as a result of the conflict, and attempting to establish facilities for basic education and health-care. In effect the United Nations High Commissioner for Refugees (UNHCR) and NGOs have replaced the state to ensure that people are not starving and homeless. Third, since 2004 the International Criminal Court has been proceeding with the prosecution of some of the warlords responsible for killing, raping and kidnapping in the region on the grounds that the DRC does not have the capacities within its judicial system to bring them to account (despite the fact that the EU has spent more than forty million US dollars reforming the Congolese judiciary) (Clark 2007). In this respect international law supplements the national judiciary, which does not have the code, the infrastructure or the personnel to deal with war crimes and crimes against humanity. There have been a couple of convictions at the ICC, but the UN has reported that just in the period between January 2012 and August 2013 nearly 1,000 child soldiers were recruited in the DRC.

Supplementing the state is controversial for a number of reasons. One of the charges against Northwestern states, especially the United States, involved in UN peacekeeping is that they are neo-imperialist, supporting missions only where it suits their interests (though in the case of the DRC, as elsewhere in Africa, they might equally be criticised for indifference). There is some justice in this argument given that there is no possibility of military intervention and state-building without US permission, even when it is decided in the UN Security Council (see pp. 78–83). A further area of controversy that is now emerging is the lack of accountability of the UN for human rights violations committed by troops and personnel employed in its peacekeeping missions. Guglielmo Verdirame argues that until relatively recently it was assumed at the UN that human rights abuses were only committed by others: UN troops and experts on peacekeeping missions arrived *to end* human rights violations. This assumption has been shaken by accusations that in the DRC 'blue-helmeted' soldiers employed by the UN were involved in sexual violence and abuse, including of very young children. The accusations have been investigated and they were apparently well-founded. It seems, however, that legally those who were responsible can only be prosecuted in the countries that 'lent' them as troops to the UN – and this has happened only in very few cases. There are no means of bringing people who violate human rights to court as agents employed by the UN itself: the 'sending' state is obliged to co-operate with the UN, but there are no sanctions if it does not. In addition to the lack of accountability of troops and personnel engaged in UN peacekeeping missions, the way the UNHCR is involved in setting up refugee camps has also been criticised as leading to routine violations of human rights – people's freedom of movement is restricted, and they are not protected from violence either by people inside or outside the camp (see pp. 146–53). UN peacekeeping missions and refugee camps supplement states by providing security and other basic services, but unlike states, the UN apparently has no legal responsibility in international human rights law to redress violations that may be committed by people acting 'in the name of the UN'. In the activities that supplement states UN personnel effectively have the power of state agents, but they apparently do not have the same responsibility to prevent human rights violations (Verdirame 2013; Verdirame and Harrell-Bond 2005).

Finally, deploying peacekeeping forces is controversial where it appears to be making the situation safer, not only – or sometimes not at all – for the people of the region, but for foreign investment that has historically been part of the problem in predatory state formation. In the case of the DRC, for example, the processes by which public/private contracts for mining its enormous reserves of cobalt (necessary for the manufacture of microchip technology) and copper have been administered have lacked transparency, and do not seem to be advancing the economic development of the DRC. The INGO Global Witness has documented secret deals granting contracts to mine resources involving offshore companies and the funding of armed conflict through trade in minerals. It has been involved in lobbying governments around the world to produce effective policies to prevent the exploitation of these resources in ways that harm people and the environment. If the economic structures of a predatory-type state are not altered, UN forces effectively become part of a strategy of 'extraversion', to strengthen the ruling elite and to help them achieve domination over their rivals rather than preparing the ground for a new form of state. In this case supplementing a predatory state *prolongs* rather than *transforms* it.

Attempts to realise human rights in predatory-type states are quite different from those employed in states that resemble juridical and post-colonial types. Despite all the human rights provisions that are now in place in the DRC, the people who suffer violence, hunger and deprivation there are as far from being able to *claim* rights as ever. Human rights in the DRC overlap with humanitarianism, with helping people to meet their immediate needs in situations of emergency – however long-term the emergency may turn out to be. When humanitarian aid is given, it is professionals employed in IGOs and NGOs who decide what is feasible, permissible and advisable. Where states are supplemented, people have rights to what IGOs and NGOs provide. In fact, Hilhorst and Jansen suggest that in such situations, humanitarianism itself produces claims for human rights that are highly problematic: people in need learn to tell aid workers want they want to hear (Hilhorst and Jansen 2012). In this respect supplementing predatory-type states leads to a distortion of the language of human rights rather than to the remaking of structures through which rights can effectively be claimed.

Developmental states

The term 'developmental state' was originally coined for Japan, and more recently it has been applied to 'Asian Tigers' (such as Taiwan, South Korea, Vietnam) and now to China, which has based its project of building market capitalism on the success of Singapore. According to Manuel Castells' definition, 'A state is developmental when it establishes as its principle of legitimacy its ability to promote and sustain development, understanding development as combining steady high rates of economic growth and structural change in the productive system, both domestically and in relation to the international economy' (Castells 1998: 276). The authority that is claimed by governments in development-type states is a mixture of expert and popular: technology and development is to be achieved to serve the people's needs, even if the means by which people outside government might contribute to influencing the agenda or setting goals are limited or non-existent as a result of repression, censorship and – very often – a lack of free and fair elections. In this type of state, Castells, argues, development is less a *goal* than it is a *means*: achieving capitalist development builds and protects the state, domestically and internationally, and this in turn enables governments to claim the authority to follow their chosen path *on behalf of* society. Developmental states involve a kind of 'enlightened despotism': officials gain and secure influence, status and wealth through acceptance of their aims to improve living standards, rebuild the nation, and safeguard patriarchal families (Castells 1998: 223–5).

China is the most important example of a developmental-type state today. Its size and rapid economic growth make it a rival to the United States as a global superpower. Chinese officials represent China as demonstrating an alternative model of human rights to those of the West. Although still run by the Communist Party, China is now a signatory to all the major UN human rights treaties, including the ICCPR. Chinese officials have not yet, however, ratified the ICCPR, and they have put a reservation on the ICESCR banning independent trades unions. In the White Papers that are published each year, officials insist that China will set its own human rights standards, defending the developmental model that privileges social and economic benefits over abstract freedoms whilst attacking Western states for hypocrisy, racism and imperialist intentions against China. They also link human rights to 'Asian values', suggesting that high rates of crime and unhappiness in the West demonstrate that the individualism celebrated in liberal democracies make a stable and harmonious society impossible.[10] In terms of foreign policy, Chinese officials insist on the value of state sovereignty and not interfering in the affairs of other peoples. The Chinese government has made important links with leaders across Africa over the last decade to secure supplies of oil, to create investment opportunities, and to open up African markets for manufactured goods. State officials justify the fact that they put no conditions on aid or investment in development projects on the grounds that they respect sovereignty, are against imperialism, and hold that domestic conflicts are better settled by those directly involved (Rotberg 2008). Both internally and externally, then, Chinese state officials promote social and economic rights over civil and political rights in ways that exemplify the developmental state.

Violations of civil and political rights by officials of the Chinese state are well known outside China. There have been legal reforms in China, but they are more concerned with regulating business contracts than with human rights. In terms of civil rights, what is especially well known is the repression of human rights activists. Whilst 'counter-revolutionary' activities are no longer a crime in China, 'endangering state security' has replaced it as the main way of dealing with dissent. Punishments include indefinite detention without trial in 'complicated cases', imprisonment in harsh 're-education camps' where hard labour is part of the regime, torture and immediate execution (often on the same day that the defendant is found guilty). Moreover, it is not just political crimes that are dealt with harshly. In general, despite legal reforms, ordinary criminal procedures do not seem to be based on rational-legal procedures. The principle that defendants are innocent until proven guilty was only recently introduced in China, torture to extract confessions is routine, conviction rates in the courts may be as high as 99 per cent, and the numbers of those executed each year is in the tens of thousands (though the actual number is a state secret). In addition, the political system in China fundamentally violates international standards of political rights because it remains a single-party state, not a democracy. State restrictions on freedom of speech and religion, censorship of the media, the persecution of members of the Falun Gong movement – these have all led to international condemnation of China for human rights abuses over the last couple of decades.[11]

Economic and social rights are also being violated in China. Whilst there has been massive economic growth over the last decade, making China the world's second biggest economy after the United States in 2013 according to International Monetary Fund (IMF) calculations, in terms of per capita income it remains a very poor country. Industrialisation is concentrated in the special economic zones of the coastal cities, where working conditions are harsh, and there is massive discrimination against rural workers – called migrants – who have only temporary permits to live and work in factories and in construction in cities. They are denied rights to housing, education and health-care, and they are not permitted to bring their families to live with them. At the same time, the construction boom has created displacement, loss of livelihood and unemployment for many. In terms of health-care, state secrecy has been a problem in controlling infections (such as HIV), and epidemics (like SARS and avian flu) have endangered massive numbers of people in China and beyond (Ching 2008; Hsing 2010). In fact, the premise of the developmental state, that social and economic rights take precedence over civil and political rights, is fundamentally flawed. As Amartya Sen has argued, in the absence of civil rights to share information and to protest against inequalities, economic growth will damage people's health and welfare, and benefits will be very unevenly distributed (Sen 1999). Without media that is free from censorship, enabling injustices and corruption to be brought to light, and without the freedom to mount sustained campaigns to achieve social and economic rights, it is not clear that the Party itself can even know about, let alone manage, the various inequalities that are being produced by the rapid marketisation of China's economy (Shirk 2011).

What are the possibilities for institutionalising international human rights norms in the developmental state? Inside China, civil and political rights do not seem to be a high priority. Although every day there are protests over corruption, working and housing conditions and also environmental damage, there is no popular movement for human rights. In addition, there is widespread suspicion amongst Chinese intellectuals that the championing of human rights masks imperialist interests.[12] Chinese development has resulted in real benefits for many people, and the state is far less intrusive into personal life than it was during communism. Though inequalities and crime have increased, it seems there is widespread optimism in China that the state will deliver benefits for everyone. Of course, this makes the Party vulnerable if economic development should slow down, but it seems very unlikely that an authoritarian Party under threat would become *less* repressive. In this respect it is notable that the People's Liberation Army, on which the capacity of the Party to retain control of resources concentrated in the state ultimately relies, continues to be well funded and to retain its status and authority (Dreyer 2010).

The Chinese state in the twenty-first century is continually reforming, politically and legally as well as economically. It is extremely difficult to predict what these reforms will create (as indicated by the huge numbers of books that have been written on this topic over the last few decades) in part because of state secrecy and repression. Certainly pressure from outside is muted. Although critical of China's human rights abuses, Northwestern states are reluctant to deal strictly with Chinese elites. Not only is China a huge market for their manufactured goods, the Chinese state is also prominent in the UN – with veto power on the Security Council – and growing in influence in IGOs like the G20 and the World Trade Organization (WTO) (China has not yet been accepted into the G8). In fact it is quite surprising when there is any discussion at all of China's human rights record in diplomatic circles and IGOs.

Transforming states

International human rights law is the focus of so much of the inter-disciplinary study of human rights that anyone approaching the study of human rights for the first time could be forgiven for thinking that establishing the rule of law is what is most important. It is in this respect that the juridical state is presupposed; not just in making international human rights agreements but also in the scholarship on human rights. The juridical state is presupposed as existing or as a necessity that must be achieved if human rights are to be realised in practice.

From the perspective of political sociology, there are a number of problems with this assumption. First, the juridical state that is presupposed in international human rights law does not exist. And even when it is approximated, as it is in Northwestern states, and when they are bound to all the relevant treaties and conventions, human rights are not guaranteed. Even the civil rights of national citizens can *legally* and routinely be breached within the territories of Northwestern states, and social and economic rights are even more precarious; while the rights of non-citizens both inside and outside state territories are more likely to be honoured in the breach than in the observance by officials of these states. 'Cause lawyers', whistle-blowers, broad-based social movements, NGOs, unions – networks of organisations and individuals that cross boundaries between the 'inside' and the 'outside' of states: these are all vitally important to the realisation of human rights by Northwestern states at home and abroad. The demands they make go far beyond limiting the state by the rule of law.

Second, the assumption that it is only through juridical states that human rights can be realised is linked to international attempts to rebuild states organised through the UN, to create the conditions for the rule of law and bureaucracy. This is problematic because it seems to suggest that technocratic solutions to systematic violations of human rights are possible and desirable. Rebuilding what are commonly thought of as 'failed' states has been a significant commitment at the UN in the last two decades.[13] It seems that attempts to do so led by experts, lawyers and bureaucrats and supported by UN peacekeeping forces have been relatively successful in Kosovo, Bosnia and East Timor – though there have also been continuing problems of human rights violations during the process of rebuilding, and we do not know how long peace will last in these states. Making a juridical state by technocratic means is, however, extremely expensive, and it has only been relatively successful in these very small territories. Generally UN 'peacekeeping operations' are more piecemeal: they are more like the measures that supplement the state in the DRC we have looked at here. Other international attempts at state-building that have been less comprehensive than those in Kosovo, Bosnia and East Timor, but still very intensive, have failed spectacularly – most notably in Afghanistan and Iraq. We look in more detail at all these examples in Chapter 4. What seems to be clear is that technocratic approaches to state-building that focus on legal code and bureaucratic procedures without transforming the structures in which states are embedded will not succeed in making violators into guarantors of human rights.

Third, most states in the world today have been formed historically through colonialisation that ended only in the mid-twentieth century. It is not clear whether they *can* be transformed to more closely resemble the juridical state. In fact, it can be argued that it is *more likely* that Northwestern states will come to resemble post-colonial states. This is the case that is made by Jean and John Comaroff in their provocative book, *Theory from the South*. They argue that fragmentation and impoverishment growing in the Northwest as a result of neo-liberalism and the shift of capitalist economic growth to Latin America, Asia and Africa will mean more people in North America and Europe living in conditions that resemble those of the Global South. If increased repression, authoritarian policing of dissent, and limited economic opportunities converge so that people become more dependent on informal networks rather than on the relative peace and prosperity that were organised for citizens through Northwestern states for a relatively brief period in the second half of the twentieth century, the Comaroffs suggest that the world will be turned upside down (see Comaroff and Comaroff 2012). Margaret Somers argues that some people in the United States who have never enjoyed the benefits of full citizenship already experience the state as 'post-colonial'. Faced with a state that barely meets the basic needs of the poor (as exemplified in the response to Hurricane Katrina), and that presents especially racialised minorities almost exclusively with its repressive face, one response is to organise locally and to demand human rights internationally to try to make national officials more responsive (Somers 2008). Finding it impossible to gain any purchase with US state officials through national channels alone, people are trying to bring them to account through international human rights commitments, especially with regard to social and economic rights.

Campaigns for human rights are innovative and creative in India and Latin America. Movements like those studied by Dreze and Sen in India, as well as the women's movement there (see pp. 128–31), the Treatment Action Campaign in South Africa (pp. 34–8), and Via Campesina in Latin America (pp. 108–10) offer creative approaches to achieving human rights in practice. They involve making changes to the content of the law and also to administrative norms by making bureaucracies more transparent and accountable. In addition they involve decentralisation, to enable people to participate more directly in what concerns them at the local level whilst at the same time addressing how the conditions of their lives are entangled in national and international structures.

We have seen in this chapter how states are situated in structures that organise resources over which state officials have some, but not complete, control. It is extraordinarily difficult to transform states from violators to guarantors of human rights because structures are rooted in everyday life and supported by people whose deeply felt interests are tied up with the status quo. I have argued in this chapter that too much of the attention of human rights scholarship has been given to international human rights law at the expense of studying the politics through which state officials try to manage the material and moral resources on which states depend. This is not to say, however, that realising human rights in practice depends *only* on states, as if they existed in isolation. Given that the structures in which states are embedded are international and transnational, international duty-bearers of human rights are also crucial to realising human rights in practice. It is to the UN as the principal international duty-bearer of human rights that we now turn.

4 The United Nations: not a world state

> [R]ecognition of the inherent dignity and of the equal and inalienable rights of all members of the human family is the foundation of freedom, justice and peace in the world.
>
> (Universal Declaration of Human Rights Preamble)

> The Organization is based on the principle of the sovereign equality of all its Members.
>
> (United Nations Charter Article 2)

In principle, we have human rights simply by virtue of being human. We have rights regardless of which state we happen to be born into, what happens to that state, where we go or where we live. In this sense – though it sounds rather grandiose – whether or not a person actually enjoys human rights is the responsibility of the world.

It was in the newly founded UN that human rights were declared to be essential to all human beings. The Universal Declaration of Human Rights of 1948 affirmed that 'All human beings are born free and equal in dignity and rights' (Article 1). The declaration is not, strictly speaking, a legal document. It is more in the nature of a promise. The Universal Declaration of Human Rights (UDHR) is the promise that the atrocities committed by the Nazis – the 'barbarous acts which have outraged the conscience of mankind' in the words of the preamble to the declaration – would not be allowed to happen to anyone ever again. The preamble goes on to herald 'the advent of a world in which human beings shall enjoy freedom of speech and belief and freedom from fear and want ... as the highest aspiration of the common people'. No longer should individuals be killed, tortured, maimed, or allowed to suffer hunger and despair simply because they happen to live in an oppressive state, or because their neighbours believe they should not be there. 'Everyone is entitled to all the rights and freedoms set forth in this Declaration, without distinction of any kind, such as race, colour, sex, language, religion, political or other opinion, national or social origin, property, birth or other status' (Article 2).

It was in the UN, then, that the contemporary social construction of human rights was inaugurated. And within the UN there are continuing efforts to construct human rights in ways that will make good on the promises of the UDHR and the conventions and treaties that have built on it. The UN remains the only organisation with responsibility for ensuring human rights globally. It is a complex, sprawling and amorphous organisation with a multitude of branches, committees and offices. Some of these are known as 'the human rights machinery'. They include the Human Rights Council, the treaty bodies, the Special Rapporteurs, and the Office of the High Commissioner for Human Rights. State-led forums concerned with security (the Security Council), and with the building of international consensus (the General Assembly), and the staff who work directly for the Secretary General are also concerned with standard-setting, monitoring – and even on occasion trying to protect human rights in practice. In addition there are branches of the UN that are more or less distinct organisations dedicated to health (World Health Organization, WHO), education and culture (United Nations Educational, Scientific and Cultural Organization, UNESCO), children (United Nations Children's Fund, UNICEF), refugees (especially United Nations High Commission for Refugess, UNHCR, which we will discuss more fully in Chapter 7), women (United Nations Development Fund for Women, UNIFEM), labour organisations (the International Labour Organization, ILO), development (the United Nations Development Programme, UNDP), food and agriculture (the Food and Agriculture Organization, FAO) and many, many more. There are ongoing projects within the UN to 'mainstream' human rights so that, in principle all these branches are supposed to be involved in trying to construct human rights in ways that will make them really effective in the not-too-distant future. In this chapter we will focus on the 'human rights machinery' and the state-led so-called 'political' bodies of the UN.

Structures of 'sovereign inequalities'

The UN was never intended to be anything like a world state. From its beginnings, it was structured to face in several different directions at the same time with regard to human rights. The UDHR and subsequent international human rights law that builds on it offer individuals and groups extensive protection against repression within states and make states responsible for ensuring that everyone has the basic necessities of life. In the 1970s, most states signed and ratified the International Covenant on Civil and Political Rights (ICCPR), the International Covenant on Economic, Social and Cultural Rights (ICESCR), the Convention on the Elimination of All Forms of Discrimination against Women (CEDAW), the Convention on the Elimination of All Forms of Racial Discrimination (ICERD) and the Convention on Torture (CAT). The Convention on the Rights of the Child (CRC) came into force in 1990. In each case these conventions go beyond the UDHR, which was never intended to have binding force, creating mechanisms to monitor and to put pressure on states to conform to the emerging body of international human rights law.

On the other hand, the UN is structured to safeguard respect for state sovereignty. The UN Charter is above all a legal agreement between sovereign states not to interfere in each other's affairs. In international law, 'sovereignty' means that it is illegal to infringe on the independence of a state, its right and power to govern itself. The UN, like other IGOs, has what Barnett and Finnemore call 'delegated authority'. Offices and branches of the UN are given tasks (known as 'mandates') by UN member states and allowed specific ways of collecting and combining the resources with which to deal with them. The delegated authority of the UN is dependent on what is required and what is allowed by states (Barnett and Finnemore 2004). In addition, the UN was structured in such a way as to accommodate what were called the 'Great Powers' at the end of the Second World War – the United States, Russia, China, the UK and France. It would not have been possible to create the UN at all without the co-operation of the leaders of the 'Great Powers', and it was built in a particular way in order to secure that co-operation (Mazower 2004, 2012). The legal equality of state sovereignty was never intended to be equivalent to equality of geo-political *influence*. In fact the UN is structured around the principle of what Jack Donnelly calls '*sovereign inequalities*' (Donnelly 2006).

Different branches of the UN are more or less formally structured by 'sovereign inequalities'. Sovereign inequalities are most evident in the UN Security Council. In the General Assembly all member states have one vote each – a structure that formally recognises their equality as sovereigns. In contrast only some states are represented in the Security Council – the only authority that can legally sanction military intervention in a member state. Nothing in the UN Charter authorises interference in the domestic affairs of states except where the Security Council unanimously decides that they represent a threat to international peace and security. The Security Council has five permanent members, the United States, Russia, China, the UK and France, who are now joined by ten other states (always including representatives from Africa, Asia and Latin America) elected by the General Assembly and rotating on a two-year cycle. A decision to intervene in the affairs of a member state, whether by sanctions or by military means, requires 'yes' votes from all ten states, and no veto from any of the permanent members. In part the 'Great Power' status of members of the Security Council is a matter of ongoing mutual and self-recognition as well as historically structured position. The UK and France have not used their veto power since 1989: they are no longer world powers as they were fifty years ago. On the other hand, there is no real prospect of Brazil, South Africa or India, rising powers in their regions, becoming permanent members of the Security Council.

Beyond the Security Council representatives of the United States, Russia and China try to shape the international human rights agenda across UN committees and offices. They do so by making alliances with the representatives of other states. Officials from both Russia and China lead bloc voting of states based in their geographical regions, with additional allies in Latin America, the Middle East and (especially now in the case of China) in Africa too. Russian and Chinese officials evade accountability for human rights violations for themselves and their allies by framing their positions as resistance to US imperialism. Representatives from the United States are most commonly allied with those from European member states, and with some from states in the Middle East (Israel, and also Eygpt) and Asia (notably Pakistan). US officials do exert exceptional influence over human rights at the UN in comparison with those from China and Russia. What is especially important is that many of the professionals who work at the UN were educated in the United States: this gives representatives of the United States an advantage in networking and in understanding the language of human rights reports and the nuances of rules and procedures through which international human rights law is monitored. It is also notable that the UN headquarters is in New York (with smaller offices in Geneva, Vienna and Nairobi), and the United States is the biggest single contributor to the UN budget. Planning for the UDHR was overseen by Eleanor Roosevelt, wife of the US president, in the 1940s, and it is not difficult to argue that human rights are a US export with little or no resonance in other 'cultures'. This was a common theme of debates over 'Asian values' in the 1990s. Accusations of cultural relativism have become less prominent in recent years at the UN (except with regard to gender, as we shall see in Chapter 6) as even Chinese officials now accept the main principles of human rights, at least in principle (see pp. 59–63). What replaced 'cultural relativism' during the US-led 'War on Terror' were accusations of US imperialism – which we will look at later in this chapter with respect to 'humanitarian intervention'. But it is interesting that the United States is notorious for *not* signing and/or ratifying international human rights agreements. It is one of the very few states that has not ratified the ICESCR or CEDAW, and nor has it signed the optional protocol to the ICCPR (which enables individuals to bring complaints against states to the Human Rights Council) (Mertus 2004; Ignatieff 2005). The fact that the 'Great Powers' dominate the UN, and that they do not support, recognise or, very often, even come close to complying with major international human rights treaties is a serious obstacle to the realisation of human rights through the UN (Freedman 2014).

Standard-setting and monitoring

The way the UN is structured does not mean that what happens there is completely under the control of the officials of the 'Great Powers' or determined by how they represent their interests. In fact the purpose of delegating authority to the UN is often to solve problems about which relatively little is known, it is unclear what can be done, and international co-operation is seen as necessary. Mandates change over time – and in general they have been expanded at the UN. Professionals at the UN create their own aims and means for dealing with the problems they have been set, establishing their authority in relation to the bureaucrats, diplomats and politicians who represent states. As Barnett and Finnemore have shown, through politics within the bureaucratic structures of the UN, officials and experts have gained a degree of relative autonomy, a certain freedom of thought and action, even from representatives of the 'Great Powers' (Barnett and Finnemore 2004).

Apart from their delegated authority, professionals in the UN are able to construct themselves as having moral, expert and rational-legal authority. They claim moral authority on the grounds that they are concerned with the values and interests of humanity, beyond the limited national framings represented by member states. They claim expert authority on the basis of their educational training and credentials, the detailed reports they produce and their policy recommendations. They also claim rational-legal authority. According to Barnett and Finnemore it is above all bureaucracy that enables the relative autonomy of the UN as an organisation. In terms of everyday practice, all the branches of the UN are hierarchically structured by offices and procedures, reports and forms that must be filled out, protocols concerning who speaks when, who makes decisions and on what basis. People who work there learn the rules and the professional terminology, and they thereby gain the authority to guide others through procedures, protocols, reports and decision-making. It is for this reason, Barnett and Finnemore argue, that what comes out of UN procedures and reports are *technocratic* solutions to the problems set by mandates. What is most important is *how* things are done, not the results of what is done. In fact, 'action' largely involves putting in place more procedures and more reports. Within what are supposed to be neutral and impartial administrative procedures, however, there is politics. The language that is used in reports is highly selective: it frames problems in certain ways precisely in order to produce or to prevent very specific ways of seeing the world, which in turn have concrete consequences in practice (Barnett and Finnemore 2004).

The cultural politics of human rights are embedded in bureaucracy at the UN. International declarations, treaties and conventions are based on consensus: they are drawn up in lengthy meetings in which what matters is attention to the detail of language. International human rights law is all about *words* – what must be put in and what must be left out in order to get agreement that is as broad as possible between representatives of member states. It is words that frame human rights 'wrongs' and the consequences for action that are to be expected from states as a result of making international agreements. Accounts of the committee sessions in which human rights documents are made emphasise the detailed scrutiny that each and every word is given. What they also show is that in the end what is most important in these committee meetings is getting agreement from all the participants. Without agreement there will be nothing to show for all the work – there will be no final document (Merry 2006). Very often, then, what comes out of the extremely lengthy processes of creating human rights agreements are documents that have been carefully and precisely crafted with wording that allows states to *avoid* taking action to end human rights abuses. CEDAW is a notorious example. Although there is no doubt that it was an achievement to have women's rights recognised when it was adopted at the General Assembly in 1979, CEDAW was accepted with very serious limitations. States are permitted to make reservations on a convention – opting out of certain provisions – provided that they continue to observe its object and purpose. The reservations on CEDAW are numerous, and in many countries they make attempts to end discrimination against women impossible. A number of states signed and ratified CEDAW only on the basis of excluding family and religious law for consideration. Eygpt, for example, signed and ratified CEDAW with the reservation that where equality between men and women clashes with Sharia law, it will not be considered relevant. In Eygpt at the time of ratification in 1981, this was understood to 'restrict[s] the wife's rights to divorce by making it contingent on a judge's ruling, whereas no such restriction is laid down in the case of the husband'. Although CEDAW has been signed and ratified by most states, ruling the family out of the remit of rights draws a sharp distinction between public and private life that is one of the main ways in which discrimination against women is naturalised. As a result, until NGOs working with the UN revived the issue of women's rights in the 1990s, CEDAW was seen as making very little difference to women's lives in practice (see Chapter 6).

How are human rights agreements *supposed* to make a difference to people's lives? The UN has no means of enforcing human rights in practice. Creating bureaucratic procedures is in part a solution to the problem of what UN officials can realistically hope to do. Once a convention has been agreed, a system for monitoring it is put in place. The main arenas for monitoring human rights on a regular basis at the UN are the Human Rights Council and the treaty bodies.[1] In these forums representatives of states present 'country reports' that detail what has been done to fulfil obligations according to international human rights law, how well they have succeeded or failed, and what officials plan to do in the future in order to end torture, raise women's literacy rates, ensure that migrants are treated fairly according to due process and so on. In most cases 'country reports' presented on behalf of states are supplemented by NGO reports too. States vary immensely in how respectfully and conscientiously their officials address these various committees, none of which has any means of enforcing compliance with their recommendations. It is on the basis of monitoring procedures like those of the treaty bodies that the UN has been called 'a paper paradise for its advocates and bureaucrats that fails to touch the world's victims' (Harry Steiner quoted in Oberleitner 2007: 17).

If UN procedures for monitoring human rights are a paper paradise, why is so much effort put into getting international agreements in the first place, and then into assessing how well they are working? There is a cynical answer: generally those involved are paid to be there and they also gain a good deal of respect and status because they work at the UN. On the other hand, setting standards of human rights does at least make 'wrongs' visible: it affirms fundamental values on which 'the world' agrees and so gives NGOs and grassroots movements support in terms of validating ideals of justice and well-being. If human rights did not exist, perhaps it would be necessary to invent them as standards to which the world *should* aspire? It is because human rights conventions can be effective at least in making violations visible that NGOs and their supporters within the UN campaign work so long and hard to create them. And it is also for this reason, and because of the symbolic weight they carry as representing a kind of 'world conscience', that those who do not find them acceptable or who are unwilling to be held to standards of fair treatment fight so hard to prevent them becoming international human rights law.

In Chapter 2 we looked at Amnesty's campaign to have the Argentinian government acknowledge the torture and disappearances of its political opponents and to change state practices that had resulted in such serious human rights violations (pp. 22–4). What this example shows is that monitoring human rights in the treaty bodies of the UN is just *part* of any successful campaign to win respect for human rights. Human rights can only be realised in practice far beyond the committee rooms of the UN. As Julie Mertus puts it: 'At its best, the process creates opportunities for governments, NGOs and other members of civil society, including, for example the media, to have a constructive dialogue regarding national priorities, successes, best practices, and challenges in meeting convention obligations' (Mertus 2005: 86).

In practice, however, many representatives of states in UN monitoring systems treat them rather as an opportunity to *evade* scrutiny of human rights violations for which they are responsible, even when they have signed and ratified international agreements. They are able to do so by failing to submit proper reports and treating the procedures with disdain, indifference or hostility. It is an irony of the UN system that the states involved in the most systematic and routine violations of human rights are also the most likely to be secretive, to practice censorship and to resist investigation by NGOs and UN special rapporteurs. According to Rosa Freedman, however, at least a *quarter* of the world's states have been complicit in torture and disappearances since the beginning of the US-led 'War on Terror'. They include not just the United States and UK but also – much more surprisingly – Sweden and Denmark (Freedman 2014: 2). What this suggests is that human rights monitoring does not work to prevent the violation of human rights in *any state* – even those that strongly support the UN, and even where what are often considered the most fundamental rights are concerned. In effect, the system is set up to make human rights effective only through the action of state officials when they care about how they appear at committee meetings at the UN. In practice, rather than resulting in universal adherence to human rights principles and genuine attempts to make them effective, human rights monitoring results in a patchy, 'layered' commitment to human rights norms as state officials pick and choose what, how and when they will observe them (Oberleitner 2007: 102).

Bureaucracy is not only limited and ineffectual as a way of producing commitment to human rights; critics of the UN also argue that it is alienating: deadening emotion and sensitivity to the suffering that is actually supposed to be addressed by documents, reports and procedures. Probably the most celebrated aspect of UN human rights monitoring, and a feature that has been hard-fought by advocates, is that in many cases it actually does enable the voices of individuals suffering violations to be heard. Individuals may make their case to the UN as a representative or a guest of an NGO that has consultative status; they may also do so through what are called 'optional protocols', agreed on as part of the monitoring system of most of the major human rights conventions. An optional protocol allows an individual to bring a direct complaint against a state on the basis that his or her human rights are being violated. In the opening pages of her book, *Failing to Protect*, Rosa Freedman gives an account of a scene she saw at the UN: Mr Gibril Hamid, a refugee from Darfur, was addressing the Human Rights Council, describing what he had seen of attacks on villagers by government soldiers, raping, murdering and setting fire to houses. While he was talking, '[p]eople wandered around the Chamber, talking on mobile phones, rustling papers or gathering up their belongings. The webcast of his statement shows people walking into and out of the row directly behind the speaker: the hum of voices accompanying Mr Hamid's words' (Freedman 2014: xiv). There is a sense in which, when suffering is framed as a matter of human rights 'wrongs' which are then dealt with at great length in meetings, reports, more meetings and more reports, it can seem to everyone involved as if some good is being done when actually – even when they are physically there – all connection with those who are actually suffering has been lost. At these moments, it is hard to avoid the conclusion that bureaucracy itself is dehumanising, stripping individuals who work in it of any real moral sense, reducing them to 'cogs in an administrative machinery' (Barnett 2003: 8). In UN human rights monitoring the risk is that bureaucratic procedures and processes not only become equivalent to action, they completely displace any real sense of connection with the people whose suffering they are supposed to bring to an end.

From headquarters to the field

It is difficult now to imagine the euphoria of the end of the Cold War and the new possibilities of genuinely realising human rights it seemed to open up at the UN (see Barnett 2003). There seemed to be a real possibility of constituting a new international order guided by principles of human rights and of going beyond talk, beyond the rational-legal procedures of bureaucracy, to actually alter practices within states to end human rights violations. Throughout the 1990s and into the twenty-first century there was hope that the UN could become something more like a world state with resources of authority, money, even military force where it was felt to be absolutely necessary, to make a difference to the conditions in which people suffer from human rights abuses.

In part these changes involved a challenge to the ideal of 'sovereignty' encoded in the UN Charter. Rather than control over territory by an independent nation-state, in the 1990s 'sovereignty' was redefined across a range of settings as a *responsibility to protect* populations from human rights violations.[2] The new definition of sovereignty as responsibility was recognised in a speech by Secretary General Kofi Annan in 1999:

> Sovereignty … is being redefined – not least by the forces of globalization and international co-operation. States are now widely understood to be instruments at the service of their peoples, and not vice versa. At the same time individual sovereignty – by which I mean the fundamental freedom of each individual, enshrined in the Charter of the UN and subsequent international treaties – has been enhanced by a renewed and spreading consciousness of individual rights. When we read the Charter today we are more than ever conscious that its aim is to protect individual human beings, not to protect those who abuse them.
>
> (Quoted in Weiss 2007: 96–7)

One of the most important challenges to state sovereignty as the right to govern without interference from other states was the setting up of international courts. In the 1990s the Security Council set up international tribunals to try military commanders and politicians accused of war crimes and genocide in the former Yugoslavia (the International Criminal Tribunal for the Former Yugoslavia, the ICTY) and Rwanda (the International Criminal Tribunal for Rwanda, the ICTR). It was the first time individuals had been held to account for gross violations of human rights under international law since the Nuremberg Trials that were held immediately after the Second World War. These tribunals also had the power to prosecute military commanders and political leaders regardless of their standing within their own states. But military leaders and politicians enjoyed diplomatic immunity during the Cold War: they could not be prosecuted for any actions they took as the heads of sovereign states.[3] The International Criminal Court (ICC) was set up in 2002 as a permanent court with a mandate to prosecute individuals, including elected politicians and military commanders who are accused of committing genocide, war crimes and crimes against humanity (see Oberleitner 2007; Sikkink 2011). The ICC goes beyond state sovereignty in that the states that have joined have agreed to compel anyone the ICC prosecutes for gross violations of human rights to stand for trial, regardless of their standing within their own state and regardless of national law at the time. It is, however, limited by the fact that the United States has refused to allow its military personnel to be subject to the court's jurisdiction, and China, India, Russia and Turkey have refused or have not yet ratified its founding statute. In fact, the UK and France are the only members of the Security Council that have joined the ICC. In addition, it is remarkable that from its beginnings in 2002 until the time of writing this in 2014, *only* African leaders have been indicted by the ICC, a fact that does not inspire confidence in its ability to administer law impartially, or to act as a world court (Mazower 2012: 399–405).

Another challenge to the ideal of sovereignty as non-interference has been the increased use of economic sanctions. Since the end of the Cold War the UN Security Council has been increasingly ready to endorse economic sanctions and arms embargoes as part of its role to maintain international peace and security. Only Rhodesia and South Africa were subject to economic sanctions before the 1990s. Sanctions against South Africa, which included boycotting cultural and sporting activities as well as trade, were widely seen as contributing to the end of the apartheid system. As a result, 'comprehensive sanctions' (banning trade, and also international flights and transnational financial transactions and seizing assets) were seen as a valuable way to make authoritarian governments accountable for human rights violations in international law. Taken against the former Yugoslavia and Iraq in the 1990s, they resulted in terrible suffering for civilians in these countries. As a result of protests against the suffering caused by 'comprehensive sanctions', 'targeted sanctions' have become more popular in the UN. They have included arms embargoes, travel bans, and embargoes on particular trades (diamonds in Angola, for example, oil in Libya, Angola and Sierra Leone). These have been accompanied too by an increasing readiness by the UN Security Council to 'name and shame' governments that find a way round the sanctions it imposes (Bellamy 2009: 139–46).

Most controversial in terms of redefining state sovereignty through the UN are humanitarian interventions, the use of military force to end gross violations of human rights. Indeed, 'humanitarian intervention' is *so* controversial that for many people it now stands for 'illegal and unjustified war in the name of human rights'. In the UN, military intervention that is legally permitted by the Security Council is called 'peacekeeping' – though the term 'humanitarian intervention' was used in debates over whether it was justified to stop genocide and ethnic cleansing in the 1990s. In 1999, for example, Kofi Annan challenged opponents:

> If humanitarian intervention is indeed an unacceptable assault on
> sovereignty, how do we respond to a Rwanda, to a Srebenica – to gross

and systematic violations of human rights that offend every precept of
our common humanity?

(Quoted in Mertus 2005: 125)

During the 1990s and into the twenty-first century, in many cases
'peacekeeping' became indistinguishable from 'humanitarian intervention'. Traditional UN peacekeeping operations were rare. In the 1970s
just three new peacekeeping operations were authorised, and there were
no more until 1988 – compared to thirty-eight in the 1990s (Mazower
2012: 382). Traditional peacekeeping operations were almost always
carried out at the invitation of a member state, after an initial agreement had been signed, and with the aim of using minimum force in
order to allow peace to be established. They remained clearly within
the remit of the UN to safeguard state sovereignty. Since the end of
the Cold War, however, there has been a far greater willingness to 'put
boots on the ground' *without* a state's consent and when peace agreements are known to be precarious and reversible or when they have
not been agreed by all parties to the conflict. In human rights terms,
where a state is in breach of what are known legally as 'peremptory
norms', or fundamental human rights to freedom from state violence,
it is increasingly understood that military intervention *without the permission of that state* is justified to protect civilians. Charges of genocide, war crimes and crimes against humanity may now justify military
intervention without the permission of the states that are held to be
responsible, either because political and military leaders are implicated
in gross violations of human rights or because they cannot prevent
atrocities.[4]

At the UN it is now understood that successful 'comprehensive
peacekeeping operations' must end with free and fair elections.
For this to be possible, states must be rebuilt. In many cases this
is a consequence of bombing from the air, which destroys a country's infrastructure and communications systems and which is the
favoured military strategy for humanitarian interventions because it
minimises troop casualties. State-building is also seen as necessary
because where state officials were implicated in or unable to prevent gross violations of human rights, politicians and judges must be
replaced, or at least closely monitored, and the failures of legislation
and administration must be addressed. In Bosnia, Kosovo and East
Timor, 'transitional administrations' involved complete control of a

territory. In 'transitional administrations' international experts take over completely, remaking governmental and juridical branches of the state, as well as creating and overseeing national security forces. UN Security Council resolutions granted extensive, and controversial, control over the appointment of state officials and the making of new laws in Kosovo and East Timor. In Bosnia it was agreement between different groups in the country that authorised the High Representative, supported by UN and EU experts and NATO troops, to have oversight of rebuilding the state.[5] 'Transitional administrations' are exceptional. They are extremely expensive; they have only been carried out in small territories, and only where Northwestern states have declared a strategic interest in the area. In Afghanistan and Iraq, state-building was far more limited. It was different too because it followed foreign invasion, not civil war. State-building was called 'light footprint' in Afghanistan and Iraq: people living in these states would be involved as much as possible; they would take 'ownership' for creating democracy and the rule of law. In both cases interim governments were appointed under the supervision of US military leaders and favoured national political figures: in the Iraqi case they were mostly exiles; in Afghanistan, they were national political figures and military allies (including militia leaders of the Northern Alliance who had helped NATO forces defeat the Taliban). Subsequently, interim governments drew up constitutions, and elections were held that were judged to have been reasonably free and fair. In both Afghanistan and Iraq 'light footprint' state-building was dominated by military priorities. Both wars were very unpopular in the United States and Europe. Consequently international troops aimed to bring insurgents under control and to establish national security forces to take over so that they would be able to go home as soon as possible.

The principal controversy over humanitarian interventions is that they are effectively imperialism justified in the name of respect for human rights. Formal imperialism – the direct rule of people inside a territory by a dominant state outside that territory – was brought to an end with decolonisation in the 1960s. But criticisms are made of the use of military force to realise human rights on the grounds that it furthers *informal* or neo-imperialism, the *in*direct rule of peoples who live in other states for the benefit of the dominant state.[6]

For critics of humanitarian intervention the most important question is 'who decides?' The answer is somehow both complex and simple. The UN has no standing army. UN peacekeeping depends on the deployment of efficient, well-trained and well-equipped forces by its members. In principle there is a clear *legal* distinction between UN peacekeeping operations, which can only be agreed by the Security Council, and those that are led by military alliances like NATO, 'coalitions of the willing' or regional organisations like the European Union or the African Union. But in terms of 'boots on the ground', the difference is a good deal less obvious. Peacekeeping operations that are UN-authorised are often led by particular forces: NATO led UN operations in Bosnia in 1992, Australia led UN operations in East Timor in 1999. On other occasions the Security Council has sanctioned peacekeeping operations and state-building *after* the forces of other states have invaded in the name of 'humanitarian intervention'. This was the case after NATO bombed the Serbian militias out of Kosovo in 1999, and after the NATO invasions of Afghanistan in 2001 and of Iraq in 2003.

There is no doubt that the United States was the dominant state at the UN at the end of the Cold War – when it was often referred to as the 'sole remaining superpower'. Building up military power that the USSR and China could not hope to match was the US security strategy during the Reagan administration of the 1980s. As a consequence, by the 1990s the United States had unrivalled fire-power and military technology. The United States continues to spend more on its military than all the other countries in the world combined (Weiss 2009: 5). The drone attacks that are still ongoing to kill people the US authorities consider a security risk in Pakistan are just the most spectacular instance of military technology today (Ayoob and Zierler 2005; Bhatt 2012). Any form of military intervention, whether sanctioned by the Security Council or not, is simply impossible without the agreement of US advisors, military commanders and politicians. It would be inconceivable to carry out peacekeeping operations *against* what US officials consider to be the interests of their state. In addition, the United States has led humanitarian interventions in which the UN has become implicated after bombing and invasion in the name of human rights. In a sense, then, the answer to the question 'who decides?' when there will be humanitarian intervention has been 'the US president'.

It is especially around humanitarian interventions in Afghanistan in 2001 and Iraq in 2003 that the UN has been implicated in furthering the military and geo-political aims and strategies of US state officials. The reasons that were given for both these invasions shifted as the occasion demanded, but human rights violations (especially of women under the Taliban in Afghanistan and of Kurds by Saddam Hussein) were certainly part of the reasoning proposed by the Bush administration (supported very vocally by UK Prime Minister Tony Blair). In fact, neither the invasion of Afghanistan or of Iraq was legally sanctioned by the UN Security Council as a humanitarian intervention. The invasion of Afghanistan in 2001 was legally permitted, but on the rather vague, and quite traditional grounds that US self-defence permitted it as the Taliban were reportedly hiding Al-Qaeda who had just claimed responsibility for the 9/11 attacks. The Security Council *refused on several occasions* to legalise the invasion of Iraq in 2003. In 2004 Kofi Annan, then Secretary General of the UN, denounced it as illegal in no uncertain terms (Sands 2005: 175). Nevertheless, the UN subsequently mandated missions to maintain security and to enable state-building in Afghanistan and Iraq after the invasions (UNAMA in Afghanistan from 2002 and UNAMI in Iraq from 2003). In this way the UN willingly contributed to 'regime change', which was undoubtedly the aim of both invasions by the United States and its allies.

Despite these ongoing controversies over humanitarian intervention and neo-imperialism, in 2005 there was unanimous agreement on 'the Responsibility to Protect' at a UN World Summit. It was agreed in the Responsibility to Protect that the purpose of a state is to protect the people within its territory, and that when it does not or cannot, people whose lives are threatened there become a matter of concern to the 'international community'. Where civilians are in immediate danger for their lives, military intervention is justified without a state's consent. In other words, when a state does not accept its responsibilities in practice, it may forfeit its sovereignty (Weiss 2007; Bellamy 2009).

It seems that agreement on the Responsibility to Protect was in part a result of the shock of the genocide in Rwanda and the role that the UN played in allowing it to happen. In 1994 UN peacekeeping forces *withdrew* from Rwanda, leaving as many as 800,000 people to be killed in just a few months (Barnett 2003). In part, however, it seems too that many state representatives voted for the Responsibility to Protect because it was seen as putting *an end* to humanitarian interventions *except* where they are agreed by the UN Security Council. It was seen as putting an end to the idea that NATO could take it on itself to act as the policeman of the world, legitimating its military activities in terms of humanitarianism and human rights. In fact, the Responsibility to Protect was seen above all as a responsibility to *prevent* gross violations of human rights. In the document there are no mechanisms specified to trigger the use of military force if a state fails to protect people in its territory. All that has been agreed is that military force is *not ruled out* where there is the threat or the actual occurrence of large-scale loss of life and massive forced migration. Military force is still *only* legally permitted where it is authorised by the UN Security Council (Bellamy 2009: 66–7). It is not clear, then, what the Responsibility to Protect actually adds to existing international law which already permits military action where the Security Council agrees that there is a threat to international peace and security given that there are now precedents for deciding that genocide, ethnic cleansing and mass human rights atrocities constitute such a threat.

In many ways the 'Responsibility to Protect' *reinforced* the UN as 'an authority' that can plan and oversee peacekeeping operations for the protection of human rights. In practice, however, the era of 'humanitarian intervention' may be over, at least when the Great Powers have an interest in a particular region or country.[7] In 2011 the UN Security Council drew on the 'Responsibility to Protect' to authorise military intervention in Libya to protect civilians from the government forces of Colonel Gaddafi's regime. The intervention was supported by the states of the Arab League. There has been no possibility of a large-scale intervention in Syria, however, in a situation that is similar to that of Libya (in that both involved uprisings against authoritarian governments as part of the Arab Spring) because of Russia's continued support for the government in Syria. There will be no Security Council resolution to sanction a peacekeeping operation as long as the Assad regime is supported by Russia, its long-standing ally (Muir 2013). Formal agreement at the UN on the 'Responsibility to Protect' has not defused suspicions that 'humanitarian intervention' is an instrument of imperialist designs, and that it will be used to undermine state sovereignty when it suits how the politicians of the 'Great Powers' construct their security and economic interests (Weiss 2007: 112–18).

Tragic dilemmas

In this chapter we have looked at how the UN was structured around safeguarding state sovereignty and the influence of the 'Great Powers' at the end of the Second World War. We have also looked at how the cultural politics of human rights at the UN has enabled professionals there to create a domain of action that is relatively autonomous of constructions of national interests by state bureaucrats, diplomats and politicians. Throughout most of the history of the UN, this domain of relative autonomy was confined to the committee rooms, offices and corridors of the UN itself. Since the end of the Cold War, however, with the collapse of the USSR and a reshaping of how US officials constructed the national interests of the sole remaining 'superpower', it has been expanded to activities that have effectively redefined sovereignty as responsibility.

Redefining sovereignty as responsibility opens up a role for UN experts to put in place practices that supplement states within their own territories. Indeed, the report on which the agreement on the 'Responsibility to Protect' was reached in 2005 explicitly lists 'responsibility to rebuild' as one of the duties of the 'international community' to prevent further human rights atrocities alongside the 'responsibility to prevent' and the 'responsibility to react' (Bellamy 2009). In UN-sanctioned peacekeeping and state-building missions, states that remain nominally sovereign are effectively replaced over at least part of their territories in order to protect people from gross violations of human rights. In the name of the 'international community' activities that were previously understood as the prerogative of sovereign states have been undertaken by foreign experts and supported by military force. In effect what state-building aims to do is to transform states that resemble predatory states into something more like the juridical-type state we looked at in Chapter 3. The aim is to end structures that support political and military leaders' strategies of extracting wealth (from foreign aid and raw materials) to fund militias, which in turn protect their wealth-making activities. The structures of predatory-type states should be replaced with structures that support administration by rational-legal bureaucracy. In the post-Cold War era, experts in peacekeeping maintain that establishing the rule of law and rational-legal administration is the best way to secure respect for human rights within states that have been torn apart by violence and repression.

Have these missions succeeded? This is of course a huge question, to which clear-cut answers are hard to find in the extensive literature on peacekeeping and state-building. Transitional administrations in Bosnia, Kosovo and East Timor (now Timor-Leste) do seem to have been successful in that armed conflict and ethnic cleansing has been ended. The main controversy concerning human rights in transitional administrations concerns political rights. In each case state-building has been extensive and long term, with international mission succeeding international mission, each having significant legal powers over the government, the judiciary and the security forces within the territories. In all these cases the UN has now left, but Bosnia and Kosovo are still international protectorates over a decade after peace was declared. Today representatives of the European Union have the final authority over elected officials in Bosnia and Kosovo, including members of government. In Kosovo the judiciary is mostly made up of international judges and prosecutors who may also be removed by the EU representative there. No mechanism for the judicial review of these decisions has been built into the new constitutions either of Bosnia or of Kosovo. Guglielmo Verdirame argues that these powers are incompatible with democracy: citizens are not free to elect their legislatures, and judges are not independent. He argues that although human rights atrocities have ended, and humanitarian intervention was an important contribution to that end, 'no autocracy can remain benign for too long' (Verdirame 2013: 268). There is a danger that even in what appear now to be successful cases, the 'top down' administrative solution to state-building is superficial, it has not really engaged ordinary people, and removal of internationally imposed limits on democracy will result in renewed human rights abuses.

The so-called 'light footprint' state-building in Afghanistan and Iraq, on the other hand, has been spectacularly unsuccessful. In part this is because political settlement was always secondary to security issues in peacekeeping missions there. The initial invasions and peacekeeping were accompanied by well-documented violations of human rights by the United States and its allies: civilian casualties have been very high (an estimated 20,000 in Afghanistan since 2001 and as many as 500,000 in Iraq since 2003); and disappearances, torture and unlawful detention have been extensive. In Afghanistan the interim government appointed by US and UN experts included the leaders of militias in the Northwestern territories who had helped NATO troops defeat the

Taliban. They were then able to win key government posts, sometimes using them to confirm a fundamentalist Islamic agenda that was at odds with women's rights (Amnesty International 2011). At the same time, the Taliban continued to operate, providing welfare assistance to Pashtun groups that the Tajik-dominated government largely ignored. In 2013 there were reports that the war in Afghanistan was escalating, not ending, with thousands of people killed each month and many more fleeing their homes to escape violence. After all the casualties and chaos, it seems that US officials now see their interests in negotiating with the Taliban (*Guardian* 2013). The failure of state-building in Iraq has been even more spectacular: in 2014 the country was split by civil war as IS (Islamic State) militias defeated the Iraqi army, which had been trained and equipped by the United States and its allies. Toby Dodge traces this civil war directly to the support of the United States and UK for the Iraqi prime minister chosen to head the interim government and still in place after a popular vote against him in the 2010 elections. Dodge argues that the IS insurrection is a symptom of many Iraqis' disaffection with the corruption, nepotism and authoritarianism of the government led by Nouri Al-Maliki (Dodge 2014). The human rights violations for which state officials under Al-Maliki's government were responsible were documented by Amnesty in 2013: 'Thousands of Iraqis are detained without trial or serving prison sentences imposed after unfair trials, torture remains rife and continues to be committed with impunity, and the new Iraq is one of the world's leading executioners' (Amnesty International 2013a).

The UN is the only organisation with oversight for the human rights of everyone in the world. It is easy to be cynical about such an ideal, and about the people who are supposed to make it a reality. If we allow, however, that people who work at the UN are generally sincere in trying to end suffering that is framed in terms of human rights violations, we might think rather that they are faced with 'tragic dilemmas'. People in official positions at the UN in which they are supposed to be able to make a difference can, on occasion, be faced with a choice between allowing terrible suffering – killing, rape, people fleeing for their lives – or trying to end it by 'borrowing' military force from willing governments. The tragic dilemma is that military intervention will itself cause terrible suffering in the short term, and quite possibly fail to end it in the long term.

Another way of looking at the problem of how the world might be responsible for human rights takes us beyond the corridors and committee rooms of the UN. There is a sense in which all of us who are citizens of wealthy and influential states are responsible for human rights. 'Great Powers' are *always already* involved in the history and politics of states that violate human rights. Legal sovereignty did not prevent the 'Great Powers' intervening frequently in the affairs of smaller states without UN authorisation during the Cold War, including by military means, in what they considered to be their economic and security interests (see McMahon 2003). 'Great Powers' continue to do so by using 'proxies' or 'clients', providing arms – to governments or to rebels – sometimes covertly, and by giving them international recognition and delegitimating their opponents as 'dictators', 'terrorists' or 'warlords'. In fact, the permanent members of the Security Council are the top five arms-selling countries in the world (Amnesty International 2013b). In many ways humanitarian interventions fall squarely within this history: they have been attempts to create states that will be friendly to governments of the United States and Europe. It is quite remarkable, however, that support given to dictatorships shielded by sovereignty is not exposed to anything like the same degree of opposition as humanitarian interventions. There were massive protests around the world against humanitarian interventions by the United States and its Western European allies in Afghanistan and Iraq, and there has been mediated public outrage at the expense and the lives of soldiers that have been lost. In addition, there are frequent – though marginal – calls for Bush and Blair to be tried as war criminals. In contrast, the routine sale of weapons and the support for leaders of states that are involved routinely in violating human rights by all the 'Great Powers' goes relatively unnoticed and unopposed.

At the same time, it is important not to over-estimate the effect that redefining sovereignty as responsibility will have on ending human rights violations where that means intervening in the territories of states in which officials are violating, or are failing to prevent gross violations of human rights. International law is still overwhelmingly made, adjudicated and enforced by states through treaties and through *national* commissions, legislatures and courts. Only very rarely is there recourse to international courts, economic sanctions and peacekeeping operations.[8] Sovereignty as the legal defence against non-interference in a state's internal affairs remains an ideal at the UN – even if it is now in tension with the ideal of 'sovereignty as responsibility'. Sovereignty as non-interference is supported by the structures of the UN and, for the most part, by the ethos of bureaucrats and experts employed there. As we have seen in this chapter, for the most part attempts to achieve human rights in practice through the UN involve *persuasion* rather than *force* and this will no doubt continue to be the case. It is only in very exceptional circumstances that invading a sovereign state is ever considered to protect civilians, and when it is, the way in which the 'Great Powers' construct their interests in the region is always an important factor in the decision to go to war.

The UN is not a world state. It has no means of enforcing human rights and it relies on states to provide moral resources of delegated authority and compliance with international norms, and material resources of money and arms. The UN was structured to accommodate the 'Great Powers', to give weight to their formal as well as their informal influence. In this context it is not surprising that people with national ties to other states are concerned about guarding sovereignty as independence, especially as in many cases it was won only relatively recently from European imperial states. How to support anti-imperialism and at the same time avoid what amounts to indifference in the face of actions by state agents that are directly causing terrible suffering? This is the difficulty for those committed to respect for human rights, both for those who work inside the UN and for those of us who are outside.

Humanising capitalism

Everyone has the right to a standard of living adequate for the health and well-being of himself [*sic*] and of his family [*sic*], including food, clothing, housing, and medical care and necessary social services, and the right to security in the event of unemployment, sickness, disability, widowhood, old age or other lack of livelihood in circumstances beyond his control [*sic*].

(Article 25, Universal Declaration of Human Rights)

There is a sense in which rapid economic progress is impossible without painful adjustments. Ancient philosophies have to be scrapped; old social institutions have to disintegrate; bonds of caste, creed and race have to burst; and large numbers of persons who cannot keep up with progress have to have their expectations of a comfortable life frustrated. Very few communities are willing to pay the full price of economic progress.

(United Nations, Department of Social and Economic Affairs 1951, quoted in Escobar 1995: 3)

The Universal Declaration of Human Rights (UDHR) clearly lays out the expectations that every individual in the world has, or should have, with regard to their social and economic rights. In addition, most states (with the notable exception of the United States) are signatories to the International Convention on Economic, Social and Cultural Rights (ICESCR), which came into force in 1976. According to Article 2 of the ICESCR:

Each State Party to the present Covenant undertakes to take steps, individually and through international assistance and co-operation,

especially economic and technical, to the maximum of its available
resources, with a view to achieving progressively the full realization of
the rights recognized in the present Covenant by all appropriate means,
including particularly the adoption of legislative measures.

The rights recognised in the ICESCR are mostly elaborations of Article
25 of the UDHR quoted at the beginning of this chapter: to food, shelter and social security. International human rights law not only specifies
in some detail what individuals are due, it also codifies the expectation
that it is the duty of states to co-operate internationally in order to
realise rights in practice for everyone. The UN Committee on Economic,
Social and Cultural Rights has repeatedly stated that, under the terms
of Article 2 of the ICESCR, states are bound to refrain from action that
might result in human rights breaches of social, economic and cultural
rights in other countries, and to help each other protect these human
rights within their own jurisdictions (Kinley 2009: 53).

The fact that social, economic and cultural rights are so well established
internationally may come as something a surprise. Expectations and
duties concerning social and economic rights contradict the dominant
economic theory of our times: neo-liberalism. Neo-liberal economists
see freeing markets from state control as a fair and efficient way of
distributing goods and rewarding hard work and ingenuity. In practice projects that are designed to free markets are not necessarily
unified, coherent or well designed to meet their stated aims. In very
general terms, however, 'freeing markets' since the 1980s has involved
the de-regulation of exchanges of money for investment and speculation within and across borders; the privatisation of nationally owned
industries; increased commodification – including of public services
like education, health, even the privatisation of prison security and
border control; and the imposition of free trade around the world to
enable corporations to take advantage of labour and resources that
are cheaper in some parts of the world than in others.

Capitalism is not just markets. There are many disputes amongst
classical and contemporary sociologists about what capitalism *does*
involve, but this is something on which all agree.[1] Neo-liberal projects
to 'free markets' stimulate economic growth that is dependent on profits made by investing capital. Investors make most profit where they
pay as little as possible for labour, machinery and materials. It is here
that *corporations* become important. Corporations plan and organise

investment, production and exchange to reduce costs and maximise profits. Transnational corporations (TNCs) are designed to take advantage of inequalities that they also produce. In terms of manufacturing goods for exchange or creating services (in office work, tourism and so on) capitalist investment creates inequalities – between workers, most immediately as a result of differences in skills and education, and also differences of nationality, ethnicity, gender, age. It also creates inequalities between whole regions. Capitalist investment creates jobs that are often relatively well paid compared to work in agriculture and local businesses in an area, but when they are no longer as profitable as opportunities elsewhere, TNCs can leave everyone there worse off than before. This is especially the case where common land that previously maintained small-scale farming has been taken over. Today much capitalist investment is not in manufacturing or services at all, but in money markets. There are profits to be made by gambling on anticipated changes in the price of stocks and shares, currencies, derivatives, futures and a slew of esoteric inventions that directly affect the possibilities of other exchanges of goods, services, labour and capital. In short, where investment is driven by profits, markets are in large part the product of corporations that successfully create the conditions of their own success.

From within the terms of neo-liberalism markets and human rights are understood to be linked in a very particular way. The 'invisible hand of the market' that neo-liberals see as fair and efficient is linked to civil rights (sometimes called 'negative freedoms') because both are marked by the *absence* of the state. Human rights are understood *exclusively* as civil rights, and we enjoy them only where the state does not interfere with people's freedoms – especially the freedom to buy, own and sell property, skills and labour, but also to freedom of movement and of speech.[2] It is especially this link between markets and civil rights that was celebrated by neo-liberals after the Cold War: when state communism collapsed, opposition to state intervention was championed both on the grounds of the value of free markets to economic development and of freedom from totalitarian government. In contrast, for advocates of social, economic and cultural rights, markets must be limited for human beings to enjoy real freedoms (sometimes known as 'positive freedoms'): states must enable more or less equal opportunities to realise the aims we set ourselves and for us to develop our full capacities.

Markets are socially constructed

Markets are part of how we live together: they do not exist outside the meaningful codes through which we make them. Neo-liberals assume that human beings are motivated *only* by individual calculations of self-interest. One of the important features of markets for neo-liberals is that they 'incentivise' people to act: by the carrot of material rewards and social status; and by the stick of insecurity, homelessness and hunger. In contrast, human rights advocates do not see human beings as solely rational, calculating creatures. Even in conditions of advanced capitalism people value experiences, relationships and other people: we do not live only to maximise our own advantage. Markets are valued for certain kinds of exchanges, but they are never without limits. Once they are established, markets are structured: they become background, taken-for-granted; to a greater or lesser extent they seem to us to be objective, social constraints on how we are able to live. However, we continue to make markets in everyday life, to frame exchanges in terms of what we value as well as what is 'normal'. Markets are structures that are constrained as well as constraining.

There are two basic types of limits on markets – formal and informal. In formal terms, markets are shaped by legislation and public policy established through states. This is one of the biggest areas of controversy today. 'Rolling back the frontiers of the state' is the most important principle of neo-liberal political projects that aim to free markets. In fact, however, it is clear that markets cannot exist without states. Although, as we saw in Chapter 3, states are very different, where capitalist markets are well established it is because states provide conditions that corporations cannot provide for themselves. It is through states that taxes are gathered, and money collected or that has been borrowed from the International Monetary Fund (IMF) and the World Bank or donated by international aid is distributed. Governments and experts employed by states are supposed to invest money 'in the national interest' to make their country competitive in the global economy. There are historic reasons why Northwestern states have been especially successful in this respect that continue to be important today (as we shall see in the next section). But state-directed economic growth has also been achieved by the 'Asian Tigers' (Hong Kong, Singapore, South Korea and Taiwan) since the 1980s. First, money is used to pay for publicly funded infrastructure that is necessary to attract investment in manufacturing,

service and extractive industries, transport and communications systems, and reliable energy supplies. Providing security for investment
by organising police and military forces is perhaps the most important part of infrastructure that states provide for investment. For the
most part violence and conflict are not good conditions in which to
organise buying and selling across any distance – at least not to do
business that is legal (with the important exception of making and selling military supplies). Second, it is through states that legal contracts
between investors, suppliers of goods and services, manufacturers and
retailers, workers and management are regulated and guaranteed. To
ensure stability and to create conditions in which corporations can plan
investment, legal contracts must be backed up by courts and tribunals
to which managers and workers can appeal to adjudicate controversies
if they break down. Third, as capitalist societies become increasingly
industrialised and profit is based on providing services and goods that
involve design, technology and marketing, corporations need educated,
well trained, flexible and healthy workforces. States that successfully
compete for investment in 'high-end' industries are those that have
national systems of education and health-care. Although 'freeing markets' in the public sector is one of the aims of neo-liberal projects,
and selective privatisation is profitable for some corporations, national
systems have to be co-ordinated. Planning and long-term investment
is needed to produce the 'human capital' that is necessary for businesses to make profits, and it is only experts who work within the
frame of 'national interests' that are in a position to project what will
be needed in terms of skills for a country to become and to remain
competitive. Fourth, although it has become much more difficult with
the deregulation of money markets, states set limits on the supply of
money to their national economies to establish a degree of stability for
investment by keeping inflation low and encouraging businesses to
borrow to support economic growth. 'Macro-economic' policies were
very evident after the financial crisis of 2008 when US and European
governments did not leave under-capitalised investment banks to fail.
They used trillions of dollars of public money to prevent the complete
collapse of banking, and to keep a degree of control over national economies. Finally, all states invest public money in areas of the economy
that are valued by governments. This investment has significant effects
in terms of the growth of national economies (on jobs and tax revenues), and it invariably produces significant benefits for investment

in other enterprises. The United States, for example, spends almost one quarter of the federal budget, billions of dollars each year, on defence, including the development of military technology. The invention of the Internet is one of the side effects of this investment: it is unimaginable that private business would have funded the long-term, 'blue skies' research that led to the development of digital technology. It is difficult to imagine what capitalist investment would be today without the digital revolution; but it was actually a by-product of state planning, not the innovation and creativity that neo-liberals see as produced only by markets (Castells 2001; Chang 2010a).

The ways in which markets are structured *informally* can be harder to pin down, but they are no less important. Informal norms are often contrasted as 'soft' compared to 'hard' law and regulation: while law and regulation compel through fear of punishment, informal norms and values compel through persuasion and consensus. In very general terms, everyone recognises certain ethical limits on what can be bought and sold. Legal limits are often in place as markers of these moral limits so that even though there certainly are markets in babies, vital organs and small arms, for the most part these are not considered 'commodities' that can be exchanged like fruit and vegetables. A classic example of the limits of markets has been norms and values concerning sex, gender and sexuality in the Northwest. With historical variations, since the nineteenth century (sometimes backed by legislation and public policy), there has been a general understanding in the Northwest that it is women who care for young people, the sick and elderly while male heads of household provide the conditions (housing, food) for that care by exchanging their labour for wages. There is no market logic for this arrangement: in fact, it is to the advantage of business to have as many people as possible compete for work in the labour market, and to be able to sell services and goods that women have provided in the home. What is considered appropriate for men and women is now changing to some extent, and what was previously done in the home is increasingly commodified. Nevertheless, care-work remains an important limit on markets: love and intimacy have never been outside market exchanges altogether, but nor can they ever be completely captured in calculations of profit and loss. Raising children to become adult workers and consumers is necessary for business to make profits, but its value to most people goes far beyond the production of workers for corporations. How people organise exchanges of time and skills for money in labour markets is still shaped by the value of care that remains gendered in many ways – even though this is completely illogical from the point of view of market exchanges to maximise individual advantage.

The cultural politics of human rights by advocates for more just and human-centred economies is part of a wide range of challenges to neo-liberal projects. The most well established opposition to neo-liberalism in terms of social and economic rights comes from social democrats. It is this tradition that is encoded in the Universal Declaration of Human Rights with its long list of articles specifying rights to freedom from state repression, democratic participation, and social and economic rights to well-being, solidarity and the meeting of our basic needs. The ideal of social democrats is something like the welfare states in Scandinavia and Western Europe that are now threatened by neo-liberalism.[3] Social democrats today, however, are far more sensitive to global inequalities than earlier generations. They advocate for *global* social democracy, the regulation of markets to benefit people in all countries, not just those who live within the national boundaries of specific Northwestern states.

Global social democrats are not against markets as such. In fact, they see the spread of markets as *necessary* to the realisation of social and economic rights for everyone. They argue that it is not capital investment and transnational markets that cause the intensity of poverty in sub-Saharan Africa. On the contrary, it is because there is too *little* trade and investment in these countries that people are suffering from the harshest deprivations. Global social democrats are not even against TNCs, as long as they are properly regulated. They do not, however, see the 'trickle-down' of wealth that neo-liberals argue will make the poor better off as a result of economic growth in general as a good way of organising markets. Nor do they suppose that each individual taking responsibility for their own well-being is a good way to make the most of the benefits markets can bring. What global social democrats want to see is well-managed economic development and state-directed investment to provide well-paid jobs with good conditions of employment, and tax revenue that is used for public goods (education, health-care) and to supplement incomes where people can not earn enough to live with dignity. What this means in practice is international regulation and state protection to realise the benefits of markets whilst moderating the inevitable insecurities, injustices and indignities they create.[4]

Alongside this social democratic construction of markets and human rights there is an alternative challenge to neo-liberalism that is constructed in terms of *cultural* rights: ways of life must be protected that can only survive if markets are far more closely regulated. Where social democrats are concerned to make the most of capital investment and markets to benefit the world's poorest, the alternative model of development is far more focused on safeguarding local, and to a lesser extent, national markets. I will call this alternative model 'local communitarianism'. Like global social democrats local communitarians address their concerns to inter-governmental organisations (IGOs) and states. But they are focused especially on non-industrialised ways of life. These are most important in Africa, Asia and Latin America, where there are still large numbers of people living in communities based on small-scale farming and on hunting and gathering. It also involves people in the Northwest who are trying to live as far as possible on self-provisioning (growing food, bartering services and so on) outside markets dominated by corporations and in environmentally sustainable ways.[5] Local communitarians are far more sceptical about markets than social democrats, and they are against TNCs. They see traditional and alternative ways of life as threatened by exchanges of money, technological know-how, and cheap goods produced in industrial processes.

In this chapter we will look at three sets of human rights campaigns that focus on altering the conditions of globalising markets today. These campaigns are mobilised at different scales and they address both the formal and informal regulation of markets. It is not always possible to separate out campaigns that aim at global social democracy from those that aim at local communitarianism. This is in part because their aims converge in particular campaigns – around the gross violations of human rights in which some TNCs have been involved, for example. In addition, human rights non-governmental organisation (IGOs) are often *reacting* to human rights abuses, to forcible evictions carried out in the name of development projects, or to the violent repression of resistance to TNCs. When they are concerned with mitigating or resolving immediate crises rather than with long-term projects, the fact that advocates may actually have very different views about how society should be organised may not be relevant.

International Financial Institutions: co-operation and competition

The ICESCR requires states to co-operate internationally to realise human rights for everyone in the world, regardless of where they happen to be born and to be living. If the UN is the organisation responsible for human rights in general, it has partner organisations that might be taken to have similar responsibilities specifically for the social and economic rights listed in the UDHR. They are the International Financial Institutions (IFIs): the International Monetary Fund (IMF), the World Bank and the World Trade Organization (WTO). The IMF and the World Bank were set up as part of the UN in 1944 as 'Bretton Woods institutions', specifically to take responsibility for the global economy: the IMF to make loans and regulations to stabilise currencies; the World Bank to make loans and give advice initially for the reconstruction of Europe after the Second World War and later for particular development projects. The General Agreement on Tariffs and Trade was also set up as a Bretton Woods institution: a forum for negotiating trade rules and settling disputes. In 1995 it was replaced by the WTO, which was intended to liberalise trade across borders.

The Bretton Woods institutions were established according to principles of Keynesian economics: to stabilise currencies and to regulate international trade and investment in order to support state-managed national economies. Since the 1980s, however, the IFIs have become notorious for promoting neo-liberal policies to 'free markets' from state controls. Officials at the IMF have attached conditions to loans that required states to reduce public spending, cut food subsidies and devalue currency to attract imports (which have had the side effect of pushing up the cost of the debt). The World Bank has made loans for large modernisation projects (like the Narmada dam we discuss later in the chapter), irrespective of their effects. And the international agreements brokered by officials at the WTO – with such acronyms as TRIMs and TRIPS – have created opportunities for corporations to earn returns on investments by reducing protections for workers and communities in the Global South.

IFIs have been the object of a variety of campaigns, some of which frame their policies as violating human rights.[6] It is difficult, however, to construct IFIs as duty-bearers of human rights in international law. Respect for human rights is not part of the articles of agreement by which they were set up. In fact, IFIs are bound to respect state sovereignty, to avoid interfering in the decision-making of national governments (Oberleitner 2007: 130). Even if IFI policies *do* quite clearly limit what can be done in national economies, IFIs were not designed to consider the human rights of the individuals and groups their policies affect. In fact, like the UN, the IFIs are structured by respect for sovereign *inequalities*. IFIs were set up to be dominated by the wealthiest states, especially the United States. The IMF and the World Bank allocate voting and governing positions to those who hold the most shares. The United States has always had, and continues to have, an effective veto in the IMF. In the World Bank, five executive directors are elected by the biggest shareholders and nineteen others are voted for by regional groups of other members. There has also been a convention that the United States chooses the president of the World Bank, while Europeans appoint the managing director of the IMF – both positions are important to setting the policy agenda. In the WTO decisions are reached by consensus; though there is the possibility of making decisions by voting, with one member one vote, it has never yet been used. Consensus building at the WTO involves a good deal of informal pressure from states with the most to offer in terms of trading opportunities on those with national economies in greatest need of investment (Woods 2003).

It is because of the formal and informal influence of US officials as representatives of the largest and wealthiest economy that neo-liberal policies have been known as 'the Washington consensus'. Neo-liberal policies have benefitted the US economy: the dollar is the global currency, which makes for a common international interest in keeping its value stable; the government has found it relatively easy to borrow money (from China especially); investment in manufacturing and service industries has been high compared to the rest of the world; and even ordinary people have found it easy to borrow from banks (though as wages have declined in real terms in the United States, it is also the case that many people there have had to borrow to maintain their standard of living).[7] It is not just the national economy of the United States, however, that has benefitted from the 'Washington consensus'. The vast majority of investment and trade has been, and remains between, the highly industrialised countries of North America, Western Europe and Japan. This is not accidental. Despite the commitments of IFIs to free global markets, the governments of the United States and Europe continue to direct investment and to protect certain areas of their economies from foreign competition. In the United States, research in public universities and the military that leads directly to developing industry and exports, including of arms and military technology, is very important. So too are subsidies to agri-businesses – which result in surpluses that end up being dumped as food aid in other countries. Subsidies to agri-businesses are especially problematic for developing countries, many of which have economies that were organised historically to grow food for export to the Northwest (coffee, sugar, peanuts). It is difficult to develop diverse national and even local markets for food when prices are kept low by subsidies paid elsewhere over which governments have no control (Hoogevelt 2001; Chang 2010a; Kiely 2010).

The structural design of the IFIs does not determine their policies. As highly qualified professionals who are employed to produce knowledge-led economic policy for development and financial stability, experts in IFIs have a degree of independence from and influence over officials employed by member states. And it is in part experts *within* the IFIs who have campaigned for human rights. The president of the World Bank between 1995 and 2005, James Wolfensohn, campaigned strongly for the organisation to become a 'duty-bearer' of human rights. In fact, it is argued that as a result of pressure from human rights campaigns both inside and outside, policy-making at the World Bank and, to a lesser extent the IMF, is no longer driven by 'the Washington consensus'. First, poverty reduction is now seen as requiring non-market means of redistributing wealth (rather than just 'trickle-down'), including social services such as education, health-care and safety nets for people without income. Second, economic growth is increasingly seen as requiring good governance, which includes transparency, accountability and citizen participation in development projects. The World Bank now requires its borrowers to consult with NGOs; and the IMF and World Bank require borrowers to produce Poverty Reduction Strategy Papers that are publicly available (Oberleitner 2007: 131; see also Scholte 2011).

It is a continuing criticism of the IFIs, however, that much of the work they do is bureaucratic, procedural and dominated by economic expertise rather than by concern for human rights. In fact, in an interesting ethnographic study of the World Bank, Galit Sarfaty argues that economists still dominate knowledge-production there – despite Wolfensohn's decade-long campaign to get human rights onto the World Bank agenda. According to Sarfaty structures of status and incentives within the World Bank contribute to the dominance of economic expertise. Economists treat human rights with suspicion as either too vague (as moral principles) or too rigid (as law) to facilitate development. Sarfaty found that what is important for the status and promotion prospects of individuals working at the bank is *making* loans, rather than monitoring their effectiveness. As a result, human rights still tend to be perceived as obstacles rather than as priorities (Sarfaty 2009). In general, critics of the IFIs argue that what we are now seeing is the 'Washington consensus augmented' rather than an end to neo-liberal policies: economic experts are still committed to 'freeing markets' from state regulation; it is just that now there is *an additional* level of bureaucratic procedures that borrowers must negotiate before they are able to access loans (Salomon 2007: 8–9; Chang 2010b).

It is above all global social democrats who call for the *reform* of the IFIs. There is a fundamental problem with this approach. Although officials at the IFIs are supposed to foster international co-operation to create monetary stability and the conditions for investment and development, investment actually depends on international competition. States must *compete* to provide the conditions to attract foreign investment, and to borrow money to build up infrastructure and to subsidise parts of their national economies. They must compete to gain 'comparative advantage', to be *more* attractive than other national economies in certain sectors (in manufacturing cars, producing parts for computers, growing coffee, extracting diamonds or cobalt). The officials of Northwestern states use their structural advantages in the IFIs to enhance the 'comparative advantages' of their national economies at the expense of those of other states.

Local communitarians are sceptical about possibilities of reforming the IFIs. They are more likely to argue that the IFIs should be *abolished* (see Bello 2004). And in practice, the IFIs may be declining in importance as brokers of international co-operation on trade and development. Many states have distanced themselves from the influence of the IMF and the World Bank, including the 'Asian Tigers' and Latin American states like Argentina and Brazil (Dieter 2008). And the Doha round of talks at the WTO ended in 2013 with very little agreement on international trade. In addition, Chinese officials are lending trillions of dollars to Latin American and African states for development without imposing conditions in terms of human rights. They do so to gain access to oil and minerals, and to provide work for Chinese citizens on large infrastructure, mining and construction projects. This undermines the attempts of human rights campaigners to get IFIs to take human rights obligations seriously. Not only can borrowers go elsewhere for development loans but the World Bank and the IMF are now in competition with China (Guttal 2008).

The changing geo-politics of international economic policy-making are likely to make the IFIs less relevant in future. Simply taking the IFIs out of the picture is not, however, in itself enough to make respect for human rights more easily realised. For one thing, state officials will still use the advantages of state wealth and the size of national markets to negotiate with other state officials. Bilateral and regional trade agreements are not necessarily fairer than those that have been brokered through the WTO, and unconditional loans will not necessarily be used to benefit a national economy. As we discussed in Chapter 3, how wealth is distributed by state officials depends on many factors, including how states are structured to enable officials to make use of moral and material resources for their own projects, and the influence of movements, NGOs and parties. Abolishing or marginalising the IFIs will not necessarily make for more of a focus on social and economic rights either *between* or *inside* states in the future.

Taming transnational corporations

Global social democrats see TNCs, properly regulated, as contributing to the realisation of social and economic rights: part of the solution rather than part of the problem. In fact, Mary Robinson, a former UN Human Rights Commissioner, has gone so far as to suggest that as well as creating jobs and opportunities that would not otherwise be available to people in developing countries, corporations should be expected to put pressure on states to draw attention to human rights abuses and to *raise* human rights standards in states that want their business (Clapham 2006: 221–2). In contrast, local communitarians see TNCs as part of the problem: they create jobs and opportunities by destroying ways of life that are the only possibility of sustaining respect for people's human rights in the long term.

In practice, the human rights campaigns of global social democrats and local communitarians converge on the human rights *abuses* of TNCs. In terms of civil rights, corporations can be directly complicit with or benefit directly from human rights violations that are committed by states, more or less on their behalf. In the worst cases this involves murder, torture and slavery. Much more common are violations of workers' rights to decent pay and conditions, and the right to unionise and strike to improve collective bargaining power. Corporations also benefit from development projects that displace traditional ways of life and livelihood. In this respect (as in the cases we look at in following section) they can impinge directly on the enjoyment of cultural as well as social and economic rights.

The most obvious difficulty in making TNCs accountable for human rights abuses is that they are not directly subjects of international human rights law. It is states that bind themselves to respect international human rights agreements, and it is on this basis that they are monitored at the UN. Effectively, transnational corporations are private actors: company directors are not legally accountable for human rights violations, which can only be committed by state officials, even if their companies benefit directly from murder, slavery and torture.

This is not to say that TNCs operate outside law and regulation that protect human rights altogether. Quite apart from laws against complicity with murder, slavery and torture, states establish regulations that detail what counts as bribery, corruption and fraud, require corporations to conform to their contracts with sub-contractors and workers, and set rates of taxation. There has been much discussion of the way in which TNCs are able to *undermine* state regulation: dictating terms state officials and workers must agree to before foreign investors will set up factories in developing countries. Legal regulation remains important, however, because even the most 'border-hopping' corporations are neither as mobile nor as global as we tend to think. In practice TNCs almost always do a high proportion of trade and even production in one country, which is usually also where they have their headquarters. Most top decision-makers in corporations are from the 'home country' in which they are based (Chang 2010a: 79–82). In addition, the vast majority of foreign direct investment (FDI) – investment in productive industries – still goes into Northwestern states and Japan. The proportion of FDI that goes to China, the Asian Tigers, Brazil and Mexico has risen in recent years, as have the size and number of the wealthiest corporations in these. Sub-Saharan Africa continues to attract the least FDI, though it too has risen proportionately in recent years – especially as a result of Chinese investment (Kinley 2009: 169–70). It is in states where there is little FDI that corporations are most likely to be associated with human rights abuses. These states are especially susceptible to pressure to lower environmental and labour standards or the tax requirements they impose on corporations. The most notorious of these agreements concern Export Processing Zones (EPZs), specially designated areas in developing states for processing imported goods to re-export, in which globalising corporations have been offered a range of incentives, including tax breaks, subsidies on rents and utilities, duty-free imports and so on. Some of these agreements restrict workers' rights to unionise whilst at the same time imposing long hours, brutal conditions, and arbitrary rules concerning who can be hired and fired. Even when workers' rights are respected on paper, in practice they may be ignored or overruled with states' complicity. We should note that this is the case *outside* EPZs too, where no formal agreements are made to suspend workers' rights, but in practice they are not respected. In fact, wages and conditions are often *worse* outside EPZs. In general, developing states that see cheap labour as an attraction to TNCs are willing to sacrifice human rights to undercut each other in order to attract foreign investment (Nam 2006).

One legal strategy to deal with corporate abuses of human rights is to try to bring TNCs to court in their 'home' states for violations committed elsewhere. TNCs are always legally incorporated in one state. In fact, human rights advocates argue that states already have the responsibility in international human rights law to prosecute their 'home companies' where they are involved in human rights abuses (see Ziammatto 2011). In reality, however, it is very difficult to successfully prosecute corporations 'at home' because of the complexity of their operations: they invariably involve long chains of exchanges with subsidiaries, sub-contractors and suppliers in other countries. It is common that courts decide a case should be heard elsewhere. The most notorious example of *forum non conveniens* (where a court refuses to hear a case on the basis that it should be heard elsewhere) is that of the Bhopal disaster in 1984 when thousands of people were killed and hundreds of thousands suffered injuries and ill-health as the result of a gas explosion in plant belonging to the US-based company Union Carbide. Despite the fact that Union Carbide was legally incorporated in the United States, American courts decided that the case would be more appropriately heard in India, where the damages eventually awarded were far less than adequate to compensate for the effects of the negligence that caused the tragedy (Amnesty International 2009; Kinley 2009: 145–8). In 2012 the Canadian Supreme Court ruled that the case against Anvil Mining, in which members of the company were accused of being involved in the Kilwa massacre, would be better heard in Australia or the Democratic Republic of Congo, despite the failure of earlier attempts to bring them to court in those countries (Amnesty International 2012).

One of the most creative legal strategies through which activists have addressed corporate human rights abuses is through an obscure US law, the Alien Tort Claims Act (ATCA), which allows any company complicit with or benefitting from human rights violations to be sued in American courts, regardless of where and against whom they were committed (Clapham 2006: 252–65). In Burma, for example, the government used soldiers to protect the gas pipeline built by Unocal, and the company was accused of complicity with murder, rape, forced labour and forced relocation (Nash 2010: 229–30). In Nigeria, Shell was accused of complicity with the Nigerian military to suppress peaceful protests of the Ogoni people through rape, killing and detention without trial (Kinley 2009: 154; see pp. 28–9). Both oil companies settled out of court. Corporations now make calculations concerning 'human rights risks', against which they can be insured, as part of their business plans. They weigh the risks of bad publicity against the financial gains to be made by doing business in ways that may lead to violations of human rights. ATCA cases are a way of raising the 'risk' side of that calculation in terms of the damage that can be done to a company's reputation if it is found guilty of human rights abuses in a US court. On the other hand, it is extremely difficult to bring such cases, and they have rarely been conclusive in legal terms. ATCA can only ever be a last resort; it cannot provide the basis for regular enforcement of international human rights law concerning corporations (Kinley 2009: 193).[8]

Given the difficulties of finding legal remedies to human rights abuses in which corporations are involved, the less formal tool of 'corporate social responsibility' (CSR) has become a way to make corporations more susceptible to pressure from human rights advocates. Technically CSR involves corporations regulating themselves; it is voluntary, and it is popular with business and governments for this reason. In practice, however, CSR is just one element in a process by which corporations' activities are monitored by NGOs and wrongdoing is brought to public attention by the media. CSR can even be understood as a continuum, with corporate codes of self-regulation at one end, and their incorporation into government regulation at the other. For example, the UK now requires pension funds to declare whether they are taking social, environmental and ethical considerations into account in making their investments (Gond *et al.* 2011). Such regulation is 'soft'; it does not make corporations accountable in court, but it does go beyond civil society monitoring, setting up procedures that may make it more difficult for governments to be complicit with corporate abuses of human rights abroad.

It is on the grounds that it is 'soft', that it is a *substitute* for law at the international level, that CSR has been criticised. Since 2000 the UN has tried to make up for the lack of international human rights law regarding corporations with its 'Global Compact', which sets out ten principles with which public bodies, local networks and corporations should comply, drawing on various international agreements concerning human rights, labour rights, the environment and anti-corruption. However, no monitoring or enforcement mechanisms have been put in place to accompany these principles. To comply with the compact companies have only to submit a brief 'communication of progress' report and to enter into dialogue with the secretariat if they raise an 'integrity matter'. Critics argue that companies are effectively gaining endorsement by the UN simply by declaring their allegiance to principles of good practice, without making any real commitment to follow them (Bruno and Karline 2000).

There is no doubt that in some cases moral pressure can be effective in ending corporate abuses of human rights, especially where it impacts on commercial self-interest. There have been notable successes in shaming corporations into giving up human rights abuses, such as the campaigns against sweatshops run by Nike and Reebok in the 1990s (Kinley 2009: 179–86). The biggest human rights international non-governmental organisations (INGOs), including Amnesty and Human Rights Watch, are now very much involved in 'corporate watch', and combined with media pressure they can make a difference. However, it is unsurprising that it is pressure on food and clothing manufacturing that has been most successful, since these are sectors where 'brands' are especially valuable. Such pressure is much less likely to be effective in extractive industries and infrastructure projects, in part because such companies do not rely on their brand names in the same way. These are also, of course, projects that can only be sited in specific places, which may be unstable or under the jurisdiction of predatory states in which governments encourage conflict for their own purposes (Wells and Elias 2005: 143–4). It has also been suggested that, with notable exceptions (like Tata), the big corporations that are emerging from China, India and Brazil will face far less international and domestic pressure than American and European companies over human rights issues (Kinley 2009: 151–2). Certainly these countries face enormous challenges in terms of poverty and inequality, and so there may be less inclination for civil society organisations to monitor TNCs that benefit the domestic economy. In the case of China, of course, the development of civil society organisations is itself very difficult. On the other hand, transnational corporations based in these states are emerging from historical traditions of socialism and paternalism that mix governance and markets in ways that are unfamiliar in the Northwest. It may be that we will see new demands made on globalising corporations, for philanthropy, or for care of workers, for example, rather than the disappearance of CSR altogether (Prieto-Carron *et al.* 2006; Gond *et al.* 2011).

Protecting rural ways of life

For local communitarians what is ultimately most important is to protect ways of life that are threatened by capitalism: by the building of big development and infrastructure projects, mining, deforestation, and intensive fishing and agriculture. Indigenous peoples' movements and peasants' movements are concerned with 'cultural rights': with preserving traditional ways of life in rural areas. In 2007, UN experts estimated that for the first time in history more people were living in cities than in the country, and the rural exodus is set to continue (UN 2007). Nevertheless, this makes for a very high proportion of the world's population that still lives in rural areas. Indigenous peoples' and peasants' movements are trying to reverse the ongoing rural exodus, as people leave or are pushed out of the countryside to escape hunger and despair and to make a better life for themselves (though once they arrive in cities, they will join the millions of people who arrived before them, and who are barely getting by in shanty towns and slums). Local communitarians support those who claim human rights to alternative, sustainable development, and argue that they should be an example to the rest of the world.

In recent years indigenous peoples have gained rights at the national and international level. In 2007, after decades of campaigning, the UN Declaration of Rights of Indigenous Peoples was finally ratified by most countries in the world – with the notable exceptions of the United States, Canada and Australia (though Australia subsequently endorsed it). At both national and international level, by far the most important indigenous claims concern issues of autonomy and the stewardship of sacred lands without which it is impossible for people to sustain their distinctive ways of life. What is most difficult for indigenous peoples is to get claims to land recognised or respected in practice, especially where those claims come into conflict with development priorities. The Narmada dam project has come to symbolise these conflicts worldwide. It involves the submersion of vast areas of land on which over 200,000 *adivasis* and subsistence farmers live to provide water to states in Northwest and Central India. There has been a very high-profile national and international human rights campaign against the project, and several rulings by the Indian Supreme Court. There was also a reversal of policy on the part of the World Bank in 1993, which withdrew the loans it had been making to the Indian government to build the Sardar Sarovar dam on the grounds that the benefits it was supposed to produce were not clear enough to justify the environmental damage and the displacement of people it involved. Nevertheless, the Sardar Sarovar dam is now built, funded by the Gujarat state and the Indian government. The people affected have been resettled, but in conditions where they can no longer live communally by small-scale farming. There are another 30 dams planned for the Narmada River, and resistance continues.[9] This situation is replicated around the world where there are conflicts over land between indigenous peoples and states that prioritise economic development over existing ways of life. Dispossession of land, poverty, violence and the criminalisation of protest are a continuing reality for indigenous peoples, and in the vast majority of cases it is as yet unclear precisely how they can use rights at the local and national level to make a difference in practice (UN 2009; Morgan 2011).

According to Edelman and James, small farmers are following indigenous peoples in claiming rights to culture to preserve traditional ways of life (Edelman and James 2011: 94–5). Small farming is threatened by neo-liberal globalisation, led by corporate activities and state policies, and co-ordinated by the WTO since the mid-1990s, that makes it increasingly difficult for small farmers to live off the land. The pressures include increased export-oriented, chemical-intensive, contract farming (for supermarkets, and increasingly of biofuels that replace oil), the 'dumping' of agricultural surpluses by Northwestern states that have been produced as a result of state subsidies, and growing speculation on land and on food as commodities. In countries subject to structural adjustment programmes since the 1980s, small farmers lost state-guaranteed prices and access to low-interest loans. For those who have to buy at least some of their food, a rural way of life is also threatened by the volatility of global food markets, which resulted in a food crisis in 2008, and which is tending to raise the cost of food generally around the world. It is estimated that 80 per cent of people who are malnourished live in rural areas (Seitz and Hite 2012: 78).[10]

It is on the basis that their way of life is threatened that Via Campesina, an INGO based in Latin America, argues for peasant-centred alternative and sustainable development. It argues that limiting large land-holdings and guaranteeing the rights of small farmers to own land and to make use of unproductive state-owned land are solutions to the immediate problems of the poorest rural people, and will contribute to stable and sustainable food production for everyone. It proposes a UN Declaration on the Rights of Peasants that includes rights to own and use land, to participate in decision-making at international and national levels, and 'to reject interventions that can destroy local agricultural values'. Via Campesina's vision of alternative and sustainable development is centred on what it calls 'food sovereignty'. By 'food sovereignty' it means the development and protection of environmentally sustainable, small-scale, local and national food production. 'Food sovereignty' is a militant concept, put forward to counteract the UN ideal of 'food *security*'. According to the UN's Food and Agriculture Organization, 'food security exists when all people, at all times, have physical and economic access to sufficient, safe, and nutritious food that meets their dietary needs and food preferences' (Edelman 2012: 437). There is nothing in this formulation about how food is to be produced, nor who participates in deciding how land should be used to produce it. In other words, 'food security' is compatible with the neo-liberal agriculture that has brought about the food crisis and that, Via Campesina activists argue, is fundamentally damaging to the ways of life of small farmers.[11]

The model of alternative development that is put forward by Via Campesina and by indigenous peoples is quite different from that envisioned by global social democrats. It requires a very high degree of government control over markets, with extensive planning and control not only over the limits of markets, over what is traded, but also over how food is to be distributed according to need. For local communitarians respecting the cultural rights of people to rural ways of life means withdrawing from transnational markets in money and technology as well as food: governments should be building national self-sufficiency and the production and consumption of products should be devolved as far as possible to the local level.

One of the main difficulties for local communitarians is that very few governments around the world now see agriculture as key to development, so that small farmers find themselves politically and socially, as well as economically, marginalised. It is worth noting in this respect that Via Campesina is strongly linked to the Brazilian landless workers movement, but even here, where it is grassroots and militant and where the government has been receptive to its demands, its gains have been limited. Sue Brandford reports that when President Lula, who had strong links to the Movement of the Landless in Brazil, was elected president in October 2002, thousands of families moved into camps in the countryside and occupied big unproductive estates, sure that they would now benefit from the massive programme of land reform that would be enacted. Eventually, some families were settled legally on land they had occupied, but despite the government's repeated support of land reform and of rural workers, far fewer have legal title than they expected. In many cases, squatters are farming these lands, in a sense realising their social and economic rights in practice; but they do not have legal titles (Branford 2009: 163–5). In fact, in recent years it seems that government policy in Brazil has moved much further in the direction of promoting industrial agri-businesses to deal with problems of chronic rural poverty and hunger and away from redistributing land to small farmers (Araujo 2010).

It is movements in Latin America that are leading the world in claiming cultural rights to preserve rural ways of life. Indeed, what I am calling 'local communitarianism' is often called 'buen vivir' – living small-scale, in harmony with nature, outside the influence of trans-national markets of money, technology and goods. Throughout the 1990s indigenous peoples' movements met with some success: most countries in Latin America now have multicultural constitutions that allow a degree of autonomy to indigenous communities to manage their own affairs. It is on this basis that Via Campesina is mobilising its claims for small farmers. At the same time, however, governments in Latin America that construct themselves as radically 'socialist for the twenty first century', explicitly against capitalist development led by TNCs, are in practice putting in place 'neo-extractivist' economic policies that undermine the rights of indigenous peoples and small farmers. 'Neo-extractivism' is so-called because it is continuation of colonial economic policies: when raw materials were shipped to the Europe to be turned into manufactured products which were then sold for far greater profits.[12] Although mining, deforestation and mono-culture of crops like soybeans and wood are now often carried out by industries that are nationalised (oil in Venezuela and Bolivia, for example), or at least controlled to a far greater extent by national governments, neo-extractivist industries are very far from enabling national economic self-sufficiency: they create products for sale on international markets and, very often, they involve foreign invest-ment, infrastructure building, and importing technology and expert-ise too. With respect to the protection of cultural rights to rural ways of life, 'neo-extractivism' is immensely environmentally damaging, it destroys ways of life as people are displaced from subsistence farm-ing and forests, and it is often associated with violence against those who resist it. If Latin American governments, which explicitly name themselves as socialist and multicultural, have strategies for economic growth that are based on such capital intensive, export-oriented and environmentally damaging practices, there would seem to be very little hope for indigenous and peasant farmers' rights anywhere (Gudynas 2010; Acosta 2013).

Human rights beyond neo-liberalism

Organisations and movements that frame inequalities and pov-erty in terms of social, economic and cultural rights are just *part* of counter-movements against neo-liberal market fundamentalism – alongside trade unions, neo-Keynesian economists, left-of-centre political parties, environmentalists and a host of others. The logic of capitalism may be the complete marketisation and commodification of all aspects of social life, but it is resisted from a multitude of directions. Whether or not a more just and human-centred global economy is possible, however, and the role that human rights advocacy may play in bringing it about, are open questions.

Both global social democrats and liberal communitarians advocate the strengthening of states to realise social, economic and cultural rights. For global social democrats the aim is to strengthen states to enable them to exercise greater control over markets in capital, labour and goods: to provide a degree of stability for investors as well as employees; to increase the resources at their disposal for public goods such as education and health-care; and to enable them to provide a reasonable standard of well-being and security for people who are not in paid work. In terms of global trade what is needed is regulation that is fair rather than 'free': that enables developing economies to protect 'infant industries' (as the United States and Europe did when they were developing their economies, and still do today) and crucial food supplies, whilst the markets of highly industrialised countries are opened up to imports in order to promote genuine competition. A fair taxation system that would close tax havens and offshore banking, and that would raise taxes on wealth is necessary. And flows of money should be slowed down (by a Robin Hood, or Tobin, Tax) to prevent it being diverted from investment in productive industries, to discourage the enormous inequalities in wealth being generated by financial speculation, and to stabilise national currencies and banking systems. Finally, 'odious debt', which has benefitted bankers and not the people who live in states to which it was loaned, should be dropped to enable governments to spend more on promoting economic growth and protecting people from global markets.[13]

Global social democrats do not believe that globalisation necessarily means a 'race to the bottom'. It need not mean undercutting wages and workers' conditions. How people fare within states depends on national public policies. IFIs and TNCs have put pressures on all states to liberalise their economies since the 1980s, but these pressures have been quite differently dealt with in different countries. In the United States and Australia neo-liberalism has led to massive changes in social provision, while in Denmark and Germany state protection for workers and citizens remains strong (Doogan 2009). South Korea stands out as an example of a previously authoritarian state which, now it has achieved a high level of development, has introduced state protection and social provision, in part as a *response* to pressures of globalisation and the Asian financial crisis (Scholte 2005: 198).

Historically social democracy has only ever been realised in a small handful of states. It has been states at the metropolitan 'core' that have – as a result of pressure from social movements, unions and political parties – provided social rights for workers and economic support and social security for those outside paid work. This does not necessarily mean that social democratic states are impossible elsewhere. Sandbrook *et al.* have studied the very particular conditions of what they see as the relatively successful welfare states 'of the global periphery': Costa Rica, Kerala, Mauritius and Chile. However, uneven capitalist development which creates and depends on inequalities may mean that social democracy is not possible everywhere *at the same time*: as some national economies develop comparative advantages over others, there will inevitably be movements of capital to more profitable regions. In fact, Sandbrook *et al.* argue that these economies are much more vulnerable than larger European states to being undermined by foreign investment today. They are similar to welfare states in Scandinavia and Europe in that they offer the comparative advantages of peace, stability and good infrastructure. However, their workers are not skilled and educated enough to compete with those in the Northwest, whilst relatively high wages, good working conditions and high taxation make it difficult for them to compete with states that offer much cheaper labour and tax breaks (Sandbrook *et al.* 2007: 32–4).

Local communitarians and global social democrats share the aim of bringing national economies under democratic control through state regulation. Ultimately, however, they have different visions of how human rights should be realised. At times these visions clash. Whilst for global social democrats capitalist investment can be managed to enable democratic, human-centred economic growth, local communitarians are opposed to industrialisation and foreign investment. In rural areas investment in industrial agri-businesses and in mining to extract natural resources displaces people who already live at the very margins of their societies: indigenous peoples and small farmers. What becomes then of their human rights to stay where they are and to continue to live in ways they value? On the other hand, if their cultural rights are respected, what is the effect of *not* allowing development projects that, with proper regulation and state regulation, could have the effect of improving the social and economic rights of those who cannot support themselves and their families by living off the land?

In a sense this has been the dilemma for governments in Latin American countries that have taken the route of 'neo-extractivism'. Eduardo Gudynas, inventor of the term 'neo-extractivism', is highly critical of the choices that have been made by left-wing governments in Latin America to invest in mining and agri-business on the basis that they are neglecting ideals of 'buen vivir'. Gudynas acknowledges, however, that unlike previous administrations that oversaw national economies built on exports of raw materials, the governments of Brazil under Lula, Argentina under Kirchner, and Morales in Bolivia have used tax revenues and income from 'neo-extractivism' to build social programmes that transfer wealth to poor families. Gudynas seems to be opposed to these programmes on the basis that they pacify resistance to 'neo-extractivism'. But where governments are using wealth to build education, health-care and social security, might we conclude rather that there is an inherent *conflict* of values between local communitarianism and social democracy? Gudynas is in favour of local communitarianism, but perhaps social democrats have a point when they argue that transnational markets, properly managed, can be to the advantage of most people.

The 'tragic dilemma' represented by the differences between global social democrats and local communitarians may not be quite as stark as the choice that has to be made for or against military intervention to prevent genocide that we looked at in Chapter 4 – though for people who are displaced by development and neo-extractivist projects, it is just as immediate. It is a real dilemma nevertheless. Humanising capitalism involves planning at international, national and local levels. In order to plan, governments need a vision of how society should be organised, and how markets are to be shaped and limited. Although global social democrats and local communitarians are allies in campaigns against repression and for social and economic rights up to a point, ultimately the visions of local communitarianism and global social democracy are not compatible. The danger then is that arguments for 'buen vivir' become as marginalised as the small farmers and indigenous people local communitarians take as exemplary. Although global social democracy is certainly more benign than neo-liberalism, it may be just as damaging for those who do not fit mainstream ideals of development.

6 Women's rights are human rights

Let us look for more allies. And to look for them, let's look for languages that cannot be rejected.

(Susan Chiarotti, quoted in Keck and Sikkink 1998: 166)

Until recently, human rights standards were set and monitored in inter-governmental organisations (IGOs) in ways that confirmed men as having greater value than women. The human rights listed by the Universal Declaration of Human Rights (UDHR) are supposed to apply to everyone 'without distinction of any kind, such as race, colour, sex, language, religion, political or other opinion, national or social origin, property, birth or other status' (Article 2 UDHR). However, foundational human rights documents, the UDHR, the International Covenant on Civil and Political Rights (ICCPR) and the International Covenant on Economic, Social and Cultural Rights (ICESCR) are not gender-neutral. They do not apply equally to women and to men. The fact that these documents use the pronoun 'he' throughout is not accidental. Rather than listing universal, gender-neutral rights, they list 'what men fear will happen to them' (Edwards 2011: 51–64). The UDHR, ICCPR and ICESCR practically never mention women explicitly, and they are above all concerned with what happens to people in the public sphere, as a result of activities and policies carried out on behalf of the state. The private domestic sphere of the family, which has at least as much impact on how women are controlled and exploited, is constructed in foundational human rights documents as a place of natural, family relations, somewhere that is itself in need of 'protection'.

It was not until the 1990s that feminists came to the question, 'Are women's rights human rights?'. The women's movements of the 1970s and 1980s took little interest in human rights. In the Northwest, radical and socialist-inclined movements were more concerned with raising consciousness and finding new ways to live in egalitarian and liberated ways outside the nuclear family than with changing laws and policies. Women's movements in what was then called the 'Third World' also had their own concerns, different in different national and regional contexts. Even when the Convention on the Elimination of All Forms of Discrimination against Women (CEDAW) was signed and ratified in the 1970s, as a result of the efforts of people involved in the UN Commission on the Status of Women that dates back to 1946, it seemed too limited and bureaucratic to hold much appeal (Reilly 2009).

The question 'Are women's rights human rights?' emerged along-side the building of a new consensus amongst feminists and women's organisations that the answer could and should be 'yes'.[1] In large part this was due to the UN decade of women, which brought thousands of non-governmental organisations (NGOs) together at global conferences beginning in Mexico in 1975. Initially activists clashed over priorities and strategies. Women from the South found women from the North patronising: unable and unwilling to understand the importance of global inequalities in women's lives. Eventually it seems that a focus on violence against women enabled agreement, and a plan of action was drawn up at the Fourth Women's World Conference in Beijing in 1995. NGOs could agree that violence against women was a very serious problem everywhere *and* that it took many different forms around the world.[2]

Defining violence against women as a violation of human rights is a way of representing women's rights as fundamental, of the same level of importance as torture, imprisonment without trial, disappearance and extra-judicial execution.[3] Although since the Vienna Conference that was held by the UN in 1993 human rights are supposed to be *indivisible* (all are supposed to be equally important and necessary for the enjoyment of each other), in fact, rights to 'physical integrity' are often treated as more fundamental than others. Rights to life, freedom from imprisonment without trial, torture and slavery are sometimes called *jus cogens* or 'peremptory norms', meaning that they may never be overruled or ignored, even during times of war or national emergency (see Alston and Goodman 2013: 163–5). It is actions by agents employed by the state, however, that are expressly forbidden: the right to life is the right not to be deprived of life by the military or police, the right to be free from torture is the right not to be subjected to pain in processes of interrogation by soldiers, police or prison guards. Traditionally, then, fundamental rights to physical integrity have been developed with men in mind (Charlesworth and Chinkin 2006). The violence women suffer, which is far more likely to be carried out by 'private individuals' – family members, members of the community or strangers – than by state agents, had been completely ignored in international human rights law.

In the twenty years since feminists asked the question 'Are women's rights human rights?' much has changed. Women's rights have been 'mainstreamed' at the UN. As we shall see, even the resolutions of the Security Council now show some awareness of women's rights. In this respect the kinds of problems that are raised by constructions of human rights that we have looked at in previous chapters are now equally important with regard to women's rights. Women's rights raise all the difficulties of neo-imperialism, elitism and empty bureaucratic proceduralism that we have considered with respect to other constructions of human rights. Because the violence women suffer is more likely to take place outside the state, however, in the 'private' sphere of the family and the neighbourhood, constructing women's rights as human rights also raises very particular difficulties. Creative constructions of human rights in cultural politics outside the bureaucratic procedures of IGOs and states in which women's organisations are involved offer insights into the possibilities, and the limitations, of human rights today.

'Gender violence' at the UN

Gender violence is violence against women *because* they are girls and women.[4] The term covers a wide range of abuses. Most violence against women is not committed by agents of the state. Rape and other forms of violence may be used as forms of torture or punishment by police, prison guards or soldiers. But rape, murder, domestic violence, sexual assault at work, enforced slavery and prostitution: these are most commonly committed by 'private' individuals and groups. In addition, some forms of violence are just as likely to be committed by women as they are by men. This is the case with regard to what are often called 'harmful customary practices'. Female genital mutilation (FGM) is typically carried out by women, for example, as part of rituals that accompany girls' coming of age, their transition to womanhood. Other gender violence, like honour-killing and dowry murders, may also be carried out with the collusion of women who fear that their family status or wealth has been damaged by the behaviour of other women and that they must be punished.

As a result of pressure from transnational feminist and human rights networks, women's rights as human rights have been 'mainstreamed' in the UN. In the UN report on the Beijing conference mainstreaming was called for 'so that, before decisions are taken, an analysis is made of the effects on women and men, respectively' (Otto 2010: 100). The idea of mainstreaming is that women's rights to freedom from violence should become as uncontroversial as fundamental human rights that apply more generally to men.[5]

In her review of how violence against women is treated in international human rights law, Alice Edwards argues that all treaty bodies of the UN do now take it into account. Edwards argues that women's issues are no longer sidelined in the 'Women's Committee' that monitors CEDAW. All the treaty bodies now report back on states' responsibilities to end gender violence against women when advising on country reports. They also respond to individual petitions that are made by women bringing complaints against their states for failing to prevent gender violence or provide redress for victims. Even the Security Council has been willing to consider violence against women as a threat to international peace (Edwards 2011).

'Mainstreaming' women's rights as human rights could be seen as an immense achievement given the complete neglect of violence against women at the UN until recently. This is not, however, how it is seen by most feminists involved at the UN. Edwards argues that rather than *challenging* the perception that human rights are actually men's rights, mainstreaming has subtly reinstated the gendered hierarchy of international law: what happens to men at the hands of state agents is still taken to be more important than what happens to women at the hands of family members and others. The problem is that advocates of women's rights must fit definitions of gender violence into criteria that were developed to deal with violence by state agents. It is always a stretch to adapt these criteria to gender violence, and Edwards argues that it is therefore impossible for women's rights to gain the status of (men's) fundamental human rights (Edwards 2011).

Edwards outlines two main ways treaty bodies have adapted established human rights law to cover gender violence. The first is by showing that states discriminate against women when they do not exercise 'due diligence' to prevent gender violence or to provide redress for victims. Discrimination on the basis of sex is prohibited by all UN conventions. Treating gender violence against women as discrimination emphasises that protecting *everyone* is states' responsibility, even when it is not the brutality of prison guards, soldiers or police that is at issue. It is complex to show that there has been discrimination in the observance of a treaty. A two-step process is necessary. Advocates have to show that violence was carried out on women because they are women, or that it is violence that affects women disproportionately. Then they must show that the violence was ignored or condoned by police, the courts, and/or in public policy and law. It is necessary, in other words, to show that gender violence is *systematic, and* that it is tolerated by the state. Given that violence against women is under-reported and under-recorded, this can be extremely difficult. In comparison it is only necessary to show that state officials have been involved in *one* case of torture or murder to decide that there has been a violation of human rights. Nevertheless, there have been some cases in which the case for understanding gender violence against women as sex discrimination has been made quite successfully. Edwards gives the example of a CEDAW report on a series of abductions, rapes and murders of young women in the Ciudad Juarez area of Chihuahua, Mexico in 2005. The Women's Committee found that hatred and misogyny were the root causes of the violence, and that they had been going on for over a decade without anyone being convicted of the crimes. The report also made it clear that the state had a responsibility to combat discrimination against women, not only in assisting the families of the women killed but also with 'specific policies on gender equality' (Edwards 2011: 187–8; see also Alston and Goodman 2013: 198–201).

In addition to the *practical* difficulties of addressing gender violence against women as sex discrimination, Edwards argues that to do so is *symbolically* more complex than a straightforward denunciation of violations of human rights. It seems counter-intuitive, she says, to think of the violence that women suffer as wrong because it is *discrimination*, rather than because it violates fundamental human rights. Discrimination is controversial in a way that *jus cogens* norms are not. It is notable that CEDAW has a large number of reservations against it. All UN conventions allow states to put reservations against at least some of their articles, to opt out of certain aspects of the provisions, as long as opting out does not go against the core purposes of the convention. The vast majority of state reservations on CEDAW concern customary, religious and family law. Effectively they are reservations that enable states to opt out of eliminating discrimination against women – the purpose of the convention – in matters concerning marriage, child-rearing and

family relations. Reservations against CEDAW aim to protect the differences in roles, and rights, of men and women that sustain structures
of gender inequality (Coomaraswamy 1994). Edwards argues that most
of these reservations are not legal, and they have been criticised by the
Women's Committee. But states have not been asked to systematically
review the reservations they placed on CEDAW when they ratified it
before it came into force in 1980 (Edwards 2011: 50). In a sense, then,
framing gender violence as discrimination *adds* levels of complexity and
controversy, rather than framing it as unequivocally wrong (Edwards
2011: 179–97).

The second way women's rights have been mainstreamed in treaty
bodies has been by considering gender violence against women as *like*
violations of human rights that are widely agreed to be fundamental.
In effect, this strategy aims to have violence against women considered
as a breach of a *jus cogens* norm. Considering rape as torture began in
the 1990s in relation to the tribunal that was set up to try war crimes,
genocide and crimes against humanity in the Former Yugoslavia under
international humanitarian law.[6] Subsequently, rape that is committed
outside armed conflict has also been defined as torture by the committees that monitor the ICCPR and the Convention Against Torture.
However, Edwards describes the approach to rape as torture at the UN
as inconsistent and superficial. Feminists have argued that many forms
of gender violence against women can be likened to torture because
they are intended to control and intimidate by inflicting pain, physical
and psychological (Copelon 1994). But according to Edwards, though
the UN Human Rights Committee and the Committee Against Torture
have equated rape with torture in a few cases, they have not presented
reasoned arguments to show *why* rape (and not other forms of violence)
is like torture, nor under what conditions (Edwards 2011: 216–62). They
have treated rape as exceptional, as 'special', without trying to show
what makes it so horrific. Under these circumstances, Edwards argues,
it seems unlikely that rape will come to be perceived as a violation of
human rights that is just as serious as torture.

Neo-imperialist feminism?

While feminists at the UN continue to find women's rights marginalised
in international human rights law, at the same time there is growing

criticism of what Janet Halley calls 'governance feminism'. According to Halley, feminists and feminist ideas are now part of global governance. By global governance she means not just legislation and policy-making, but also the way experts working for NGOs and IGOs have won authority to influence the development of international human rights law (Halley 2006: 341). Far from powerless and marginalised, Halley represents feminists as influential in international non-governmental organisations (INGOs), at the UN, and in charitable foundations and in governments. As such, according to Halley, feminists are valid targets of criticisms: they may be elitist, technocratic, and the way they construct women's rights may have colluded with and furthered a specific vision of US national interests since the end of the Cold War.

One of the main areas of criticism of governance feminism as neo-imperialist is in relation to humanitarian intervention. Karen Engle argues that feminists – like other 'human rights hawks' at the UN – have contributed to the idea that humanitarian intervention is justified where violence against women is systematic. As an example Engle discusses an article called 'Women's September 11th' published by Catherine MacKinnon in 2006 in which she asks why humanitarian intervention can be justified to protect *men* from violence carried out by other *men* (when both sides are engaged in armed conflict) when systematic violence against *women* in armed combat continues to be ignored. In terms of her contribution to international law, MacKinnon made the case in the early 1990s that rape in Bosnia should be considered genocidal because Serbian soldiers were targeting Bosnian women to achieve their aim of 'ethnic cleansing'. In the International Criminal Tribunal for the Former Yugoslavia (ICTY) some soldiers were prosecuted and convicted of rape as a crime against humanity. Engle considers MacKinnon's focus on horrifying atrocities to be problematic because it contributes to the kind of 'emergency thinking' that make calls for 'something to be done' virtually irresistible. At the same time focus on what is happening 'right now' allows people in the Northwest to ignore longer-term structural problems in which their states have been implicated (Engle 2007).

In fact, there is now an international legal agreement that women should be protected from gender violence in situations of armed conflict. In 2000 the Security Council passed what is considered the landmark Resolution 1325, the first to deal with women, security and peace. Article 10 of this resolution requires state parties that sign it to take 'special measures to protect women and girls from gender-based violence, particularly rape and other forms of sexual abuse, and all other forms of violence in situations of armed conflict'. The resolution also, however, has several articles on the importance of including women as active participants in building peace. Historically, peace has been a central concern of many women's organisations. As Dianne Otto points out, there is a range of feminist voices and positions on women, war and peace that are represented in the organisations that lobby and advise the UN Security Council (Otto 2010; see also Cohn 2008). Given that 'humanitarian intervention' is so highly contested (as we saw in Chapter 4), even after the agreement on the Responsibility to Protect in 2005, and that getting agreement on it is so complex, it seems very unlikely that where feminists had any influence at all they would all speak with one voice. The complexities of winning a resolution to intervene to protect any civilians would not be reduced by considering the views of feminists concerned with violence against women. There would surely be some feminists 'for' and others 'against' if protecting women against sexual violence were to be raised as a real option at the Security Council.

The second area of controversy over feminists in global governance is the amount and the direction of funding for combatting gender violence since the 1990s. Janet Johnson notes that in Russia alone, millions of dollars funded women's organisations between 1997 and 2006. Some came from the EU, Scandinavian countries and the UN, but the vast majority came from the United States: from the government and from philanthropic organisations like the Ford Foundation (Johnson 2009: 57–60). This was the period following the collapse of communism and the Soviet Union. Johnson suggests that the United States Agency for International Development was part of the foreign policy of the Clinton administration: a way of securing US interests in the former rival superpower. Funding NGOs could be seen as 'soft' US imperialism: as an attempt to remake Russian society from within, to 'build democracy' to safeguard the region for US security and prosperity. Johnson argues – in contrast to Keck's and Sikkink's analysis of US funding in Latin America as helping to create a 'boomerang effect' – that so great were the flows of funding and expertise into Russia during this period that the relationship between foreign money and local organisations was more like 'catch': '[g]lobal actors (donors, transnational activists, and governments) tossed the ball (funds, norms, diplomacy) at Russia (activists, policy-makers, social workers, and law enforcement officials) and waited to see if Russia would drop it' (Johnson 2009: 155).

A number of problems have been identified with international funding to human rights organisations that are relevant here. They reiterate the more general problems of NGOs we looked at in Chapter 2. First, where it is the only source of income to which organisations – and often also the individuals who work for them – have access, funders can impose priorities that are quite different to the work people see as important locally and nationally. According to Valerie Sperling and her colleagues, the end of communism in Russia saw a flourishing of women's organisations concerned with a range of issues. Many women's activists in Russia in the early 1990s saw crime, corruption and the collapse of the welfare state as more pressing problems than violence against women (Sperling *et al.* 2001: 1169; see also Hyrcak 2002). Second, funding can contribute to what is sometimes called the 'NGO-isation' of politics. It is only credible organisations that receive funding: those that are formal, hierarchical and bureaucratic. This can be problematic where such organisations displace more fluid, inclusive and responsive grassroots activity, and political organising becomes dependent on professionalism and expertise (Alvarez 1998; Menon 2004: 219–20).

However, NGO-isation is not a simple one-way process in which the poorest women always lose out. In fact funding creates a situation where what counts as an NGO *itself* becomes a matter of politics. As Dorothea Hilhorst found in her study of NGO-isation in the remote highlands of the Phillipines in the mid-1990s, in practice funding can give some scope to women with informal claims on those who are employed by NGOs, especially as funders often make 'reaching the grassroots' a condition of donating money (Hilhorst 2003). In addition, from their fieldwork in Latin America in the late 1990s, Maxine Molyneux and Sian Lazar found that NGOs tried to select donors who shared similar values, and who would allow them to pursue strategies for longer-term structural change not just short-term projects. In fact, Molyneux and Lazar found that some NGOs *welcomed* the new focus on gender that was being imposed on all NGOs at this time, arguing that as a result many people who had been resistant to thinking about women were now 'beginning to change their way of seeing reality' (Molyneux and Lazar 2003: 97). On the other hand, Sperling and her colleagues found that the vast amounts of funding flowing into Russia in the 1990s had the effect of *dividing* organisations from each other, creating competition and personal jealousy (Sperling *et al.* 2001).

Despite the dangers of international funding, Johnson argues that money that went to NGOs to deal with rape and domestic violence in Russia did have some valuable results. For her, the important question is not where funding comes from and why, but whether and how it is effective. Johnson argues that up until 2002 many NGOs were able to make use of the funding in ways that were productive for women. Adapting the norms and models that came from transnational feminist networks (in which, of course, many Russian women were themselves involved) to the local context, funding enabled women's organisations to help women resist and escape violence in the home. In particular, the crisis centres that were set up before 2002 were very useful to women. They followed the 'global model' in that they provided shelters for women to leave homes in which they were subject to violence, as well as offering legal help and public education on domestic violence. They were also responsive to the particular needs of the women they served, emphasising the housing needs of women in Russia at this time, for example, where it was often abusive husbands who were registered as having the only legal entitlement to the family home. In this way, Johnson argues the crisis centres worked on immediate problems as well as the more long-term goals of altering gendered hierarchies (Johnson 2009: chapter 3).

On the other hand, and using the same terms of evaluation, Johnson considers US funding following 9/11 to be much more problematic. This funding was focused on combatting people trafficking and enforced prostitution. After 2001, the Bush administration was concerned above all with the securing of borders in Eastern Europe and elsewhere against flows of money, weapons and people associated with international terrorism. States that did not comply with US standards were threatened with economic sanctions: the termination of non-humanitarian and non-trade related aid. In addition, US aid was denied or withdrawn from women's organisations that were seen as supporting the legalisation of prostitution – principally as a result of pressure from religious groups. Many of the crisis centres that had been funded by the United States had to close down or commit themselves to campaigning against prostitution (Johnson 2009: 60–3). Prostitution is a difficult and divisive issue for feminists. There are those who feel very strongly that any form of prostitution involves violence because sex cannot be sold as a commodity – and anyone who thinks they are choosing to do so freely is mistaken. In contrast there are others who think that prostitution can be a form of work, and all workers should have rights – especially where their work makes them vulnerable to abuse. Although, as Chantal

Thomas argues, many people probably take a mid-way position (prostitutes should have rights, even if they are mistaken in thinking that they have freely chosen their line of work), the division amongst feminists made it particularly difficult to engage with the Bush administration, which had its own agenda in pursuing anti-trafficking (Thomas 2006: 349–58). In this instance, it seems that US funding that was ostensibly to be used to combat gender violence actually resulted in the harassment and imprisonment of women who may, or may not, have been trafficked into prostitution. At any rate, as Prabha Kotiswaran argues, the flow of US funding surely altered 'national conversations' everywhere as positions became polarised, sex worker organisations came under increasing pressure, and organisations pursing an abolitionist line with regard to prostitution were strengthened (Kotiswaran 2006: 370–1; see also Kapur 2005). Johnson argues that Russian womens' organisations, supported by transnational feminist networks, did make some impact on domestic legislation regarding prostitution. She also suggests, however, that the heavy-handed approach to sex trafficking resulted in a nationalist backlash in Russia against foreign intervention (Johnson 2009: chapter 6).

Criticisms of feminist constructions of human rights are very similar to criticisms of human rights in general: advocating human rights no longer involves supporting those who are *resisting* abuses of power; claiming human rights also comes from *within* powerful organisations. Claiming women's rights no longer involves just moral authority. Where human rights advocates are making use of the moral and material resources of institutions like the UN and states, they are engaging in Politics with a capital 'P'. Halley surely over-states the case when she suggests that feminists have a 'will to power' that they do not acknowledge, disguising it by adopting a victim status (Halley 2004). Feminists have certainly achieved footholds in the making of international human rights law and public policy. But feminists do not all take the same position, even at the UN. And although feminists have far greater influence than ever before, they do not control the way in which women are represented in the making of international human rights law.

Vernacularisation

In this section we will look in some depth at a third criticism of advocacy for women's rights as neo-imperialist. This concerns how 'culture' is constructed at the UN, and how it is to be understood if women are to enjoy human rights in practice. 'Culture' is especially important to women's rights because the violence women suffer is often closely linked to how gender and sexuality are structured. That is to say, much of the violence that women suffer is not really exceptional. It is on a continuum of how women are assumed to be inferior in various ways, and as therefore rightly, and for our own good, as in need of protection and instruction from men. This means that violence is often normalised – even by women who have been subject to terrible brutality – as a matter of punishment and control that is justified by their own inadequacies and imperfections *as* women. The cultural politics of human rights, the construction of violence against women as wrong, must therefore go far beyond matters of governance through IGOs and states, policy-making and law. If human rights to freedom from gender violence are to be realised in practice, advocates must address how men and women understand themselves as gendered: as human beings who have particular relationships to others in ways that are invariably normalised by being male or female, masculine or feminine.

There are two main ways in which 'culture' is linked to neo-imperialism by critics of women's rights. First, framing violence against women as a 'human rights wrong' tends to be at the same time a construction of some cultures as backward. Sally Engle Merry argues that activists and officials at the UN tend to work with outdated and unhelpful conceptions of 'culture', seeing it in essentialist terms as fixed, bounded and uniformly repressive for women (though at the same time she found that cultural differences and variety are, paradoxically, also considered to be valuable in themselves). Women are seen as 'prisoners of culture'. The Beijing Platform for Action, for example, states that 'Violence against women ... derives essentially from cultural patterns, in particular the harmful effects of certain traditional or customary practices and all acts of extremism linked to race, sex, language or religion that perpetuate the lower status accorded to women in the family, the workplace, the community and society'. It is common to refer to 'customary practices harmful to women and girls' in UN documents on gender violence (Merry 2006: 64). 'Culture' is seen either as 'traditional customs', which supposes that some people are the inheritors of a history that is untouched by the effects of imperialism and capitalism; or as 'national culture', which neglects the enormous differences and range of understandings within a state's territorial boundaries – especially between the educated representatives of nations who participate at the UN and the very many others who do not. In either case, 'culture' is associated with 'tradition' and with violence against women that can, and should, be eradicated through processes of modernisation: through law, regulation and education.

The essentialist view of culture – or rather culture*s* – as bounded and complete is shared both by those who advocate women's rights *and* those who *oppose* women's rights on the grounds that traditions must be defended. According to 'cultural relativists', ideals of human rights are Western: they impose a set of values that women from other cultures do not accept and do not want to live by. It is this kind of reasoning that is embedded in reservations to CEDAW, when states opt out of eliminating discrimination in the family on the basis that communities – which of course include women – have their own religious and customary law. Human rights advocates find cultural relativism unacceptable because it justifies precisely the 'harmful customary practices' to which they are opposed. From the perspective of human rights advocates, cultural relativism is the same as indifference to violence that should be intolerable to *anyone.* The difference between cultural relativists and women's rights advocates is that the latter do not see human rights as 'cultural', but as universal: appropriate to all human beings. It is the failure of human rights advocates to acknowledge that human rights are *also* 'cultural' – what Marie Dembour calls the arrogance of universalism – that enrages those who see 'culture' used only to denote what are considered primitive, backward traditions (see Dembour 2001; see also Cowan *et al.* 2001).

Merry's concept of 'vernacularisation' suggests a way to analyse constructions of human rights that does not begin either from the assumption that values are always and necessarily *either* relative to cultures, *or* that they of the same importance to every human being regardless of their background. The concept of 'vernacularisation' is similar to the way we are thinking about culture in this book in terms of *politics*, emphasising that social constructions are created, sustained *and* transformed as they are lived in everyday practices. Merry argues that human rights activists appropriate global norms and models to bring about change within states, but they must also *translate* them into terms that make sense to people who live in quite different situations. At the same time, human rights will only be useful as long as they continue to *challenge* existing norms. In other words, human rights cannot become *too* close to local understandings, because they then risk losing their critical force. Merry argues that what human rights mean must stay close to the framings of international law, to individual rights to protection of the body from violence, to choice, and to equality. Human rights can only work insofar as, drawing on international norms that emphasise the freedom of the individual and the obligations of states, they are able to disrupt local, established common sense. They must *displace* local understandings of kinship, religion and community whilst being intelligible in terms people understand in order to be genuinely useful (Merry 2006).

What this means in practice is that an emphasis on womens' freedom to choose their relationships must be embedded in 'common sense' assumptions about what it is to be a gendered human being. This is the second way in which critics link 'culture' and women's rights to neo-imperialism. It is precisely the emphasis on *autonomy*, on the freedom of women as individuals to choose how they will live their relationships with others, that those who are suspicious of human rights see as most problematic. Radhika Coomaraswamy, the first UN Special Rapporteur on Violence Against Women, names the kind of person constructed in international human rights law as 'the Enlightenment individual'. This is a woman who defines herself as a free, choosing individual, rather than through her connection to family, community or religion (Coomaraswamy 1994; see also Merry 2006: 220–1). It is an image with which few women in the world would identify, and which many – perhaps especially those who see religion as a source of strength in difficult times – would reject outright (see Abu-Lughod 2013).

'Vernacularisation' suggests that the 'translation' of international human rights norms does mean seeing oneself *in some ways* as an 'Enlightenment individual'. Framing violence against women as a matter of human rights is meant to raise questions that are not otherwise considered important in everyday life. It is meant to challenge the ways in which women are prevented – and women do not allow themselves – to choose relationships that are not abusive. Dealing with and escaping violence, even in the family, need not, however, mean giving up on relationships in which women find themselves. On the contrary, 'vernacularisation' means adapting strategies to combat violence against women to particular conditions and contexts, to particular ways in which women live – as all humans do – in relationships with others.

Women's movements in India offer a valuable example of 'vernacularisation'. Indian feminists are attentive to differences in what women's rights mean to different communities at different times in a multicultural society. At the same time, the women's movement in India has been working to encode the ideal of 'the Enlightenment individual' in Indian law.

A democracy since the 1940s, with a constitution that is in many ways exemplary as encoding human rights, India also has a pluralist legal system in which Hindu, Muslim, Christian, Jewish and Parsi communities have their own family laws governing marriage, divorce, inheritance, maintenance, guardianship, succession and custody. It is on this basis that the Indian government filed a reservation against Article 16 of CEDAW: government officials undertook to end discrimination against women as long as those measures were compatible with 'non-interference with the personal affairs of any community without its initiative and consent' (Merry 2006: 105). The women's movement in India had long campaigned against religious family laws, and for a uniform secular code to secure equal rights for women. But this changed in the 1980s with the rise of Hindu nationalism, which has used the issue of women's rights to attack Muslims as backward and oppressive. It is not that feminists in India now accept that different religious communities must live by different laws. It is rather that for political reasons they have decided to pursue less divisive strategies. Some maintain that to focus on legal reform is misguided altogether because the law is ineffective at best, dangerous at worst (see Menon 2004). We will explore some of these arguments in the final section of this chapter. But those feminist organisations in India that do try to reform law now focus on codes of feminine virtue that date from the British Empire in Victorian times. One example is the law against 'outraging the modesty', which is the only legal redress for women if they are sexually assaulted in India. 'Outraging the modesty', as it is dealt with in Indian courts encourages judges to give attention to ideas of 'womanly propriety', 'shame', 'chastity', 'decency', 'freedom from coarseness, indelicacy and decency' in addressing the validity of a women's case. It focuses attention on women's behaviour on the assumption that any deviation from accepted norms of femininity is unacceptable and legitimates predatory masculine sexuality (Kannabiran and Kannabiran 2002: 82–3). Rajeswari Sunder Rajan sees legal reform feminists as challenging codes that construct sexuality as dangerous to women and replacing them with law that values the 'Enlightenment individual' constructed by transnational feminist networks: the aim is to win recognition in law of women's sexual autonomy and rights to bodily integrity (Rajan 2005: 127).

At the same time, maintaining relationships is very important to women who try to escape from domestic violence. Unless their children are being harmed, it seems that women in India very rarely seek divorce (Merry 2006: 155). What women *do* contest is that they are 'rightfully' under the command of husbands who treat them violently. To be able to remain in their homes whilst escaping, or at least reducing, the violence to which they are subject, women in India try to engage organisations outside the family. They bring to bear a range of methods: from reporting to what are called 'dowry' police stations (though they deal with domestic violence more broadly than the name would suggest), to involving 'women's courts' and 'women's councils', which are groups of women who travel from place to place in rural areas trying to name and shame and alter the behaviour of men who abuse their wives. Although women's courts are unpaid and do not involve professionals, they do use official, headed notepaper, they call on police, and they cite laws that forbid violence against women. Ultimately their authority is not backed by the force of the state; it is informal: they do not bring cases to state courts, but they do cite laws to support their actions. Research by the International Center for Research on Women found that women who had been helped by these organisations had a sense of rights and 'were able to speak up' (Merry 2006: 156–7).

The question of whether people are ever freely choosing individuals is a philosophical one (see Butler 2005). In reality there is no one who is self-sufficient for the whole of their life. There are of course differences in how people see themselves as individuals. Some societies, and some sectors of all societies, are more individualist while others are more communitarian: more oriented towards the group, towards shared values and activities. In all societies families tend to be seen in communitarian terms to a greater or lesser extent. But the form that is taken by 'the family', who it includes, what is expected of its members in terms of obligations and its relevance, or otherwise, to public life, varies enormously at different times and places. In Northwestern societies, the question of individualism as a consequence of de-traditionalisation has been widely discussed in sociology (Beck and Beck-Gernsheim 2001). And whether the idea of the 'autonomous person' or individual is appealing, whether it should be repudiated, or whether it might usefully be accommodated without either being accepted or rejected outright – these are all ongoing debates elsewhere too.[7] Ideals of the individual and its limits will surely continue to be quite differently constructed around the world given the very different contexts and histories out of which such debates emerge. The ideal that women should be free from violence is an issue in the cultural politics of human rights through which what it is to be a person – which is always to be in some kind of relationship to others – is currently being constructed and reconstructed.

The gendered limits of law

How human rights are effective, and what they mean to most people – including women suffering gender violence – depends far more on how they are taken up locally and nationally than it does on agreement between state officials at the international level. Nationally based NGOs, bureaucrats and lawyers understand gender violence, and develop strategies for dealing with it that draw on international agreements, models and resources. They may bring pressure to bear on their states using those agreements. Ultimately, however, beyond legal and policy changes, making violence against women unacceptable depends on changing gendered structures in everyday life.

We have been discussing the various ways in which law and bureaucratic procedures are limited as a resource for achieving human rights throughout this book. These limitations are very evident when we consider gendered structures that sustain violence against women. In states that are close to the ideal type of the post-colonial state, many people are afraid of the law and it is difficult, even dangerous, to try to have it applied to deal with gender violence. In India, one of the most important and long-standing campaigns of women's organisations has been against the sexual violence to which women are quite regularly subjected *by the police* (Coomaraswamy 1994; Rajan 2005). In states that approximate juridical states, women generally have rights that are *formally* equal to those of men in law as a result of feminist campaigning, but this does not necessarily make it easier for women to make use of law to take control of their lives. Making use of state agencies can be especially problematic for women who are seen as belonging to racialised minorities and for those whose legal status as migrants is unclear or who do not have rights to remain in the territory. Even for white women who are citizens and whose formal rights are clear, the law is not always benign. The way in which the law codifies conflict between the innocent victim and the guilty perpetrator can be problematic. It is an opposition that does not always sit easily with women's own understandings of the violence they experience, however unacceptable it may be. As a consequence women are often reluctant to turn to the police and courts. Where domestic violence is concerned, for example, women often say they want to end the violence and keep the relationship. As a consequence, women whose partners have been charged with violence towards them often decide not to press charges, or to withdraw charges before they reach court. As Merry notes, this does not make women ideal, rational subjects in the eyes of the police and the judiciary who may as a consequence treat women who try to involve them to stop violence as lacking seriousness and as unworthy of respect (Merry 2006: 189–92; Goldfarb 2011).

Perhaps the most glaring example of the limitations of the law in terms of the binary opposition of victim and perpetrator is female genital mutilation (FGM, or, more neutrally, 'female genital cutting'). FGM is illegal in most countries of the world, including throughout Africa, but it is still very widely practised and it is rare that the women who carry it out are prosecuted. The types of cutting involved in FGM vary from a pin prick in the clitoris to infibulation, generally carried out on older children, which involves the cutting of the labia, allowing it to heal through scarring, and the creation of a small hole for urine and menstruation. Infibulation leads to problems for women's health when they come to have sex and to give birth. Although infibulation seems cruel to those outside the communities in which it is practised – especially as it is carried out on children – the opposition between guilty perpetrator and innocent victim is not so clear-cut in these cases. Those who carry out FGM, and who have it done to their children, do it for reasons of love, not hate. The reasons people give for continuing the practice are tied up with the belief that a girl cannot become a proper woman without the ritual of FGM, they will not find a husband, and their lives will be ruined as a result. Marie Dembour has traced some of the cases that have been taken to court in France, one of the few countries in Europe in which women have been prosecuted for carrying out FGM. The accused have accepted that they have broken the law – they knew FGM was illegal – but their defence lawyers have represented them as unable to avoid breaking it. The argument in their defence is that people should feel sympathy for the decisions they must take in the difficult situation in which they find themselves, rather than condemning them outright. This does not necessarily mean that there should be no law against FGM. Making FGM as such illegal (rather than having it covered by other offences, like assault) is surely important symbolically as a standard to which societies aspire. It may be more appropriate, however, to try to make rituals of transition to womanhood less damaging through education and health-care, through persuasion rather than by criminal prosecutions that do not address the root of the problem and that punish people whose intentions are misplaced in law but supported by the families and communities in which they live (Dembour 2001; Gunning 2002).

Finally, law can always be enforced in conservative ways, and this is perhaps especially likely where sexuality is, or appears to be, an issue. Indeed, what 'progressive' and 'conservative' mean can be highly problematic when it comes to gender violence. As an example of the conservative interpretation of women's legal rights that appeared to be progressive, Ratna Kapur relates a case in which the judges in the High Court of Mumbai ruled in 1999 in favour of a victim of rape. On the face of it the ruling looks progressive: not only was the woman's right to redress where she had suffered sexual violence upheld, the judges did not insist on circumstantial evidence to support the prosecution; they took her word for it that she had not consented to sex with the accused. Proving that a victim did not consent to sex is often a problem in rape cases because juries do not like to convict men accused of rape where there is the slightest doubt. A good deal hangs on how 'consent' is interpreted. In many cases anything less than evidence that a woman resisted with all her physical force is taken as indicating that she did consent and later changed her mind, falsely accusing the man of rape. Despite the fact that they were not conservative in this respect, however, Kapur argues that the interpretation of the law given by the Mumbai judges (one of whom was a woman) was problematic for women's rights. The judges ruled that supporting evidence was not required to prove rape in India: the woman's word was good enough because 'an Indian woman attaches the maximum importance to her chastity' (Kapur 2005: 113–14). As Kapur points out, although the victim no doubt received legal justice, the problem is that the case was won at the expense of confirming constructions of gender that work against equality between the sexes: women are seen as worthy of justice *only* if they are virtuous, authentic victims. In addition, sexuality is seen as especially dangerous to women. The judgment, and indeed the judges' summing up, made it quite clear that if women are *not* chaste (if they are like Western women), they cannot be believed: it is understood that because of the value placed on women's chastity in India such women are likely to lie if they are found in a 'compromising situation' in order to safe-guard their reputations (Kapur 2005; see also Menon 2004: 130–1).

Women find it difficult to make use of law to take more control over their lives and to gain redress for violence in all kinds of states. Reforming the law is never enough, though it may be important symbolically – whether it is a matter of gaining formally equal rights for women that are like those of men, or of enforcing rights that women already have 'on paper'. In add-ition to legal redress what is necessary are agencies that support women to confront violence: special police units, women's organisations that can advise women about their rights and offer emotional support, accommo-dation for those who have to flee their homes. But how genuinely willing and able to help women are the people who work for state agencies likely to be without changes in the gendered structures of everyday life? Where women are not respected, where the particular difficulties of the situations in which they find themselves are not recognised, and where families and communities – even women themselves – are inclined to think that they brought the violence on themselves or that it was in some way necessary as a punishment or in order to regulate women's sexuality, it is extremely difficult for women to try to take control of violent relationships that may affect them very personally.

The cultural politics of defining women's rights to freedom from violence as a human rights issue involves steering a difficult course between cultural relativism/indifference and universalist arrogance; between the 'horror' of some forms of violence that are truly shocking and the fact that gendered sexuality is not only lived as violence – it is also about pleasure, love, communication; and between the banality of many forms of violence against women, its use as a means of regulation and chastisement, and the fact that this ties it in to relationships that women themselves want to preserve as intrinsically valuable. Tackling violence against women need not be done through the language of human rights: there are other ways of condemning violence against women. Constructing violence against women as a violation of human rights has some symbolic force – though, by the same token, it is also resisted as Western imposition. It enables activists to put pressure on states, and – at least sometimes – to make use of international resources, of ideas and expertise as well as of money. Perhaps above all, the notion of the autonomous, choosing individual that is encoded in international human rights is part, if only part, of what is necessary for women to ref-use and remake relationships of violence in which they find themselves.

7

Do migrants have rights?

Everyone has the right to leave any country, including his own, and to return to his country.

(Article 13, Universal Declaration of Human Rights)

The conception of human rights, based upon the assumed existence of a human being as such, broke down at the very moment when those who professed to believe in it were for the first time confronted with people who had indeed lost all other qualities and specific relationships – except they were still human. The world found nothing sacred in the abstract nakedness of being human.

(Arendt 1979: 299)

According to the UN Declaration of Human Rights (UDHR) 'everyone' is entitled to life, liberty, political participation, and a degree of economic and social security. 'No-one' is to be arbitrarily deprived of their liberty, tortured or subjected to 'cruel and unusual punishment'. In principle, universal human rights are 'de-territorialised', applicable to every*one*, every*where*. In this respect human rights seem to be made for migrants, since most (though not all) can also be said to be de-territorialised inso-far as they travel to live outside the states of which they are citizens.[1]

In terms of the situations migrants leave behind them, it is not hard to see the relevance of human rights: people flee their homes because they are afraid of being attacked by armed militias or of being bombed; they are displaced from their homes and livelihoods by devel-opment projects or environmental damage; they move to find a better way of life for themselves and their families, trying to escape poverty, ill-health and economic insecurity; and they flee violence that is threat-ened or that they have suffered at the hands of state agents or from which their state has failed to protect them. Given that people are suffering from poverty, lack of opportunities *and* violence in some parts of the world, very often their reasons for moving to another country are mixed. In terms of the human rights they may enjoy migrants fall into quite different legal categories. In Europe and North America, authorised migrants are workers who have been recruited for their skills, people who have come legally to join other family members, or who have been granted political asylum as refugees or who are waiting for a decision on their application for asylum. If they are not authorised, migrants are 'irregular': they are living and working illegally – they have overstayed their visas, they have not left or been deported though their asylum claim has been rejected, or they have never been registered as entering the country at all. Elsewhere, especially in the states around the Persian Gulf and the 'Asian Tigers', migrants are recruited as unskilled workers and considered to be living only temporarily there – even though they very often seem to consider themselves as settlers (Ruh 2013: 11). Where people find themselves in camps managed by the United Nations High Commissioner for Refugees (UNHCR) their legal status is clear – they have been classified as refugees – but their immediate and longer-term prospects of enjoying anything more than the most minimal human rights are very uncertain.

International law covering migrants' rights has been developing since the UDHR. In principle, migrants should be entitled to all the human rights covered by the major Conventions, the International Covenant on Civil and Political Rights (ICCPR) and the International Covenant on Economic, Social and Cultural Rights (ICESCR). According to these Conventions all human beings living in the territory of a state, irrespective of their national origin and whether they are migrants or citizens, must have *the same rights*.[2] Migrants' rights have continued to be neglected, however, to the point where a separate Convention covering them was felt to be necessary at the UN. The Convention on the Protection of the Rights of All Migrant Workers and their Families (CPRAMW) eventually entered into force in 2003, and it now has a Committee that explicitly addresses states' treatment of migrants around the world. Very few states have signed the Convention, however – it is the least ratified human rights treaty in the UN – and all those that have done so are countries from which migrants typically move. None of the states that *receive* large numbers of migrants (in the Northwest or elsewhere) have signed it (Grant 2011).

The most well-established international law with respect to migrants' rights is the 1951 UN Convention relating to the Status of Refugees.

It is far more limited than the ICCPR and the ICESCR in the range of rights it accords to migrants. Above all, the 'Refugee Convention' encodes the right not to be sent back to a country where a person has a well-founded fear of persecution (often called the right of *non-refoulement*). Typically asylum was conceived of as offering protection from persecution where a person was seen as an 'enemy of the state': it was state agents they feared. In recent years NGOs have campaigned against the conventional (male) image of the person suffering persecution, and to have people who fear gender violence from which their state does not protect them (women in some countries, and also gay men) included as eligible for asylum (see Bhabha 1996, 2002). These campaigns have had some success in the United States, Canada and the UK (Musalo *et al.* 2011). What is most striking, however, are the difficulties that must be overcome by *anyone* who seeks refugee status.

In fact, although globalisation generally concerns the facilitation of flows *across* borders, the regulation and securitisation of borders *against* flows of *human beings* is more highly prized than ever. In large part, as we shall see, the control of migration is a product of framings of state sovereignty. However, control of migration also, at least in part, represents attempts by public policy-makers to manage popular sentiments concerning what people of different nationalities and ethnic backgrounds are due, and what they are worth. In the Northwest, the role that is played by the mainstream media in creating scares over migrants as criminals, terrorists, or as simply too numerous – as 'flooding' across borders and overwhelming national and local public services and communities – cannot be over-estimated. Human rights may be de-territorialised in principle, but in practice it is officials acting in the name of states who decide migrants' fates. Migrants must be constructed as bearers of human rights in a world that continues to be structured by state sovereignty and the priority of 'national interests'.

In this chapter we will consider first the control of state borders as raising a number of issues of human rights. Northwestern states recognise the right to seek asylum, but since the 1970s, and especially since the numbers of people seeking asylum in these states rose sharply in the 1990s, all these states have had public policies that are designed *to keep people out* (Gibney 2005). The tightening of borders has had a negative impact on peoples' possibilities of actually enjoying human rights in practice. We then consider the rights of migrants who have legally settled in Northwestern states. We might expect that they would enjoy the same rights as citizens given international rights law. Post-national citizenship would seem to be a logical consequence of adopting inter-national human rights law insofar as it abolishes the distinction between citizen and migrant. There are now some aspects of EU policy that do go some way towards post-national citizenship – but it remains a distant dream for many migrants. In fact, what we will mostly be concerned with in this chapter is how the regulation of migration *creates* human rights abuses. This is nowhere more evident than in the treatment suf-fered by refugees in camps managed by the UNHCR.

Crossing borders: regulation without rights

Migrants cross state borders. In some places borders are 'porous'. The border between Pakistan and Afghanistan, for example, runs through high mountains, the people on either side of it often speak the same dialect and identify as sharing ethnic origins and customs. It is a border they are used to crossing, and it is virtually impossible to police (Macleod 2008). In contrast, and especially since the events of 9/11 in the United States, there has been a tightening of bor-ders in many states, and concerns over security and terrorism have risen up the agenda in the Northwestern states that dominate inter-national policy-making. The securitisation of borders has had serious impacts on migrants' human rights. It is important not to over-state the novelty of this development. The right to *enter* a country was never included in the human rights conventions of the twentieth cen-tury: immigration remained under the control of the state parties to these conventions in principle as well as in practice. In recent years, however, there has been analysis of 'Fortress Europe': as borders have been opened *within* the European Union they have been tightened around it to keep people out. 'Fortress America' is also being con-structed – literally in the case of the 'Border Fence' along the border with Mexico – as the United States, once famous for welcoming the 'huddled masses' of the world at Ellis Island, becomes increasingly difficult to enter, even as a visitor.

The increased securitisation of borders is problematic for migrants' rights to life. Most migrants actually cross borders legally (most irregu-lar migrants overstay visas), but there are those who are desperate enough to try to cross them without permission. People trying to get to Europe from North Africa are loaded onto boats that cannot carry them to their hoped-for destination, especially in bad weather. People trying to cross the border from Mexico into the United States perish in the desert (Golash-Boza and Menjivar 2012). All the clandestine routes across borders are made more *dangerous* as a result of attempts to make borders more *secure* when people are desperate and determined enough to continue trying to cross them.

The securitisation of borders is one part of the 'non-arrival' measures Northwestern states are taking to try to make borders impossible to cross without authorisation. These measures include vetting travellers at airports to prevent people *leaving* their countries if there is a suspicion that they may be trying to emigrate, and setting up detention centres in countries of 'transit' (Spain and Italy have established them in North Africa, for example, the UK and the Netherlands in Turkey, the United States in Guantanamo Bay) (Troeller 2008; Flynn and Cannon 2010). Mathew Gibney reports that in 2003 UK immigration officials prevented Roma boarding flights to Britain in Prague, where it was understood that they would claim asylum (Gibney 2005: 10). Such measures are clearly at odds with the principles of the 1951 Refugee Convention and with international human rights law. They effectively expand the borders of Northwestern states into the territory of other countries. How can a person seek asylum if they are prevented from fleeing a state, or from entering another? Although the Refugee Convention stops short of giving people the right to enter a country of which they are not a citizen, Article 13 does require states to recognise that people fleeing persecution may have to enter another country illegally, without a visa or a valid passport. What would otherwise be an illegal activity is justified by the Refugee Convention because of the situation in which the person finds themselves. And indeed, illegal actions that people have taken to escape oppression in the past are now celebrated: we have only to consider the runaway slaves who fled the South of the United States, helped by people in the 'underground railway'. Non-arrival measures, on the other hand, are intended to prevent people crossing borders, to enable the prosecution of the smugglers who help them, and even to bring sanctions against the transport companies that do not prevent them from travelling.

People who are caught crossing borders without authorisation are punished. Crossing borders without a visa or a passport now invariably results in detention in Europe and the United States where a person cannot be immediately returned to the country of which they are a citizen. The right not to be imprisoned without due process is probably the most well-established in international law. According to a ruling of the European Court of Human Rights (*Saadi* v. *UK* 2008), however, it is legal to detain 'asylum-seekers' for up to eighteen months, without guaranteed legal representation, and with only a very tenuous right to appeal against being detained, or against being deported once it has been decided (Webber 2012: 136). In effect, to detain someone who is seeking asylum is to treat them as guilty until they are able to prove – against all odds – that they are innocent. Asylum-seekers appear to be an exception to the absolute and fundamental human right not to be imprisoned without trial.

In order to be granted the right to stay, asylum-seekers must overcome suspicions that they are economic migrants, criminals, even terrorists. In the UK (as elsewhere) the system by which they are required to do this falls far short of the ideal standards of the law as impartial, as administered in the same way for everyone in the same situation. To be granted refugee status, you must show that you would have suffered persecution had you remained in your country. Clearly this is difficult to do: often, unless a person has already been subjected to violence that has left lasting marks, the only evidence available is the person's own testimony. The evidence is heard in special immigration tribunals where it is accompanied by 'country reports' that detail ongoing human rights violations and the groups that are most at risk of being tortured or killed for their political activities, their beliefs, their ethnic identity, or their gender and sexuality in different parts of the world. In the great majority of cases, the reason a judge gives for refusing an application is that s/he simply does not believe that an applicant is telling the truth – even if there are well-documented violations of human rights going on in the countries from which they are fleeing. Given that assessing asylum claims is all about the *credibility* of the person making the claim, the context in which 'illegals' are judged is crucial, and a good deal rests on a judge's personal feelings, their intuition about the evidence before them, even their sense of what might actually count as reasonable evidence concerning, for example, persecution in Iran or the Congo. As a consequence, judgments in asylum cases are extremely unpredictable. In fact they are so arbitrary that Toby Kelly argues that asylum law cannot really count as law at all. It is a system designed to deter applicants, and it pays only lip service to ensuring human rights (Kelly 2011).[3]

Finally, 'the shadow of the border' is also felt *inside* Northwestern states (Bosniak 2011). That is to say, states increasingly police migration *within* their own territories, trying to catch 'illegals' to deport. Policing migration within states impacts on the human rights of citizens as well as migrants. The most glaring example here is the way in which Arizona effectively legalised racial profiling in 2010. Arizona SB 1070 made it a crime not to carry immigration documents, and gave the police powers to stop and search anyone they suspected of being in the country illegally. Those who were most subject to these measures, predictably, were Hispanics – whether or not they were citizens (Archibold 2010; Howe 2012).[4] More generally, the securitisation of borders is associated with increased surveillance and control for everyone. In the UK a range of actors are now required to report on individuals so that state officials can check for illegal migrants: marriage registrars are required by law to report on 'suspicious marriages' between EU and non-EU citizens; landlords who rent out private property may be asked about their occupants; employees must check migrants' rights to work, and cafés, restaurants and supermarkets that serve 'ethnic' food are subject to spot checks; even college lecturers are expected to report to the UK Border Agency if their foreign students miss classes (the college's licence to teach non-citizen students may be removed if they do not) (Webber 2012). Effectively, policing migration 'in the shadow of the border' means greater surveillance and control for everyone, and racialised minorities especially are treated with suspicion, guilty until proved innocent.

The control of borders by Northwestern states – their concrete territorial frontiers but also the more abstract 'borders' within *and* outside states – clashes with both the letter of international human rights law and its spirit. Claims to asylum by people who make it across borders are dealt with formally, according to the letter of refugee law, but the public policies of these states are designed to keep people out, and many of the practices of officials involved in monitoring border crossing also work to this end. Politicians and publics fear 'floods' of migrants, it is widely assumed that 'asylum-seekers' are really '*bogus* asylum-seekers', and crossing borders illegally is associated with criminality, 'human trafficking' and terrorism. As a consequence, the law is administered to *regulate* and *manage* migration, not to uphold human rights. Officials sort, count and control people who cross borders, and the system is designed to demonstrate to the adventurous or desperate that they are likely to be punished, humiliated, even to lose their lives, if they try to enter Northwestern states without authorisation. Guaranteeing individual human rights is not the primary purpose of states' control of borders. Human rights are far down the list of priorities for those who manage the 'migration-asylum industry', and the securitisation of borders has dangerous consequences for the human rights of both migrants and citizens.

(Some) migrants into (post-national) citizens

Not all migrants who are non-citizens are without rights. Skilled workers who have been recruited from other countries as scientists and technicians or to work in health-care; people who been granted refugee status – judged by immigration authorities to be in fear of persecution if they are returned to the countries of which they are citizens; and people who have been allowed to stay on the grounds of family reunion: all these groups of people have rights in Northwestern states. In fact, it is sometimes argued that because discrimination on the grounds of national origin has been abolished for at least some migrants in at least some places, we might think of citizenship itself as becoming *post-national*.

It is especially within Europe that post-national citizenship is seen as a real possibility. In the first place this is because European citizenship is itself post-national. Although European citizenship is only allowed to those who are already citizens of the member states of the European Union, it does grant people rights that go beyond those of any specific national state. Above all, European citizenship enables people to move to work in any member state without having to apply for a permit. European citizenship has enabled the legal migration of hundreds of thousands of people from Eastern Europe to work in Western Europe since the accession of those states to the European Union in the early twenty-first century, and there are also significant numbers of young French people working and living in London, Italians in Amsterdam, and so on (Castles *et al.* 2014). Second, *all* individuals under the jurisdiction of member states of the Council of Europe (not just citizens of those states) are entitled to respect for fundamental civil rights. This means that people who are *not* European citizens (as well as those who are) may take any member state to the European Court of Human Rights to ensure that their rights are upheld. This is a long drawn-out process (cases have to go through national court systems first), and the results are not always satisfactory; but it does mean that all those within the jurisdictions of European states have access to a court beyond the national state in which they live (see Dembour 2006). Third, with respect to the social rights of non-citizens, Yasemin Soysal argues that drawing on discourses of international human rights non-governmental organisations (NGOs) have won rights to housing, education and social security benefits that are equivalent to those enjoyed by citizens. Increasingly, Soysal argues, rights in Europe are attached to *personhood*, enacted through the law and public policies of national states for both citizens and non-citizens alike (Soysal 1994). According to Christian Joppke, although Soysal was somewhat premature in drawing this conclusion when she was writing in the 1990s, as a result of the rulings of the European Court of Justice, which are binding on member states of the European Union, states are increasingly required in European law to treat citizens and legally resident non-citizens as the same with respect to social rights (Joppke 2010).[5] In fact, in general, the project to make Europe into a united political (as well as an economic) community is often seen as involving integrating states into peaceful co-operation and respect for human rights (Held 2004; Beck and Grande 2007). Human rights can be seen as bringing 'we the people' of Europe together to overcome the bloodiness of our recent history.

There are, however, reasons to be sceptical about the optimistic view that European states are moving towards 'post-national citizenship' in terms of equalising rights between citizens and non-citizens. First, there are continuing *inequalities* in legal rights. Non-citizens who are resident in a country (even where they are European citizens) have nowhere gained the same *political rights* as citizens. Although migrants within Europe have won rights to vote in local elections (and for members of the European Parliament if they are European citizens), only national citizens are allowed to vote in elections for national governments. This is a serious limitation if political rights to vote and stand for office are valued as part of what it is to live in a democracy. Lack of political rights for non-citizens can be seen both as a sign of their marginalisation and as contributing to it. What is surely more immediately worrying for non-citizens, however, is the insecurity of their status. If non-citizens lose their employment or are convicted of a crime they may lose their right to remain in the country in which they have made their lives. In the UK, non-citizens suspected of terrorist activities who cannot be deported (ironically because they are in danger of being persecuted by the state of which they are citizens) may find themselves dealt with in secret immigration courts with far lower standards of legal process than other courts. Non-citizens who have been through these courts have been sentenced to a form of house arrest for several years, with practically no possibility of proving their innocence.[6] Non-citizens may also have fewer rights to bring family members to live with them than citizens. In this sense they have a kind of 'quasi-citizenship' status (Nash 2009b). And even where the rights of quasi-citizens are protected in law, it is hard to be oblivious to anti-migrant sentiment mobilised by the media and politicians in Europe. Given these conditions, and especially given that many countries now allow dual citizenship, it is unsurprising that many 'quasi-citizens' opt to become citizens by naturalising, taking on the nationality of the country in which they are settled (Kivisto and Faist 2007)

In addition, those who hope we are moving towards post-national citizenship tend not to consider the situation of irregular migrants who have *no* legal right to remain in the territory in which they live. Although of course the figures are very uncertain, it was estimated that there were 3.8 million undocumented migrants in Europe in 2011 (far fewer than in the United States, where there were eleven million in 2011) (Morehouse and Blomfield 2011). This is a fall in numbers relative to the early 2000s, and it is not an enormous proportion of the population of Europe, which is 500 million. Nevertheless, what being an irregular migrant means is quite dramatic in terms of human rights: it means living without any of the legal protections most of us take for granted. If you are an irregular migrant you will not have a legally valid contract with your employer, and you will be negotiating hours and conditions of work with someone who may know you fear deportation (though they too may face criminal proceedings if they knowingly employ someone illegally); similarly, renting accommodation will probably be a precarious arrangement; you may fear calling for emergency care; you will not be able to drive legally, with a driver's licence (a serious limitation in most of the United States); and you may be exploited by people to whom you are indebted because they helped you enter the country. Women employed as domestic workers in the private sphere of the home, or who work in the sex trade (whether willingly or not) may be especially vulnerable to exploitation and violence (Koser 2005; Bloch and Chimienti 2011).

Nevertheless despite these difficulties and dangers there have been mobilisations of 'irregular migrants' – often calling themselves 'sans papiers' in Europe – that have campaigned to have their situation regularised: to gain legal protection for the lives they have established for themselves. Some irregular migrants have been able to win a degree of understanding and sympathy in the cities in which they live that enable them to access services like education and health-care despite their lack of authorisation (Nyers 2008). And in both Europe and North America there have been collective amnesties in which millions of people have been granted legal rights (Castles *et al.* 2014: 218–20). There are also 'mechanisms' of regularisation, bureaucratic procedures through which individuals can try to prove themselves worthy of being granted legal status. In the UK, for example, individuals who can show that they have been resident for fourteen years, or seven years if they have children enrolled at school, are eligible to win legal rights to remain in the country. European economies depend just as much on the *unskilled* work of migrants – in agriculture, catering, cleaning and care-work – as on the knowledge and expertise of those doing skilled work, and as birth rates fall and the relative numbers of older people increase, this will become even more evident. Regularising the situation of migrants makes sense if the goal is ultimately to integrate people into the state; not just to end the legal vulnerability of migrants themselves but also the criminal activities of employers and property owners who take advantage of them. On the other hand, regularisation is often seen as encouraging more illegal migration, and few politicians within states or at the EU-level endorse it today (Brick 2011).

In fact, the relationship between migration and human rights can be interpreted in quite the opposite direction to those who argue that we are beginning to see 'post-national citizenship' developing in Europe: migrants and human rights may be associated with injustice precisely because *both are seen as eroding citizens' rights*. This framing of both human rights *and* migrants as destructive is very evident in the UK. Although UK governments tend to be 'Euro-sceptic', the UK is bound by European law. In fact, the European Convention of Human Rights was incorporated into British law as the Human Rights Act in 1998, giving the UK – for the first time in history – something like a written national constitution. Since then, however, the populist media – sometimes in conjunction with conservative politicians and public figures – has run any number of scare stories linking the protection of migrants – invariably represented as criminals – to human rights imported from Europe. An example is this fragment of a speech from a Tory minister, Theresa May, in 2011:

> We all know the stories about the Human Rights Act. The violent drug dealer who cannot be sent home because his daughter – for whom he pays no maintenance – lives here. The robber who cannot be removed because he has a girlfriend. The illegal immigrant who cannot be deported because – and I am not making this up – he had a pet cat.

May later admitted that she got her information from a newspaper report: the pet cat had actually been mentioned briefly in a court case as one piece of evidence of the settled and permanent nature of a relationship, which was the main reason the man in question was allowed to stay in the UK (Curtis 2011). The fact that May was able to make such casually researched remarks – which were widely repeated across the media – show just how problematic human rights have become in the UK. In fact, the Conservative government is committed to repealing the Human Rights Act and replacing it with a 'British Bill of Rights' if it wins the election in 2015. Rather than gaining respect and value by being framed as the bearers of human rights, both migrants *and* human rights have come to be trivialised and associated with *injustice* for British people. There is contestation of the framing of human rights as opposed to national interests in the UK, especially through NGOs and in the courts (Morris 2010; Nash 2010). But human rights are certainly not celebrated by everyone in the UK and when politicians play to populist sentiments about 'national interests' it is difficult for non-citizens to frame the difficulties they face as 'human rights wrongs' in order to gain respect and fair treatment.

United Nations refugee camps: humanitarianism without rights

Up to now we have mostly been considering whether migrants have human rights in Northwestern states. In a sense these are critical cases: they are states in which governments, bureaucracies and courts are committed in principle and by their treaty agreements to upholding international human rights law; they more closely resemble the juridical state supposed by international human rights law than anywhere else; and there are NGOs and 'cause lawyers' dedicated to defending migrants' human rights in these countries. Non-citizens *should* be able to enjoy human rights in Northwestern states, given these conditions. It is misleading to focus on Northwestern states, however, if that leads us to suppose that the majority of migrants are living there. In fact, the vast majority of migrants are in the territories of states of the Global South. In this section, in order to get an idea of the difficulties migrants face in gaining respect for their human rights in the rest of the world, we will look at the situation of people who have been granted refugee status, a group of people whose rights, in principle, are protected by the UN and by international human rights and refugee law.

In 2013, it was estimated that there were 38.7 million people 'of concern to' the UNHCR. This number includes internally displaced persons (IDPs) and people who had returned to their homes after fleeing violence.[7] The majority of those who had crossed borders were in countries immediately neighbouring armed conflicts. About 1.3 million people had fled the conflict in Syria to Jordan, Lebanon, Iraq and Turkey. There had also been mass displacements of people in central Africa, fleeing conflict in Sudan and the Democratic Republic of Congo, mostly to neighbouring countries Burundi, Rwanda and Uganda. Longer-term refugees from Somalia and Sudan remained in Kenya, Uganda and Tanzania. In terms of overall numbers of refugees in 2013, the countries that had received most were Pakistan (with 1.6 million) and Iran (with 862,000), most of whom had come from Afghanistan, or had been born to Afghan parents in exile since 1979. Palestinians remain the largest (and growing) group of refugees, and they have been in exile the longest; they live in Jordan, Lebanon and Syria (though many there have now been displaced or killed) (UNHCR 2013; UNRWA 2014).[8]

One of the biggest problems for the safeguarding of refugees' human rights in the Global South is forcible encampment. In setting up and managing refugee camps, the UNHCR, assisted by international non-governmental organisations (INGOs) like Oxfam, CARE, the Red Cross and Médecins Sans Frontières, effectively acts as a kind of supplementary state. The UNHCR takes over many of the functions of the 'host' state, with which it formally works in partnership. It appoints officials to sort out and categorise migrants, granting them a 'letter of protection' if they qualify for refugee status (with arbitrary outcomes similar to those we have looked at in Northwestern states as a consequence of ill-conceived and poorly managed procedures: it is not known how many people fleeing their homes are simply turned back at borders). The organisation takes charge of ensuring that the refugees' basic needs are met, working with INGOs to provide food, shelter and varying degrees of health-care and education. And professionals employed by the UNHCR represent the interests of refugees to 'host' governments, 'donor' states who provide its funding, and at the UN. Territorially distinct from the surrounding countryside, fenced off and identified as UN operations by flags and logos, refugee camps even take on the look of 'states within states'; Verdirame and Harrell-Bond 2005; Slaughter and Crisp 2008).

What human rights do refugees enjoy in camps? As an agency of the UN, and as a supplementary state, the UNHCR could be expected to be committed to safeguarding human rights – as indeed it claims to be on its website and in its policy documents. According to international law, once someone is granted protection under the 'Refugee Convention', they have extensive rights, including to freedom of movement, employment on terms that does not discriminate against them as refugees, and to seek redress for violations of their rights in law. This is in addition to the full human rights to which they are in principle entitled as a person – refugee or not – according to the ICCPR and the ICESCR (Verdirame and Harrell-Bond 2005; Ferris 2008).

In fact, however, it seems that human rights are violated in refugee camps as a matter of everyday routine. In their in-depth ethnographic study of refugee camps in Kenya and Uganda in the 1990s, Verdirame and Harrell-Bond found that people were prevented from leaving the camps without permission – which could be very hard to obtain and without which they were liable to be arrested as aliens and deported. This made it practically impossible for people to work outside camps. In some cases they were not being paid for work they did inside camps. Families were separated – sometimes as a result of negligence, sometimes wilfully by spiteful officials. In many cases people were not being allowed enough food and they were suffering from malnutrition. Even peoples' rights to life and to basic physical safety were not being respected: they were not protected from violence by the police and armed bandits outside the camp; nor from murder, violence and rape by people inside it. Verdirame and Harrell-Bond found that the UNHCR was effectively allowing the camps to be policed by armed militias, who were administering justice according to their own rules, and who were also forcibly recruiting young men and boys to join them, even abducting young women to be 'army wives'. Numbers of reported rapes (and of course many were not reported) were very high, and Verdirame and Harrell-Bond found that when they were reported, rather than safeguarding the human rights of the victims or enabling them to seek redress, UNHCR officials often allowed 'elders' to apply 'customary law'. The judgments and punishments that resulted fell far short of international human rights standards. In one case, for example, a Kenyan police officer was ordered to pay a fine to the father of a teenager he had kept imprisoned in his house and raped over several days. Nor were UNHCR officials simply negligent, Verdirame and Harrell-Bond suggest, in allowing violations of human rights. In some respects, UNHCR officials were themselves actively involved in those violations. On one occasion, food distribution was stopped to all 40,000 people in a Kenyan camp to punish a small number who had rioted, resisting a 'headcount' by UNHCR and NGO staff. In addition, according to Verdirame and Harrell-Bond, bringing a complaint about any aspect of treatment people had to put up with in the camps was extremely difficult and when it did happen it could lead to further ill-treatment in retaliation (Verdirame and Harrell-Bond 2005; see also Lischer 2005; Kagwanja and Juma 2008; Kaiser 2008).

Verdirame and Harrell-Bond see many of the violations of human rights to which refugees are subject as a consequence of encampment. Camps are, they suggest, 'total institutions', like prisons or asylums: the 'inmates' are completely subject to the bureaucratic definitions and control of the staff, and – in part as a reaction to the immense suffering which they are tasked with alleviating – they become overwhelmed, even callous. As one UNHCR staff member exclaimed as they were telling her about a woman they feared would take her own life – pregnant from a gang-rape, whose family members had all been killed – 'You know ... There are just so many of them!' (Verdirame and Harrell-Bond 2005: 293). As advocates of human rights, what Verdirame and Harrell-Bond see as missing above all in camps are checks and balances, any possible means refugees might have of making UNHCR staff accountable. Effectively camps are supplementary states but there is no rule of law and they contain no courts or National Human Rights Institutions, no public fora or media in which breaches of human rights might be exposed and officials called to account. Without safeguards, refugees are subject to arbitrary and unjust rules, to insecurity and danger, and they are prevented from accessing what they need at the most basic levels.[9]

Other scholars who have studied how the UNHCR deals with refugees are more sympathetic to the problems that are faced by its staff.

What is most obvious in this respect is that although the UNHCR acts as a supplementary state in setting up refugee camps, it is *only* supplementary. The UNHCR was set up to fit the state-centric structures of the UN. It is states that retain sovereign control over their borders and over the territories in which the UNHCR operates, and the UNHCR is almost completely dependent on 'donor' governments for its funding. The organisation receives only a small subsidy annually from the UN. For the work they do with refugees UNHCR staff must raise money from 'donor' governments each year: it is the United States, the EU and Japan that donate most money for work with refugees. Furthermore, staff could not begin to assist all the refugees in need without the help of INGOs, which also raise the money they need from donations. In a sense, camps are not only the most obvious way of managing large numbers of refugees who need immediate assistance with food, shelter and medical care, they also make visible the human needs to which donors are asked to respond with funding. In addition, the fact that the UNHCR effectively depends on goodwill for its funding also means that its officials find it difficult to be self-critical in public, or to criticise the priorities or strategies of governments – whether donor or host (Loescher 2001; Crisp 2003).

Set up within the state-centric structures of the UN, as well as being dependent on 'donor' governments, staff at the UNHCR are constrained by the priorities of 'host' governments. Today this means working with refugees who are often seen in geo-political terms as a security threat or as potential allies of the states that 'host' them. This is especially the case in Africa. African countries were much more hospitable to refugees in the 1960s and 1970s, but now refugees are associated with armed conflict along borders that states often have difficulty in controlling (Slaughter and Crisp 2008). In fact, refugee camps have become militarised in a number of cases, often with the support of the 'host' state. It is virtually impossible for the UNHCR to control the militarisation of camps.

The most dramatic example of refugee militarisation were the camps in Zaire (now the Democratic Republic of the Congo) into which armed Hutus – fleeing the consequences of the genocide of Tutsis they had committed in Rwanda – drove refugees in 1994. The militias then used the camps as bases from which to conduct further raids. According to Sarah Lischer's research, officials of UNHCR and NGOs working in these camps knew they were supporting war criminals by giving them food and allowing them to recruit and train new soldiers – effectively accepting them as camp leaders in a 'don't ask, don't tell' policy. In part this fitted the humanitarian framework of staff in camps who were committed to helping everyone in need, not just 'the innocent'. But the problem was also that the UNHCR does not have the legal authority to use force on the territory of a sovereign state. At best the UNHCR can co-operate with the police and/or armed forces of a 'host' state, or with UN peacekeeping forces if they are available in sufficient numbers. In Zaire, President Mobutu more or less supported the Hutus. According to Lischer, although Mobutu's army did make a token gesture of disarming militias in the camps for the UN, their weapons were returned to them shortly afterwards. Later, with the economic collapse of his regime, and with the United States shifting its allegiance to the new president of Rwanda, Paul Kwagame, Mobotu's army lost any possibility of controlling what happened around the borders of Zaire. Eventually, in 1996, Rwandan-led troops dispersed the refugee camps on the borders of Rwanda and Zaire, killing as many as 200,000 people in the process (Lischer 2005).

For the most part, then, the UNHCR is limited to providing humanitarian assistance to save the lives of refugees in ways that are generally understood to be temporary at a time of 'complex emergency situations' (Loescher *et al.* 2008; Calhoun 2013). In fact, many of these temporary crises have been going on for decades now. In addition to providing humanitarian relief to refugees, the UNHCR is also – in principle – mandated to find what are called 'durable solutions' to the difficulties it faces. Perhaps it is in finding solutions that refugees may enjoy human rights?

The solution to the difficult situation in which refugees find themselves that is most favoured by the UNHCR is voluntary repatriation. Many refugees have been able to go home – and have done so. For others, however, home is still unsafe, or has changed so much that it no longer seems like home at all. It is difficult to return when people do not have the resources to begin their lives again. One of the major difficulties for the UNHCR is that it is funded only for relief work, and it has no control over decisions about development – whether by UN agencies or by governments. At the same time, agencies that deal with development in the UN are not directly concerned with the welfare of refugees. In such a situation, when they have been in camps for many years, refugees may even become dependent on the UNHCR, building the resources it provides into their survival strategies (Crisp 2003).

The second possible durable solution to the difficulties of refugees is integration into the 'host' state. This presents the obvious difficulty that 'host' states generally do not want refugees to stay. Those refugees who do not live in camps are already somewhat integrated into localities in their everyday lives, but this does not mean they are accepted, or that they enjoy human rights. The plight of Afghans in Iran – some of whom have been there since the Soviet invasion of Afghanistan in 1979 – is especially telling in this respect. Afghan refugees have been relatively integrated into Iranian society, in part because of the government's resistance to international interference. The Iranian government has accepted very little help from the UNHCR, and very few Afghans have been held in camps. They have, however, been discriminated against as a group since the 1980s, allowed to work and live only where there are shortages of manual labour, on construction sites and in agriculture (Macleod 2008). Even though many Afghans speak Farsi, many are Shia Muslims, and they are presumably useful to Iranian businesses, the Iranian government now insists they must leave – they cannot be naturalised as Iranian citizens even if they were born there, and however long they have lived in the country. In 2013 Human Rights Watch reported mass deportations of Afghans from Iran, with the aim of meeting targets that had been set by the president, under conditions which fell far short of respect for their rights as refugees (Human Rights Watch 2013b).

Finally, a third durable solution is resettlement in a third country, usually in the Northwest. Many of the conflicts that have forced migrants to flee from their homes and livelihoods have either been initiated by the foreign policies of Northwestern governments (like the bombing of Afghanistan and Iraq), or they have been proxy wars in which 'the Great Powers' have had a stake (as in the ongoing conflicts in the Great Lakes region of Africa). The main difficulty here is that Northwestern states only accept very small numbers of refugees for resettlement. In fact, the United States is the only Northwestern state that came in the top ten of countries receiving refugees in 2013 (taking an estimated 262,000 refugees) (UNHCR 2013). Given the very high levels of public mistrust of migrants in these countries and constructions of asylum-seekers as 'bogus' in the populist media, it would be very difficult for any government that was aiming to be re-elected to accept larger numbers.

The UNHCR was created for humanitarian work: to provide 'care and maintenance' to meet the immediate needs of refugees in 'complex emergency situations', and to negotiate durable solutions with member states of the UN. In order to fulfil their organisation's commitments, its staff must raise money and compromise with state officials in ways that leave little room for consideration of refugees' rights in international law. The UNHCR and NGOs give refugees humanitarian aid, which is charity not justice. In general the best refugees can hope for is decent conditions in which to live in exile, and the possibility of returning home, sooner rather than later. In practice, in many cases even these minimal hopes are not fulfilled.

The right not to have to migrate?

How people are treated when they are crossing borders without authorisation or when they have crossed them to seek sanctuary or to create a better life for themselves and their families is a test case for the cultural politics of human rights. National laws generally permit non-citizens to be treated less favourably than citizens, even though international human rights law does not. In practice, migrants' rights are being constructed by NGOs and human rights lawyers in a world that continues to be structured by state sovereignty and by increasingly determined efforts to control and police territorial borders. As we have seen in this chapter, it is a world in which what are framed in political rhetoric and the media as the 'national interests' of citizens have led to the treatment of irregular migrants and refugees as not really human at all. While some migrants are able to gain the status of 'quasi-citizens' – a status that gives them more rights than other foreigners but less than citizens – many suffer the most extreme dehumanisation and violations of rights in detention centres and camps, while others die trying to cross borders.

It is precisely *because* migrants and human rights are de-territorialised that it is so hard to construct migrants as worthy of human rights. It is state officials that are in charge of public policies concerning how borders are patrolled and immigration managed *and* of ensuring that commitments to international human rights law are respected. This does not mean that states are monolithic, that state officials all think and act in the same way. Courts in the Northwest have been far more responsive to claims to better treatment that are framed in terms of migrants' human rights than national governments (Nash 2009a; Morris 2010). And

Verdirame and Harrell-Bond found judges to be responsive to claims for human rights in the tiny number of cases that refugees in militarised camps managed to bring to 'mobile courts' in Kenya and Uganda (Verdirame and Harrell-Bond 2005). Judges tend to frame refugee rights differently from elected politicians who are far more likely to respond to populist media portrayals of the dangers that migrants present to 'the nation' and to the benefits of citizenship. There are such difficulties in bringing cases to court, however, and (as we have noted in relation to the unauthorised crossing of borders in particular) the administration of law is often so arbitrary and unpredictable in relation to migrants, that it hardly seems to count as law at all. While some individuals who are well represented in courts do win justice in specific cases, and the pressure of NGOs is sometimes effective in changing public policy, international human rights law enables the regulation, categorisation and control of migrants rather than ensuring their human rights.

There is no easy solution to the problem of guaranteeing the human rights of migrants given how the world is territorialised into states, how borders are policed and fought over, and how difficult it is for non-citizens to mobilise to protest their marginalisation. A simple solution that may seem logical is to open borders. But this is not really a solution that will enable anyone's rights to be safeguarded. As Stephen Castles notes, it is interesting that the ideal of open borders is shared by neo-liberal economists, who are in favour of a free market in labour across borders, business leaders, who are in favour of cheap labour, and a small section of the Left, who see open borders as a way of preventing the violation of migrants' human rights. It seems evident, Castles argues, that markets for unskilled labour in the Northwest cannot absorb all those who would like to enter from the South, and that uncontrolled migration would lower wages and the standards of working conditions. There would be competition between unskilled workers which would surely be linked to racism and violence, and probably to right-wing gains in elections. In addition, the provision of social services cannot be achieved without planning: of taxation, buildings and equipment, the training of professionals in health-care and education. Planning is only possible where the numbers of people who will need a particular service can be reasonably accurately predicted. As Castles puts it: 'The elegant simplicity of the open borders slogan is deceptive, as it would create many new problems. In the current global context it could lead to an anarchic situation in which the weakest – in both sending and receiving countries – would be even more disadvantaged' (Castles 2004: 874). Open borders would undoubtedly lead to more human rights violations, for both migrants and citizens.

It is human rights abuses, including grinding poverty and violence, that lead people to try to make a new life for themselves in far-off lands. In this sense, the most important human right of all could be the right not to have to migrate to escape human rights abuses. Although this makes no sense in legal terms, as a political aspiration it effectively encompasses all the issues we have been considering in this book – and more. In previous chapters we have looked at how human rights are being framed and mobilised to regulate states, the conduct of war, the globalising economy, and gendered structures of power. In this chapter we have effectively seen the difficulties non-citizens face in enjoying the same fundamental human rights as citizens. If all states were well regulated, peaceful, fair and responsive to claims for justice; if they managed economies for the development of the capacities and well-being of everyone; if they policed violence against women that is already illegal, there would be no need for people to risk their lives crossing borders, and to risk the kinds of humiliation and dangers to which they are likely to be subject if they do manage to cross. In a sense, the right *not to have to migrate* is implied in claims for human rights that are made on all states everywhere. In practice, of course, given the difficulties that we have been looking at throughout this book in framing injustices as 'human rights wrongs' and then in finding ways to address them in practice, the right not to have to migrate is an ideal that looks as far out of reach as ever.

8 What works? Paradoxes in the human rights field

The cultural politics of human rights is pragmatic: claiming authority to define human rights is intended to make a difference in the world. Although they are idealistic, utopian even, human rights are also supposed to be realisable in practice. As we have seen throughout this book, contemporary human rights are not just claims for freedom from state violence. Today human rights are claimed in an expansive and inclusive set of inter-related demands that include rights to freedom from *all kinds* of violence: from hunger and homelessness, the destruction of marginalised ways of life, discipline and punishment for being a woman. Transforming structures of geo-politics, of globalising capitalism, of gender and sexuality, and of the legacy of colonialism: these are all potentially radical aims in that they are meant to alter the conditions of our lives and so make a fundamental difference to people who are treated with less than equal respect. But however radical they may be, framing suffering as a 'human rights wrong' invariably situates demands as reformist too. Whether they mobilise people at the grassroots or not, claims for human rights address duty-bearers: officials in organisations who may be persuaded to make use of the moral and material resources over which they have influence to support demands for greater justice, less suffering. The pragmatism of the cultural politics of human rights is both radical in its aims to fundamentally transform structures, and reformist in that it tries to achieve these aims through existing organisations.

Given their pragmatic, reformist dimension, we might conclude that the most important question about human rights is: 'do they work?' Has the explosion of human rights claims since the end of the Cold War made any difference to human suffering?

Measuring human rights

Perhaps unsurprisingly the most focused and coherent attempt to answer this question comes from analysts of statistical data. Statistical

analysis of the effects of international human rights treaties is a growing area now in political science, international relations (IR) and
International Legal Studies.[1] Statistical analysis of the effects of campaigns is also becoming more important to non-governmental organisations (NGOs) and inter-governmental organisations (IGOs), especially
when they must justify their activities to donors. And statistics are also
growing in significance through the work of international tribunals and
courts: lawyers must demonstrate genocide, crimes against humanity
and war crimes if they are to successfully prosecute perpetrators – all
of which rely to some extent on the *numbers* of people killed or raped
as well as on who committed the violence. However, there are a number of problems with quantitative analyses of human rights. Although
they are represented as producing objective, unbiased certainty about
human rights violations, the numbers on which statistical analysis
build are actually very shaky foundations on which to base scientific
knowledge.

Statistical analyses of human rights can be complex, but most of us
are familiar with the underlying principles. Statistics are numbers that
count the same 'event': the number of people tortured in a country over
a certain time period; how many people were killed and who did the
killing; how many are imprisoned and for what reason. There are differences in how information about events is collected and organised.
Events can be counted directly (the number of bodies exhumed that
show how many were killed in a particular conflict, for example), but
this is comparatively rare for statistics on human rights. Most commonly people are asked to report on what they know: in effect it is
categorisations people make (that person was killed or died of hunger
rather than of natural causes, that person is pregnant because she was
raped) that are being measured. There are also differences in how the
numbers are analysed. In the social sciences, complex analyses are now
made of statistical information to model causes and effects: variables
are isolated and linked to assess what factors make most difference to
respect for human rights in practice.[2] But however sophisticated, ultimately all quantitative analysis is based on counting events.[3]

There is generally very little discussion of how statistics are collected
in NGO reports and social scientific analyses of human rights. The most
cited human rights statistics, and those which have been of most interest to political scientists, deal with gross violations of civil rights: to
life, and to freedom from arbitrary imprisonment and torture.[4] One

immediately obvious difficulty in collecting statistics on gross violations of civil rights is that the people carrying them out generally go
to great lengths to try to keep them secret. And even when they are
carried out in plain sight, gross violations of civil rights can be difficult to measure. The numbers of Tutsis killed by Hutus in the Rwandan
genocide are still only estimates, even though the killing was carried
out over a very short period of time in 1994, and in full view of surviv-
ing witnesses. The enormous variation in estimates of who was killed is
astonishing. Human Rights Watch reports that in one parish estimates
of the numbers of Tutsis killed range between 500 and 5,000. In part
these variations are related to the conflict itself: some of those killed
were said to be Hutus who were mistaken for Tutsis. In part it is because
ethnic divisions do not seem to have been as clear-cut in everyday life
in Rwanda as they were made to be in the killing, whilst at the same
time it is clear that some people already feared racialised hatred: it
is said that many Hutus registered with the government as Tutsis to
avoid discrimination and mistreatment. Most importantly it seems to be
because 'untrained observers' in Rwanda were – quite understandably –
unable to take in what was happening (Human Rights Watch 1999).

With the best will in the world, then, long-term endemic abuse, con-
fusion and heightened emotions of hatred, fear and desperation do
not make for the calm rule-following that is necessary to count violent events. And the best will in the world is generally in short supply
in such situations. Statistics concerning human rights violations are
very often Political with a capital 'P'. Numbers are important to arguments for the direction of resources – even if for the most part they
are the only resources of expert interest, bureaucratic monitoring and
media attention. Statistics are important, for example, to the framing
of extreme violence as 'genocide'. 'Genocide' is the destruction of a
nation or ethnic group. It depends on numbers because to be sure that a
conflict is genocide it has to be shown that those being killed are identified by those doing the killing as belonging to a group that they are
trying to destroy. To denounce the conduct of a conflict as amounting
to 'genocide' is to demand international action – in particular, military
intervention to protect civilians. As we have already seen, numbers
are far from the only consideration when the possibilities of humanitarian intervention are being debated. However, 'genocide' is one of
the very few words that make UN action practically unavoidable (and
it is for precisely this reason that US and UN diplomats avoided it in
the build-up to the massacre in Rwanda (Barnett 2003)). It is also one

of the grounds on which military leaders and politicians may be prosecuted in the International Criminal Court (ICC). In 2009 the Sudanese
President Omar Bashir was accused by the ICC prosecutor, Luis Moreno
Ocampo, of genocide, crimes against humanity, and war crimes during
the conflict in Darfur. The charge of genocide has proved especially
controversial. Even judges of the ICC initially challenged Ocampo's
prosecution of Bashir as based on too little evidence. Then in 2010 they
judged that there *was* enough evidence to charge him with genocide.
Bashir is still president of Sudan at the time of writing, and since the
charge was made prosecutors have been prevented from interviewing
Sudanese officials to verify their claims, NGOs have been expelled from
the country, and his political opponents have been imprisoned. In addition, although the African Union (AU) has co-operated with the UN on
repeated peacekeeping missions in Darfur since 2004, and it continues
to do so, in 2009, it was agreed by the majority of states in the AU
that members should not co-operate with the ICC to arrest Bashir. Part
of the objection was that it is unjust that the ICC has only prosecuted
African leaders. Although the evidence is just part of this continuing
controversy, then, debates over genocide in Darfur have not been, and
are unlikely ever to be, settled by statistics alone (Arieff *et al.* 2009).

  The collection of statistics is also 'political' with a small 'p'. It
depends on how people interpret and report on events in which they
are involved, how they understand what has happened to them, and
what accounts they give of what they are doing. The gap between how
people involved see events and how they are categorised in survey data
is well documented by critical sociologists. A controversial example
that makes the significance of this gap very clear is the attempt by
feminists at the UN to construct trafficking women for sex work as a
very serious violation of human rights. They argue that sex trafficking involves kidnapping and slavery when women and young girls
are forced to sell sex. Events of trafficking women for sex are inherently difficult to count because they are hidden. They are also, however,
inherently difficult to count because sex trafficking is mixed up with
prostitution and illegal migration: women who have been forced or
tricked into sex work live and work alongside others who have chosen
it as a way of making a living – though not necessarily in circumstances that would make alternatives appealing. Who is counted and
who counts themselves as having been forced or having chosen to cross
borders illegally to sell sex for money is inherently tied up with feelings
of shame and pride and with how people see themselves as victims or as

individuals actively in charge of their own fate (Shamir 2006; Andreas and Greenhill 2010).

It would surely be wrong to dismiss attempts to measure human rights violations altogether. Statistics are a valuable part of making standards visible, though they are always embedded in arguments and interpretations. In general long-term planning and the equitable distribution of resources in large-scale, complex societies is unthinkable without measurement and calculation. In part we are all familiar with the basic building blocks of statistical analysis because we are used to states gathering and organising information *about us*: planning for education, health-care, welfare, all depend on statistics. In relation to human rights violations, however, it seems there has been a turn to measurement that is problematic. Sally Engle Merry argues that what are only ever partial and contentious numbers appear as measurements of objective reality that have become increasingly important to NGO workers and officials in IGOs as part of a general shift towards auditing, benchmarking and 'accountability'. Merry argues that statistics reinforce the authority of experts and bureaucrats, as debate shifts from how to actually influence compliance with international human rights treaties to how to devise good indicators to measure violations. In fact, given the centrality of bureaucratic procedures and expertise to human rights monitoring at the UN that we looked at in Chapter 4, it might be more reasonable to argue that the new emphasis on measurement fits in very well with the structures that are *already* established in IGOs. At any rate, Merry argues that statistical indicators are contributing to the replacement of political debate over the possibilities, prospects and limitations of human rights by measurement, assessment and comparisons that 'fix' constructions of reality in ways that are very difficult for non-experts to contest or even to understand (Merry 2011).

Mapping the human rights field

In this book I have taken a very different approach to the study of human rights. When I first began systematically reading the vast literature on human rights to write this book, I was especially interested in finding 'critical exemplars'. By 'critical exemplars' I had in mind case studies of campaigns that had successfully brought about social change in order to realise a particular set of human rights demands in practice. There are some case studies in these pages that can be thought of in this way. One is the Treatment Action Campaign we looked at in Chapter 2, in which a South African NGO successfully mobilised people with HIV at the grassroots, lobbied the government directly, brought pressure on politicians through the national courts, and liaised with international non-governmental organisations (INGOs) to put pressure on multi-national corporations. I still think of this campaign as exemplary in many ways, not least because of its multi-scalar approach and the role it played in keeping tactics from the anti-apartheid struggle relevant in post-apartheid South Africa. However, what we know about the campaign comes largely from its leaders, who are relatively educated and experienced activists: we know very little about how framing health as a human rights issue moves people to action at the grassroots; and nothing at all about how they understand themselves as having human rights that enable them to make claims on health services, how they combine that understanding with knowledge of 'folk medicine', and how the campaign has shaped their assumptions about human rights more generally (see pp. 34–8).

In fact, one of the main things I have learned from writing this book is that thinking of human rights campaigns in terms of success is itself problematic. There are no value-free, objective criteria of success for human rights campaigns. Over what time-frame is 'success' to be assessed: in the short- or long-term? Who considers a particular campaign a success? Does it have unintended negative consequences for other groups? And how do we find out who they might be and how they might be affected? It is surely important to hear inspiring tales of campaigns that have worked: that have successfully mobilised people, and that have won better treatment for people suffering injustice. But because human rights campaigns are inherently political, and very often Political too, there is no vantage point from which we can conclude that a campaign has been clearly and definitively successful for *all* those people whose lives it may have affected.

Now I am near the end of the book, what interests me is less 'critical exemplars' of successful campaigns and more the way concepts of cultural politics, structures and duty-bearers direct our attention to inherent tensions in the human rights field. The political sociology of human rights I have developed here helps us understand the *range* of activities and themes in which advocates are engaged, and the tensions that are intrinsic to framing suffering as a 'human rights wrong'. Political sociology helps us to map the paradoxes of the global human rights field.

A field is a symbolic space bounded by the limits of co-operation and competition. What is shared, and what actors orient themselves towards in the global human rights field, is the *value of the authority to define human rights*. The human rights field is not *just* a space of conflict: of strategic attempts to advance interests and to gain benefits (whether professional or private, individual or collective). Competition in the human rights field involves strategic, organised action between actors who aim to win authority to interpret and decide what human rights are and should be. But the human rights field also involves co-operation across organisational boundaries. In fact, conflict *itself* requires a degree of co-operation. Coalitions across organisations can be small-scale and local: as they are when NGOs work with grassroots movements. They can be multi-scalar, involving NGOs, state officials and advocates at local, national and transnational scales – as they were in the Treatment Action Campaign. In addition, co-operation can emerge more spontaneously: taken-for-granted assumptions become established as a result of historic world-changing events or the circulation of stories, images, understandings that become more or less accepted as truth by everyone involved.[5]

This mixture of co-operation and conflict in and between the organisations in which human wrongs are framed is what gives rise to the paradoxes of the global human rights field. According to Joan Scott, one meaning of 'paradox' is that it is a sign of the capacity to balance completely contrary thoughts and feelings. And in ordinary usage, a 'paradox' is an opinion that challenges but does not displace orthodoxy (Scott 1997: 4–5). I follow Scott's classic analysis, using 'paradox' to understand the global human rights field as constituted by inescapable tensions that pull in opposite directions. These paradoxes can be *evaded* – they do not divide advocates and activists in each and every campaign to make human rights effective. But ultimately, we cannot escape the paradoxes of the global human rights field as it is constituted today. The meaning of 'human rights' is ultimately indeterminate: it cannot be fixed once and for all. Today there is such a wide variety of actors involved in trying to define human rights, and such a range of meanings of human rights across the world that it is impossible to eliminate one pole of any of these paradoxes either in thought or in practice.[6]

Citizenship/humanity

Human rights are at the same time the rights of citizens and of human beings. As we have often noted throughout this book, human rights are state-centric: international human rights law is overwhelmingly concerned with what states should and should not do. Even where movements and NGOs address IGOs, it is generally with the longer-term aim of putting pressure on states. States are the guarantors and the violators of human rights. In a sense this is an artefact of international human rights law since only 'State Parties' are recognised as its subjects. But the importance of states goes beyond responsibilities that are accepted as binding in international human rights law. It is only states that have the capacities to deliver the extensive range of rights that are already encoded in international human rights law, as well as in demands that have not yet reached that status.

It is *citizens* who have priority in national states. The priority of citizens who are members of the national community of a state is built-in to international human rights law itself. Article 1 of the International Covenant on Economic, Social and Cultural Rights (ICESCR) makes explicit the link between the national, citizenship and human rights:

> All peoples have the right of self-determination. By virtue of that right
> they freely determine their political status and freely pursue their
> economic, social and cultural development.

The priority of citizens with political rights to self-determination is written into international human rights law, but it is also embedded as a far more deeply rooted assumption in international relations as well as in public life inside states. The ICESCR came into effect at the UN in 1976, and Article 1 is in large part a product of decolonisation, which was already well underway by this time. It codifies respect for the national self-determination of citizens in *all states*. That state and popular sovereignty are one and the same thing had already been stated in the great eighteenth-century declarations of human rights – though citizenship was not extended to all adults within Northwestern states until the nineteenth century, and people in states that were European colonies never had citizenship rights.[7] The statement of the ICESCR was, then, both a confirmation and an extension of the priority of citizens over non-citizens for all the world.

At the same time that international human rights law privileges citizens, it also binds politicians, bureaucrats and judges appointed in national states to make public policies and legal judgments that *do not* privilege citizens over non-citizens. Article 1 of the International Covenant on Civil and Political Rights (ICCPR) states that:

> Each State Party to the present Covenant undertakes to respect and to ensure to all individuals within its territory and subject to its jurisdiction the rights recognized in the present Covenant, without distinction of any kind, such as race, colour, sex, language, religion, political or other opinion, national or social origin, property, birth or other status.

Human rights are for *humans*: for non-citizens just as much as for citizens. They are intended to be a resource for citizens suffering from repression and poverty as a result of state policies. But equally they are intended to improve the treatment of *non-citizens*. Migrants are subject to the administration of states in which they do not have citizenship, and claiming human rights is one of the few ways by which they can hope to have any influence on those states. Another less well-known and somewhat more complex example concerns public policies made by state officials that directly affect the life chances of non-citizens *outside* their territories and even outside their legal jurisdiction. In Chapter 5, we looked at the demand for international co-operation to ensure that *all* states have the capacities to realise social, economic and cultural rights that are encoded in the ICESCR. According to Article 2 of the ICESCR:

> Each State Party to the present Covenant undertakes to take steps, individually and through international assistance and co-operation, especially economic and technical, to the maximum of its available resources, with a view to achieving progressively the full realization of the rights recognized in the present Covenant by all appropriate means, including particularly the adoption of legislative measures.

In principle the ICESCR binds states that have ratified it to help each other to protect a full set of social, economic and cultural rights for *everyone*, regardless of where they live in the world.

At its most acute, the tension between citizen and humanity leads to disrespect for both citizenship and human rights. In crisis situations of war and hunger, human rights shade into humanitarianism. In principle and historically humanitarianism has been quite different from human rights. In very basic terms, humanitarianism involves a compassionate response to people in immediate need. It is associated with relief in emergency situations: for refugees, victims of natural disasters and war. In comparison, human rights are demands for the regulation of resources for the long-term benefit of everyone in the world. But just as humanitarian NGOs have increasingly taken up human rights, so human rights are increasingly invoked in situations of desperate need. This is not such an odd development: the overlap between human rights and humanitarianism is implied in the protections that are promised to people in international human rights law. Humanitarianism and human rights are on a continuum in this respect. It is problematic, however, where the overlap results in *violations* of human rights. This is very obvious in the examples we have looked at in this book in which states that are violating or that cannot ensure respect for human rights are *supplemented* using resources provided by the 'international community': states and NGOs organised through the UN. In part this is because in these situations there are none of the juridical structures (like courts) citizens might demand of states that have adopted international human rights law (as we saw in the refugee camps managed by UN High Commissioner for Refugees (UNHCR) in Kenya in Chapter 6 (pp. 146–53)). There is also the risk of distortions of human rights as such. Where humanitarian aid is delivered in the name of human rights, human rights are no longer claimed by a person who is recognised as legitimately making demands on a political community. Humanitarian aid is more a matter of charity than of rights. As Monika Krause puts it very neatly, when humanitarian aid is delivered in the name of human rights: 'people's right to relief can become the right of those who are served by the relief agency to the services the relief agency has to offer' (Krause 2014: 149). The fact that ultimately fieldworkers are themselves employed and directed by people based in offices far from disaster areas – most commonly in the capitals of Northwestern states – who also direct the resources allocated to them, only makes it all the more obvious that food and shelter are being *given out* in these situations: they cannot easily be claimed as a matter of universal *rights*.[8]

Ultimately there is no possible resolution of the citizenship/humanity paradox in the human rights field. Ideally it is citizens who would claim rights in their own states: they would 'give the law to themselves' through democratic participation. But what if states violate or neglect citizens' rights? And what about the rights of non-citizens, inside and outside state territories? Given economic and geo-political competition between states, and the continuing importance of nationalism, people are quite likely to oppose the equal treatment of non-citizens where it is seen as damaging the privileges they enjoy as citizens. Efforts to guarantee human rights for everyone, everywhere, will tend to be in tension with the aim of empowering citizens to realise their own human rights through their own states.

Emancipation/governance

Human rights are emancipatory in that they involve demands for equality of freedom for all. But the global governance that is needed to realise human rights in practice itself produces inequalities.

As the very first line of the preamble of the Universal Declaration of Human Rights (UDHR) puts it:

> [R]ecognition of the inherent dignity and the equal and inalienable rights of all members of the human family is the foundation of freedom, justice and peace in the world.

'Emancipation' is people being freed to create the conditions of their own life, to take control of their own fate. Human rights can be emancipatory for individuals. This is very evident when we consider, for example, the rights of women we looked at in Chapter 6 to choose relationships that are not abusive and violent. They are rights for women to have a far greater degree of control over their own lives than is currently the case. Human rights can be emancipatory for groups too. Group emancipation through human rights is demanded by indigenous peoples and peasants. These groups are demanding rights to a greater degree of collective control over the conditions of production and consumption that make such a difference to peoples' everyday lives.

The emancipatory role of human rights depends on grassroots organisations through which people bring definitions of human rights into their everyday lives, becoming empowered to demand recognition and respect from others. Even to realise their emancipatory possibility, however, it is almost always the case that people who demand human rights must engage with global governance. By global governance I mean the technocratic and bureaucratic procedures and norms through which cross-border organisations operate in a globalising world – from INGOs to corporations, states and IGOs. In part this is more or less a definitional issue. If the empowerment of individuals and groups does *not* involve engaging with governance there is very little reason to use the language of human rights. Where politics is solely a matter of intra-community, or even intra-national negotiation, framing suffering as a 'human rights wrong' may not have any particular value. More substantively, however, lack of respect and poverty from which people suffer invariably involve relationships of power with elites. Elite power is almost always backed by law, bureaucracy and expert authority. Elites may be local: village elders, landowners and employers, people employed by local government or even by NGOs (as we saw so vividly in the story of Chikondi in Chapter 2). Relevant elites are very often national: employed by states or the managers and shareholders of territorially based corporations. And more often than not the frameworks of law and regulation through which national elites operate involve international elites: people employed in IGOs or by states in far distant territories; or the managers and shareholders of transnational corporations with headquarters in another state. Demands for human rights most commonly address elites to persuade (very occasionally to compel) them to alter their behaviour. Human rights advocates engage with rational-legal and expert authority in forms of governance at local, national and international scales to challenge justifications for the power of elites that are built into states, corporations, INGOs and IGOs.

In addition, elites have a further, and more positive, role to play in the realisation of human rights. If we consider social, economic and cultural rights that are demanded to alter conditions of disrespect and poverty permanently, long-term planning, management and administration is needed. This means governance at all scales to foster conditions of security from violence and freedom to flourish for everyone. Even demands for local communitarianism engage with global governance. This is very evident in the demands of Via Campesina for a UN Declaration of Peasants' Rights: though focused on increasing the autonomy of small-scale rural communities, it goes into some detail about national and international regulation. Consider some of the Articles of the Declaration of Rights of Peasants:

> Article II (4): Peasants (women and men) have the right to actively participate in policy design, decision making, implementation, and monitoring of any project, program or policy affecting their territories.
> Article III (15): The right of peasants (women and men) to life and the fulfilment of their basic needs should be protected by the law and

by the state, with the assistance and cooperation of others, without discrimination of any kind.

   Article VI (1): Peasants (women and men) have the right to obtain funds from the State to develop agriculture.

   Article VII (1): Peasants (women and men) have the right to obtain impartial and balanced information about capital, market, policies, prices, technology, etc, related to peasants' needs.

Via Campesina's demands are for emancipation through local communitarianism: greater control by and for rural people over the conditions of their lives by the preservation of small-scale farming. Local communitarianism is unusual in the global human rights field – and the Declaration of Peasants' Rights has not (yet) been established as international human rights law signed and ratified by states. Some of the appeal of local communitarianism – especially perhaps for those who see it as linked to alternative lifestyles in the Northwest – is surely that it seems to sidestep difficult questions of global governance. In practice, however, as the Declaration of Peasants' Rights makes clear, what human rights advocates demand is not *an end* to governance: it is *good* governance. And demands for good governance are even more evident in constructions of social and economic rights associated with global social democracy. Most of the efforts of global social democrats are concerned with establishing better governance: improving international regulation of markets in goods, money and labour; state planning and investment to develop national economies; and the redistribution of wealth through public goods, including services of education and health-care.

   Human rights demands are, then, made *against* elites. But they are also made *through* elites. There is an inherent tension here between the aims of emancipatory human rights demands and the governance that is necessary to realise human rights: bureaucratic and expert authority also work *against* the realisation of human rights. Technocrats at all levels, from 'street level bureaucrats' through the directors of Amnesty and Human Rights Watch to Nobel-winning economists at the World Bank can and do become caught up in proceduralism: in technocratic solutions to problems that actually serve them as professionals, providing them with relatively well-paid, respected jobs, status and power over others. 'Insider politics', manoeuvring to build a career and access to greater wealth and status: these can very easily become ends in themselves for professionals employed in offices that are quite distant from those they are supposed to be helping. And even when professionals are dedicated, hard-working and idealistic, it is always difficult to influence technocratic structures set up and maintained in the name of expert and rational-legal authority. It is difficult for 'outsiders' to make themselves heard and understood when they have to address 'experts' in the languages in which they have been trained. And it is difficult even for high-ranking 'insiders' to influence hierarchical, bureaucratic organisations when responsibility for decision-making is diffused through rigid procedures that constrain thought and action.

There is no possible resolution of the emancipation/governance paradox in the global human rights field. The 'purity' of human rights demands that is sometimes conjured up by the word 'grassroots' is illusionary. Mobilisation at the grassroots is vital: very often it simply is not possible to realise human rights unless people have a sense of entitlement that enables them to refuse, resist and to demand better treatment from elites at the local level as well as those who have influence from a greater distance over the conditions of their lives. This is the emancipatory promise of human rights. But ultimately, realising human rights always also requires regulation, expertise and planning – at all scales from the most local to the most global.

Universalism/diversity

The value of human rights is that they set standards for governance, and especially the regulation of states, that are supposed to be universal. The first line of the preamble of the UDHR refers to 'the inherent dignity and the equal and inalienable rights of all members of the human family'. But human rights are increasingly diverse. There has been a proliferation of framings of human rights in recent times – in part a product of the appeal of human rights as a language for global justice. And human rights must always be adapted to particular circumstances and groups if they are to be effective.

Human rights encode universal standards. Their universalism gives human rights critical purchase in relation to structures of injustice and suffering. We saw this very clearly in the discussion of women's rights to freedom from violence in Chapter 6. Feminists at the UN argue for women's rights to be free from gender violence *regardless* of how people understand the role of women in local understandings of kinship obligations, religious duties and community norms. More generally, the universality of human rights enables advocates to make abuses visible where internationally agreed standards are not being met: it is never right to turn a blind eye to rape, whatever people may think, regardless of the circumstances, and despite the difficulties of applying national law in particular cases.

As we have also already noted, however, to be really effective in practice human rights must almost always be taken up by grassroots movements. This is because what is appropriate in terms of persuasion depends on what people already accept as normal, true and right. The necessity of working at the grassroots is also very evident with respect to women's rights to freedom from gender violence. In part this is a question of *means*: the arguments and the techniques of protest and advocacy that are used to win authority to define human rights must be appropriate to their particular circumstances. It is also, however, a question of *aims*. Women's rights to freedom from violence were not included in the UDHR or even in the Convention on the Elimination of Violence against Women (CEDAW): developing an interpretation of human rights that includes forms of violence from rape in armed conflict to domestic violence has meant altering the aims of international human rights law as well as finding new means by which women's suffering can be addressed internationally, nationally and locally. The local communitarianism of indigenous movements and of demands for the protection of peasant ways of life also represents new objectives in the cultural politics of human rights. Building campaigns across borders to develop new forms of international human rights law is seen as necessary to gain recognition and respect for ways of life that are quite different from those that are dominant in industrialised and industrialising states.

The proliferation of frames of human rights in recent decades makes *competing* definitions of what human rights are and should be in any given situation inevitable. There are still clashes between human rights advocates and *opponents* of human rights. Debates over cultural relativism remain important, especially to questions of gender and sexuality. As we saw in Chapter 6, the clash between advocacy for women's rights and accusations of neo-imperialism on the grounds of the protection of 'cultures' is entrenched internationally as well as within states. What is also far more evident, now, however, are debates over the relative value of *different definitions of human rights*. Competition over the priority of civil and political rights or of social and economic cultural rights has become a staple of the cultural politics of human rights at the UN. And we have also noted that within demands for social and economic rights there are conflicts over priorities for development that seem to benefit city-dwellers at the expense of small farmers and indigenous peoples.

The paradox of universalism and diversity – the construction and defence of universal standards which must at the same time be adapted to local contexts – is irresolvable. Human rights must encode universal values if they are to be used to draw attention to suffering that everyone agrees, at least in principle, is always wrong for all human beings – regardless of what anyone thinks. Human rights enable advocates to make abuses visible and to militate for respect and redistribution in the name of what *all human beings* need to flourish wherever they happen to have been born or to be living. Recognising and agreeing on universal definitions of injustices is a long way off for most definitions of human rights. In fact, there are still challenges even to those norms that are considered most fundamental: government officials still defend torture and summary executions as necessary for national security.[9] Even if it were to be accepted, however, that some conditions are abhorrent for everyone everywhere, definitions of human rights would still always have to be contextualised. People have to make sense of human rights in their own ways of life, and given that these are so varied, inevitably so too definitions of human rights have to be diverse. A proliferation of definitions of human rights will inevitably lead to debates over what counts as a violation of universal human rights as well as over the relative weight of definitions that are recognisably different and their value in particular cases. In order to become effective, human rights must become at the same time more universally accepted *and* more contentious.[10]

Are human rights the answer?

Throughout this book we have been looking at the complexities of the cultural politics of human rights. 'It's a human right' may sound, on the face of it, like an *answer* to the question of how to represent and address suffering and injustice. And indeed, winning acceptance for framing suffering as a human right and establishing it as a part of international human rights law is in itself a triumph for campaigners where it enables them to achieve visibility for their cause. What mapping the paradoxes of the human rights field makes very clear, however, is that the answer 'it's a human right' is always and only ever situated in a wider set of questions about political action, organisations and structures. Who are the relevant duty-bearers? What are their responsibilities? How can existing structures be altered that will really make a difference? With respect to actually achieving better treatment, more fairness and less cruelty, 'it's a human right' isn't an answer at all: even when it is accepted as the right kind of response, it only opens up further questions.

Do these complexities mean that human rights can never be realised, that they have no value in the contemporary world? Human rights are often criticised for addressing, and in the process strengthening, elites and expert authority at the expense of radical alternatives. However, we never learn what those radical alternatives might be in the work of critical theorists. In fact, what we have seen in this book is that today the language of human rights actually includes within it a range of possibilities, some more radical than others. Today human rights are the dominant language of radical *and* reformist politics. For better or worse, human rights seem to many different groups to be the most appropriate way of trying to achieving a greater degree of justice in our globalising world. As we have seen in this book, it is not just the cosmopolitan elites and experts of the UN, Amnesty International and Human Rights Watch that advocate human rights. The most marginalised and mistreated groups of people on the planet also use this language. As it is the contemporary language of global justice, it seems to me to make no sense to refuse the validity of human rights *as a matter of principle*. However, the cultural politics of human rights should not be understood as a solution to the world's problems; it does not transcend conflicts, and it brings its own problems and dilemmas. What I have been outlining in this book are the conceptual tools with which to explore the possibilities *and the* limitations of the ways in which people are using human rights in practice to transform structures that produce inequality, insecurity and violence. Political sociology helps us develop the conceptual tools with which to carry out our enquiries with an open, enquiring mind.

Notes

1. The social construction of human rights

1 For well-argued examples of theoretical critiques of human rights, see Brown 1995a, 1995b, 2002; Kennedy 2002; Douzinas 2007.

2 See Held 1995, 2004; Benhabib 2004, 2007; Blau and Moncado 2005, 2007.

3 For accounts of human rights 'from below', see Santos 2002b, 2006 (discussed in pp. 32–4); Rajagopal 2003; Kurasawa 2007.

4 On social constructivism in IR with respect to human rights see Donnelly 1999, 2013. With respect to the role of NGOs, see Keck and Sikkink 1998; Risse *et al.* 1999; Risse, Ropp and Sikkink 2013. We look at this work in more detail in Chapter 2.

5 The overlap is very evident in the work of Kathryn Sikkink: Keck and Sikkink 1998; Lutz and Sikkink 2001; Sikkink 2011. See also Donnelly 2006.

6 There is now a huge range of work in this area. I will draw on some of it in this book. For influential discussions of anthropological rethinking of the relationship between concepts of 'culture' and 'human rights' see Wilson 1998; Cowan *et al.* 2001; Merry 2006. On the relationship between the sociology and anthropology of human rights, see Short 2008.

7 For specific references to this debate as the beginning of the sociology of human rights, see Sjoberg *et al.* 2001: 25; Morris 2006; Somers and Roberts 2008: 386; Hynes *et al.* 2012: 789;. Other accounts of the sociology of human rights also situate themselves explicitly as social constructionist: Stammers 1999; Morgan 2009. Still other sociologists take a more eclectic approach to the value of different theoretical traditions, though they are still social constructionists insofar as they see human rights as historically specific rather than as 'natural' moral universals: see Madsen and Verschraegen 2013.

8 The idea of 'framing' originates in Erving Goffman's work, which was a founding source of inspiration for social constructionism (Goffman 1986). The classic reference, however, is Berger's and Luckmann's *The Social Construction of Reality*, first published in 1966 (Berger and Luckmann 1991). Berger and Luckmann talk about constructions as 'meanings' instead of 'frames'. 'Frames' is a good word here because it suggests very clearly what is *excluded* from what is seen as well as what is included. 'Meanings' is better in that interpretation of what we 'see' is not always as obvious as 'framing' suggests. In addition, 'meanings' suggests a less instrumental, more expressive understanding that is closer to how most

social interaction works: we communicate with each other regularly, and only on some occasions is communication strategic. 'Meanings' is preferable to 'framing' then in most situations – but it is far less vivid as a metaphor than 'framing'.

9 Critics of human rights are inspired by Marxism (Brown 1995b; Zizek 2005; Williams 2010), feminism (Brown 2002), post-colonialism (Matua 2002; Asad 2003), or a combination of all of these strands of thinking (Spivak 2002). This book can be read, in part, as response to such critiques.

10 Upendra Baxi makes the useful distinction between *modern* and *contemporary* human rights. Modern human rights were focused on the universality of individual rights, where 'the individual' resembled a white, male, heterosexual citizen of a nation-state. They are typified by the human rights constructed in the eighteenth century in the constitution of the newly independent United States and the Declaration of the Rights of Man of the French Revolution. In contrast, contemporary human rights are far more diverse. They include social, economic and cultural rights, and 'the individual' is much more fully characterised in a variety of ways. A 'human' can be female, poor, indigenous, resisting imperialism. Where modern rights were marked by exclusion, Baxi argues, contemporary rights are marked by attempts at *inclusion* (Baxi 2008).

11 On the sociology of practice: see Bourdieu 1979; Giddens 1984. I follow Sewell's influential interpretation of the sociology of practice, which stresses that structures do not just involve cultural norms, they also organise resources (Sewell 2005).

12 Although they differ in the details of how they theorise links between culture (as representations, meanings), and social structures, traditions as diverse as British cultural studies and the cultural sociology of Jeffrey Alexander as well as recent work on human rights in anthropology are all concerned with how to study culture as a *dimension* of social life (see Turner 2002; Alexander 2003; Ortener 2006). It is these accounts that have influenced my understanding of culture: culture and social structures are inextricably entwined in the social construction of reality.

13 I have developed the concept of authority I use in this book drawing on Michael Barnett's and Martha Finnemore's *Rules for the World* (2004). As I am concerned with human rights advocacy across the whole range of organisations involved, I have adapted and supplemented their typology – which they developed to theorise the relative autonomy of IGOs from states – to encompass the authority that is constructed by representatives of NGOs and states. For Weber's classic discussion of 'authority' on which Barnett and Finnemore draw, see Weber 1948: 294–5.

14 In fact, the European system of human rights (in which the Council of Europe and the European Union overlap, especially since the Lisbon Treaty 2009) is

commonly regarded as the most effective at reforming states, incorporating as it does legal pressure (through the European Court of Human Rights) and political pressure (to be a member of the EU states must show that they comply with the European Convention on Human Rights). The Inter-American system of human rights is well established and older than the European, though less effective. The Inter-American Commission makes country reports where there are grounds to suspect gross violations of human rights, but only where the state in question has granted permission, and they tend to have very little direct impact. The Inter-American Court is limited to advising states that they are in breach of international human rights law: it has no sanctions and very little influence in practice. The African system is the newest and least developed regional system of human rights law, and it has had very little impact on member states to date. However, the African Union and also the Economic Community of West African States have been very active in organising peacekeeping operations. For brief, up-to-date sketches of regional systems of human rights (which are continually changing), see Alston and Goodman 2013.

2. (A) human rights movement(s) and other organisations

1 This argument has been made very effectively by Neil Stammers 1999, 2009. However his arguments are entirely conceptual; they are not based on empirical research.

2 There is an enormous literature on social movements. For good general discussions see Diani 1992; Della Porta and Diani 2005.

3 There has been an enormous growth worldwide of human rights NGOs since the 1970s. See Keck and Sikkink 1998: 90; Keck and Smith 2002.

4 NGOs also vary with respect to their independence from government. In China, for example, only GONGOs (Government Organised Non-Governmental Organisations) are legal – though there are also a number of illegal and tolerated NGOs there too (Spires 2011).

5 The difference between NGOs and grassroots organisations is not always clear. As Dorothea Hilhorst shows in her study *The Real World of NGOs*, very small local organisations – which might be considered GROs – may name themselves 'NGOs' in order to attract funding (Hilhorst 2003). In very general terms, however, we can say that in GROs unpaid volunteers are likely to play more of a leadership role than in NGOs; they are smaller and 'flatter' in terms of their bureaucracy and decision-making than NGOs; and – above all – they involve people in their localities who make human-rights claims on their own behalf (Batliwala 2002; Molyneux and Lazar 2003).

6 'Northwestern' is the term I prefer as an attempt to generalise in a way that gets beyond West/East, North/South dichotomies that over-simplify complex and overlapping historical, cultural and economic interconnections between states and diversity within regions. I use 'Northwestern' to refer to Western European and European settler states, the United States, Canada, Australia and New Zealand. This categorisation lumps together states that share broad similarities in the history of their formation with regard to citizens' rights and capitalist industrialisation; and with regard to twentieth-century geo-politics.

7 It is notoriously difficult to track INGO funding, less because they are not transparent than because of the complexities of their budgets: it can be difficult to know what they turn over each year because money is collected in a number of different countries for different branches, and from different sources (membership, fund-raising, individual donations, governments, foundations, etc.). The best data-driven discussion of the funding of human rights INGOs in a global context is James Ron's edited series on Open Democracy: 'Funding for Human Rights': www.opendemocracy.net/openglobalrights/funding-for-human-rights (last accessed 1 September 2014).

8 This is a change of policy that was in part based on the need to gain more popularity in the Global South. But neither Amnesty nor Human Rights Watch is involved in delivering humanitarian relief in emergencies, and it is difficult for either organisation to really engage in development issues, especially as there are already huge INGOs devoted to it (Stroup 2012: 166–8). Aryeh Neier, one of the founders of Human Rights Watch, who is currently chair of the George Soros Foundation that funds it, has argued that it is well suited only to campaigning for civil rights (Neier 2012). Kenneth Roth, the current director of Human Rights Watch, has argued that the methodology of 'naming and shaming' only works for violations of social and economic rights where there is clear evidence of violence or discrimination so that specific authorities can be held accountable (Roth 2004). The focus of campaigns in which both Human Rights Watch and Amnesty are engaged with respect to social, economic and cultural rights tends to be on forced evictions from housing or land, and on discrimination against particular groups with respect to housing, education or medical care.

9 According to the Edelman Trust Barometer, a global survey produced regularly, NGOs are consistently the most trusted type of organisation, far ahead of governments and business, in every region of the world: www.edelman.com/insights/intellectual-property/2012-edelman-trust-barometer/trust-in-institutions/ngos-most-trusted-institution-globally/ (last accessed 1 September 2014).

10 A good example is Mahmood Mamdani's *Saviors and Survivors*. Mamdani is critical throughout the book of the international interference in Sudan, including challenging the statistics produced by human rights NGOs about how many

people were killed in Darfur. However, at the same time he draws on reports by Human Rights Watch to support his argument (Mamdani 2009: 215, 225).

11 It is primarily anthropologists who have explored issues of legal pluralism: see Merry 1988. In more recent times, the discussion has become more inter-disciplinary, especially around questions of transnational legal pluralism: see Michaels 2009. These discussions have become prominent with the growth of multiculturalism in the Northwest as a reality and (to a lesser extent) as state policy, and debates over religious law, especially Sharia law for Muslims (Possamai *et al.* 2015).

12 In Chapter 5 I explore anti-capitalist campaigns for self-determination on the part of movements of indigenous peoples and peasants that have been framed in terms of human rights, as 'local communitarianism'. Like Santos, these movements insist on the value of definitions of human rights 'from below'.

13 Beyond the example of Sharia law, Santos does not raise any questions about how we should understand local meanings of human rights as emancipatory when they are *not* obviously progressive, and where they clash with international human rights law. For example, there are vigilante groups in favelas in Brazil who see lynching as an expression of their human rights, a matter of security in areas that are neglected by state police (Goldstein 2007). Another example is that of a pueblo in Columbia which – with permission from the constitutional court – has imposed punishments that could well be considered 'cruel and unusual' (Jackson 2007). We return to this question in Chapter 8 where we consider universality and diversity in human rights (pp. 169–71).

14 Respect for women's rights may not have been quite as ideal in practice as Santos supposes. Compare Belausteguigoitia 2000 on women's rights in the Zapatista movement.

15 In their study of local mobilisations for equal rights in New York City, Sally Engle Merry and her colleagues found that grassroots activists defined human rights differently from the lawyers they worked with, stressing values of human dignity over norms of governance, and linking them with ideas from the women's movement, and national and religious ideologies (Merry *et al.* 2010). Although it is not directly on human rights, Susan Watkins and Ann Swidler's fascinating study of 'brokers' who work between NGOs addressing the spread and of treatment of AIDs in Malawian villages and the villagers they hoped to reach is also important. Watkins and Swidler show how everyone involved was quite happy despite the way they misunderstood each other because the different meanings people gave to 'fighting stigma', 'orphans and vulnerable children' and 'vulnerable women' did not interfere with the shared understanding that, whatever the theme, the solution would be 'training' (Watkins and Swidler 2013).

16 The Treatment Action Campaign is committed to financial transparency, and provides an unusually complete record of donations it has received each year on its website: www.tac.org.za/community/finance (last accessed 8 August 2013).

3. States of human rights

1 In very basic terms, human rights law has three sources: international treaties and conventions, which are made between states at the UN; constitutional law, generally made by governments, sometimes in consultation with NGOs; and international customary law, which are legal standards on which there is consensus amongst states even though this may not be reflected in existing treaty or domestic law. Not only is it states that *make* international human rights law, it is states that are *subject* to international human rights law. It is very rare that non-state actors (corporations, IGOs) may be found in breach of human rights in international law, and this is only possible where they have acted in conjunction with states: where they have been delegated public functions by state actors, or where they have colluded with state actors in committing human rights violations (Alston 2005; Clapham 2006).

2 This is the approach that has been taken up most recently and thoroughly by Foucauldians: see Rose and Miller 1992; Mitchell 1999; cf. Curtis 1995.

3 On the importance of looking at the history of state formation as a matter of international politics in the context of colonialism, rather than just as the power struggles within a state territory, see Bhambra 2007; Go 2013; Steinmetz 2013.

4 For excellent accounts of the long history of Marxist thought on the state see Jessop 1982, 1990.

5 The development of law and bureaucracy as a feature of the modern state has been one of the most important topics in sociology from its origins in the work of Weber. Poggi's account is a classical statement of the Weberian perspective (Poggi 1990).

6 For good examples, see Crouch 2011; Therborn 2013.

7 Foucault *et al.* 1991; Brown 1995a; cf. Fraser 2008.

8 Constitutional courts are almost never asked to review human rights violations outside national territories. The case of the prisoners in Guantanamo Bay, which was brought before the US Supreme Court, is an exception due in large part to the ambiguity of the territory within which the prison is located (though it is on Cuban soil, it is under US jurisdiction). In *Al-Skeini and Others* v. *the United Kingdom*, a landmark ruling in 2011, the European Court of Human Rights found that the UK's human rights obligations apply to its acts in Iraq, and that the UK had violated the European Convention on Human Rights by failing to investigate the circumstances of the killing of Iraqi civilians by British troops. Again, however, this case is exceptional in that the judges ruled that because the UK was actually occupying Iraq, it was responsible for the actions of its military on that territory (Cowan 2012). Furthermore, all that was required by the European Court was that the UK investigate the allegations. In this respect it is notable that although the Council of Europe and the European Parliament investigated and condemned the role of European states

in co-operating with the CIA to kidnap terrorist suspects ('extraordinary rendition') to take them to be interrogated (and tortured) following 9/11, they only required that states investigate these actions, and the only country in which legal proceedings have followed as a consequence of the investigations is Italy (Committee on Legal Affairs and Human Rights of the Council of Europe 2006).

9 Brock *et al.*'s book is a very interesting study of what, using the language of US security documents, they call 'fragile states'. From the perspective outlined here each of the cases they examine in detail – Afghanistan, the DRC and Haiti – approximates the 'predatory state'. I find 'predatory state' preferable because it emphasises the interplay of external and internal structures and actors, and the ongoing importance of economic and social factors to the historical formation of states. It also separates sociological analysis that is necessary in order to properly understand the difficulties of realising human rights from security discourses that refer to 'fragile' and 'failed' states as justifications of 'humanitarian intervention'.

10 For a discussion of Asian values see Langlois 2001; Ching 2008.

11 On the Chinese state, repression and human rights, see Ching 2008; Dreyer 2010; Kinzelbach 2013.

12 For discussions of the impact of Chinese intellectuals on human rights activism in China, see Hsing and Lee 2010; Wright 2010.

13 For an influential account of 'fixing failed states' written by UN advisors who have worked on state-building in Bosnia and Afghanistan, see Ghani and Lockhart 2009.

4. The United Nations: not a world state

1 Monitoring practices at the UN are complex and they are continually being reformed. For reasonably up-to-date overviews and more details see Alston and Crawford 2000; Flaherty 2002; Bayefsky 2011; Cherif Bassiouni and Schabas 2011; Keller and Ulfstein 2012; Alston and Goodman 2013. For a comprehensive and critical account of the Human Rights Council (set up in 2006 to replace the Human Rights Commission), see Freedman 2014; for a sympathetic view of the special procedures it has established, see Piccone 2012.

2 The definition of 'sovereignty' as control by a *nation-state* over its territory was itself a *re*definition created and sustained during decolonisation in the mid-twentieth century. When the UN was founded in 1948 'sovereignty' was accorded by international law to imperial states which ruled over colonies and protectorates in most of the world. There were originally fifty-one member states of the UN in 1946; by 1980 that number had risen to 157 members as a result of decolonisation; and with the break-up of the USSR, to 184 members by 1992 (www.un.org/en/members/growth.shtml).

3 The Pinochet case is often seen as a turning point in this respect. It was the first time that it was decided that a head of state did not have diplomatic immunity where crimes against humanity were concerned. Although General Pinochet managed to escape being tried for his part in the murder, 'disappearances' and systematic torture of his political enemies, he was under house arrest for two years in the UK waiting to hear if he would be extradited to Spain to be tried for crimes against humanity (Nash 2007). When he returned to Chile, he was eventually charged with crimes against humanity there despite the fact that he had ensured an amnesty for himself when he eventually stepped down from government. He died before the case came to trial. The Pinochet case was a turning point in part because he was such an epitome of the military dictator. According to Katherine Sikkink, the symbolic effects of his arrest were felt round the world as opening up new possibilities for dealing with heads of state with blood on their hands (Sikkink 2011: 121–3).

4 There is a vast literature now on all aspects of humanitarian intervention, peacekeeping operations and state-building. For surveys of the differences between different forms of peacekeeping operations see Doyle and Sambanis 2006; Bellamy and Williams 2010. For discussions of differences in state-building, see Chesterman 2004; Brahimi 2007; Call and Wyeth 2008; Paris and Sisk 2009.

5 Bosnia was different from Kosovo and East Timor because it remained nominally independent: state-building was initiated by a peace agreement between the warring parties. The success of state-building in Bosnia is also more questionable than in the other cases in that it is often said that the Dayton Agreement was suitable for making peace, but not for building a new country. In fact the state of Bosnia-Herzegovina reifies ethnic divisions in its design, and communities do not mix socially, so that conflict is a recurrent danger. On the specificities of the 'transnational administration' in Bosnia, see Chandler 2006; Belloni 2008.

6 For critiques of humanitarian intervention in general as imperialist, see Douzinas 2007; Williams 2010; Orford 2011.

7 Interestingly it may not be finished in Africa. In 2005 the African Union incorporated the Responsibility to Protect into what is known as the Ezulwini consensus, which also involved a commitment to building up regional peacekeeping forces and establishing a permanent African presence on the UN Security Council. African states have been involved in numerous peacekeeping missions in Africa since the 1990s (Bellamy and Williams 2010).

8 Not all the efforts that came out of the UN in the 1990s challenged and displaced sovereignty as the legally protected right and power of a state to govern itself without interference from others. Extending human rights monitoring and capacity-building into the field *with* states' permission has also been important. This has been the focus of the expansion of monitoring through special rapporteurs and working groups on a range of specific topics, especially after the High Commissioner for Human Rights was established in

1994 (see Alston and Goodman 2013: 99–100). Capacity-building has been undertaken with the worldwide project, in part financed and supported with technical assistance by UN professionals, to set up national human rights institutions (Mertus 2009). Both these initiatives are limited, however, by the willingness and the capacities of state officials to reform practices within their territories.

5. Humanising capitalism

1 For a very readable introduction to neo-liberalism from a social democratic perspective, see Chang 2010a. David Harvey's neo-Marxist introductions to neo-liberalism are very popular: Harvey 2003, 2005. There are useful introductions that weigh up Marxist and non-Marxist accounts: Tonkiss 2006; Ingham 2008. For a collection of sociological analyses of globalising capitalism after the financial crisis of 2008: Calhoun and Derluguian 2011.

2 In fact civil rights themselves require extensive moral and material resources organised by states to prevent the arbitrary use of force, and so that people have legal redress against the abuse of state offices. In addition, in the UN it has been agreed since the Vienna Conference of 1993 that rights are indivisible. Civil and political rights cannot be realised without social, economic and cultural rights and vice versa. People cannot easily exercise freedoms of speech and association if they are living in chronic fear of hunger, homelessness and poor health; in today's complex societies literacy is necessary: we need to be able to read to be well informed; and governments can avoid taking the needs of poor people into account where their protests are met with violence and repression rather than respect.

3 This ideal was shared by the US government at the end of the Second World War – though US politicians and economic experts have been at the forefront of neo-liberal projects since the 1980s. Cass Sunstein's *The Second Bill of Rights* explains the place of social and economic rights in the United States during the Roosevelt administration in the 1930s and 1940s (Sunstein 2006).

4 From a human rights perspective, the most detailed and comprehensive arguments for social democracy are Rhoda Howard-Hassman (2010) *Can Globalization Promote Human Rights?*, and David Kinley (2009) *Civilising Globalisation*. In part they make the connection between capitalism and human rights on the basis of statistical evidence: respect for human rights is statistically linked to economic development. The argument is not that capitalism *causes* human rights to be realised. It is rather that where there are the social and political conditions that enable organised and democratic demands for rights to be effective, capitalism is an excellent way to produce wealth, goods and services to enable everyone to live in relative security and comfort. In this respect, specifically sociological

arguments about human rights overlap with other well-known arguments for global social democracy, like Amartya Sen's philosophical work on capabilities (Sen 1999), the economic theory of Joseph Stigliz, former chief economist at the World Bank (Stiglitz 2010), and the political theory of David Held on the possibilities of transforming global governance (Held 1995, 2004).

5 An interesting theorisation of alternatives to what they call 'capitalo-centrism' is the work of Gibson-Graham (2006). Manuel Castells and colleagues have carried out preliminary research on how people in Spain are turning to self-provisioning with the collapse of the economy (Conill *et al.* 2012). With respect specifically to human rights, the work of Boaventura De Sousa Santos, Walden Bello, and others who have been involved in the World Social Forum is directly relevant as exemplary of what I am calling 'local communitarianism' (Santos 2006, and see pp. 32–4; Bello 2004; Santos and Rodríguez-Garavito 2005).

6 Many campaigns that have addressed the IFIs have mixed human rights concerns with others, including for the environment: see Fox and Brown 1998; O'Brien *et al.* 2000; Gready 2004. Human rights frames were part of anti-globalisation campaigns that were so prominent after the 'Battle of Seattle' in 1999, when around 50,000 demonstrators protested against the WTO. This and other protests are often seen as having successfully exposed the IFIs to far greater public scrutiny than those who work for them had been used to: Della Porta 2007; Smith 2008.

7 For discussions of how US imperialism has benefitted from 'the Washington consensus' see Harvey 2005; Kiely 2010; Calhoun and Derluguian 2011.

8 In April 2013 the US Supreme Court seems to have further limited the scope of the Alien Tort Claims Act. Judges hearing a case brought by Nigerians against the Dutch company Shell concerning the violent repression of the Movement for the Survival of the Ogoni People ruled that such cases should only be heard in US courts where claims 'touch and concern the territory of the United States'. It is yet to be seen how this ruling will be interpreted in future, but it looks as if it will have a significant cooling effect on ATCA cases (European Coalition for Economic Justice (2013); www.corporatejustice.org/-about-eccj,012-.html?lang=en).

9 There is an extensive literature on the Narmada dam campaign which takes the perspective of those mobilising against it. For discussions see Khagram 2002; Kothari 2002; Rajagopal 2003: 122–7; Wood 2007; Nilsen 2010.

10 On the world food crisis, see Holt-Gimenez and Patel 2009; Howard-Hassman 2010: 76–82; Paarlberg 2010.

11 There is a growing literature on Via Campesina and human rights. On Via Campesina as a social movement see Desmarais 2007; Martinez-Torres and Rosset 2010; Edelman 2012. More specifically on Via Campesina's approach to the UN, see Borras and Franco 2010; Edelman and James 2011; Claeys 2012. Situating Via Campesina in demands for social and economic rights more generally, see Patel *et al.* 2007.

12 In *Rethinking Imperialism*, Ray Kiely reviews post-1945 theories of political economy which argued that over-development of capitalist industrialisation in North America and Europe was directly related to the continued
under-development in the South because of the primacy of raw materials and
monocultures (of coffee, sugar, etc.) to these economies, whilst investment in
manufacturing was dominant in the North. Kiely argues that they over-stated
the dichotomy between (what was at that time called) 'First' and 'Third' Worlds
when, in fact, there was substantial capitalist development in Africa, Asia and
Latin America as states pursued 'import substitution' policies in the 1950s and
1960s. In Kiely's view, what these theories neglect is politics: the role of the
United States at the international level, and also the importance of national
public policies. What has become widely known as the 'resource curse' is
important, but it is only part of an explanation for capitalist under-development
in particular places (see Kiely 2010; cf. Hoogevelt 2001). Gudynas' theory of
'neo-extractivism' is better seen as an intervention in ongoing political debates
rather than as an economic *explanation* for the continuing reliance of Latin
American countries on the export of raw materials: it has similarities to theories of under-development, but he is far more interested in making a political
argument for local communitarianism (Gudynas 2010).

13 For more detail see Kinley 2009; Chang 2010a, 2010b; Howard-Hassman 2010.

6. Women's rights are human rights

1 There is some difficulty of terminology in this chapter because many women's
organisations around the world do not describe themselves as feminist, seeing
'feminism' as too closely related to Western values. This can be the case even when
they have greater gender equality as their aim, at least as far as getting women's
perspectives on the agenda is concerned. Women's organisations also work on a
range of issues that are not connected to gender inequality at all (see Basu 1995).
An example is the celebrated Madres de la Plaza de Mayo who have campaigned
for many years for truth and justice for their children, 'disappeared' by the repressive regime in Argentina in the 1980s. In this chapter I am concerned only with
organisations that work to end violence against women. As they also tend to aim
at gender equality in the long term, for the purposes of the analysis in this chapter
I will refer to them as feminist and women's organisations interchangeably.

2 For histories of the development of global feminism, see Moghadam 2005; Ferree
and Tripp 2006; Merry 2006. Specifically on women's rights as human rights,
see Keck and Sikkink 1998: chapter 5; Reilly 2009. What Moghadam calls transnational feminist networks of organisations began to overlap with transnational
advocacy networks working on human rights once the possibility of defining
violence against women in human rights terms was being explored. According

to Aryeh Neier, when Human Rights Watch set up a women's rights project in the late 1980s, the Ford Foundation, its longest-term and very valuable supporter, protested by reducing the donation it made to the organisation. Today Human Rights Watch works on women's rights and the Ford Foundation is fully supportive of its position (Neier 2012: 228). The first report Amnesty published on women's rights, 'Women's Rights are Human Rights', was in 1995; today it too works on women's rights.

3 The focus on violence against the individual has been criticised as too simplistic; as ignoring more complex questions about the impact of international economic policies and military interventions on women's lives (see Grewal 1999). Indeed, structures of gender and sexuality are entwined with all the human rights issues we are concerned with in this book, and more. Both women *and* men are peasant farmers, work for TNCs in Export Processing Zones, are slum-dwellers, migrants, activists, politicians and lawyers, international bureaucrats and experts employed in the UN and by the World Bank.

4 What I am here calling 'gender violence' is sometimes called 'gender-specific violence' or 'gender-based violence' at the UN to distinguish it from violence that is directed at people *regardless* of their (assumed) sex, gender or sexuality. An example of gender-neutral violence would be the murder and disappearance of activists, both men and women, who were treated identically because of their political activities. There is also 'gender violence' against men – those who are seen as gay, or as otherwise not fitting gender norms, and in armed conflict, to humiliate and defeat 'the enemy'.

5 On mainstreaming gender see Rai and Waylen 2008; Walby 2011.

6 There is an extensive literature on the importance of the ICTY for pioneering prosecuting crimes of sexual violence against women, most of it in legal studies: see De Brouwer 2005. For a broader approach, see Leatherman 2011. Despite being celebrated as a major achievement of the ICTY, Kirsten Campbell argues that the way in which rape has been prosecuted in this forum may also be seen as confirming rather than as challenging hierarchical gender relations (Campbell 2007).

7 For example, Jean and John Comaroff relate in some detail debates amongst the Tswana of Southern Africa over how 'personhood' is to be understood in a post-colonial context (Comaroff and Comaroff 2012: chapter 2).

7. Do migrants have rights?

1 This chapter does not deal with internally displaced persons (IDPs) or people who are called 'migrants' though they have only travelled within the borders of the country of which they are citizens (like those who go from the country to cities in China to work). There are far larger numbers of IDPs than there are of

migrants who cross borders, and they often face very difficult circumstances, including hostility from people where they settle as well as discrimination and repression by state agents. Their situation is not covered by any specific international human rights agreement, though there is increasingly a body of 'soft' international human rights law that does cover it (Goodwin-Gill 2007).

2 According to Article 2 (1) of the ICCPR, each state that has ratified it has undertaken: 'to ensure to all individuals within its territory and subject to its jurisdiction the [civil and political] rights recognized in the present Covenant, without distinction of any kind'. It is not permitted to discriminate in the rights listed in the ICCPR on the grounds of national origin. Similarly, Article 2 (2) of the ICESCR outlaws discrimination based on national origin in the enjoyment of social, economic and cultural rights.

3 Frances Webber has made a list of reasons for refusing asylum that she has heard in her years of experience as an immigration lawyer in the UK. They range from 'not being fervent enough', 'left the country too quickly' (so the risk of persecution is not clearly established) and 'didn't leave the country quickly enough' (so the risk is not real) and even 'still alive' (threats that have not been backed up are not real) (Webber 2012: 41–3).

4 Arizona SB 1070 was ruled unconstitutional by the Supreme Court in 2012: police no longer have the powers to stop anyone they suspect of being an illegal immigrant and to ask for their papers because it is the federal government that has control over immigration, not states (Howe 2012).

5 There is now an extensive literature discussing 'post-national citizenship': see Sassen 2006. David Jacobson has argued that post-national citizenship also applies in the United States (Jacobson 1997). In fact, in the United States, distinctions between citizens and resident non-citizens have been drawn *more* sharply in recent years. As a 'country of immigration' the United States has tended to separate out questions of who is and can be a member of the society, which is covered by immigration law, from questions of individual rights, which are allowed by the status of 'resident alien'. Since 1996 'resident aliens' have been denied access to federal welfare benefits to which they previously had access; now it is only US citizens who have rights to federal welfare. International human rights law is very *rarely* allowed in US courts so that migrants only have recourse to *national* law, and their rights are, therefore, particularly vulnerable to changes in the political regime (Baubock 2002).

6 The courts are held under the title: 'Special Immigration Appeals Commission' (SIAC). The law under which suspected terrorists have been held without trial (and initially without even their lawyers being allowed to know the evidence against them) has changed a number of times. Currently, as a result of a UK Supreme Court ruling against 'control orders' in 2005, terrorist suspects who cannot be deported are subject to the Terrorist Prevention and Investigation Measures (TPIMs) introduced in 2012. In fact, TPIMS differ very little from the

previous regime of 'control orders': in practice those assessed as terrorist suspects have no chance to prove their innocence, and they may be confined to a
narrow range of activities (including restrictions on where a person goes and
who they speak to) for an indefinite period by SIAC (Webber 2012: chapter 11;
Liberty,   www.liberty-human-rights.org.uk/human-rights/countering-terrorism/
tpims (last accessed 2 September 2014)).

7 IDPs have human rights within the states in which they live, and of which they
are citizens: they are migrants who have not crossed international borders. The
UNHCR takes responsibility for IDPs who can be just, if not more, vulnerable
than people who flee violence across borders.

8 Palestinian refugees are in a unique position. The UN body responsible for those
who have registered as refugees is the United Nations Relief and Works Agency
for Palestine Refugees in the Near East (the UNRWA, not the UNHCR), which was
set up after the Arab-Israeli war of 1948. And it is not being sent back to the
country of which they are citizens that is the problem for Palestinians: it is that
they have no right to return to the lands and houses they have lost.

9 In the refugee camps studied by Verdirame and Harrell-Bond, mobile courts
began to be used in the late 1990s, especially for cases involving sexual violence.
Verdirame sees them as having been quite successful in prosecuting serious violations of human rights in the very few cases they were able to hear (Verdirame
2013: 273–4).

8. What works? Paradoxes in the human rights field

1 According to Ann Marie Clark and Kathryn Sikkink, quantitative studies of
human rights are one of the fastest growing fields in research on world politics
(Clark and Sikkink 2013: 540).

2 The beginning of the recent turn to statistical analysis of human rights violations in the social sciences seems to have been discussions of what has come to
be known as 'the compliance gap': the fact that a state signs and ratifies international human rights treaties has very little effect on actually ending human
rights violations in that country (see Hathaway 2002; Hafner-Burton and Tsutsui
2005, 2007). Now statistical analyses are concerned more broadly with causal-
ity: with what makes international human rights treaties more or less effective. The conclusion so far seems to be that domestic mobilisation is key, and it
is especially likely to be effective in transitional democracies (Simmons 2009,
2013; Dai 2013; for a discussion of this conclusion rooted in qualitative methodology, see Moyn 2012).

3 Clark and Sikkink show that most statistical analyses of human rights violations are based on just two sources of information: yearly reports by Amnesty

International and by the US State Department. The information used by Amnesty is collected by local NGOs, other observers and sometimes on-site missions. The US State Department collects information from embassy staff, NGOs and other observers. This information is not intended for social scientific analysis, and in fact, the indicators that are used by social scientists – the Political Terror Scale (PTS) and the Cingranelli-Richards Human Rights Data Set (CIRI) – are even less precise than the data provided by Amnesty and the US State Department. The PTS and the CIRI are developed using indicators to organise the numbers of events in Amnesty and US State Department reports: they order those numbers on scales to compare countries over time. In effect, scales *re-categorise* events, making the gap between what actually happened and how it is interpreted even wider than it is in the original data sets (Clark and Sikkink 2013; see also Landman 2006).

4 For accounts of the way in which human rights indicators have been developed, see Landman 2006; Merry 2011. For a detailed discussion of how social and economic human rights indicators might be developed, see UN Human Development Report 2000.

5 There is not room here to discuss the extensive social theory of 'fields'. All field theory is influenced by Bourdieu, but for my purposes his understanding is limited by his emphasis on *competition*, on strategic action that is intended to advance individual, and especially professional interests. For research from a Bourdieuian perspective on the human rights field, see Madsen 2004, 2011. The other influential strand of work on fields in this area is on 'world culture' and the diffusion of norms, which is influenced by, and has influenced, neo-institutionalism (see Fligstein and McAdam 2012: 28). Work by Meyer and his colleagues has been very influential on the study of human rights, most importantly through social constructivism in IR (Madsen and Verschraegen 2013). The problem with this work, in contrast, is that it is too focused on *co-operation*: the diffusion of norms is seen as the result of mimesis, and questions of power and interpretation are completely neglected (see Nash 2010: 59–63).

6 My approach to the paradoxes of human rights has been influenced by Joan Scott's classic study, *Only Paradoxes to Offer* (Scott 1997); and more recently by Michael Barnett's mapping of the history of humanitarianism (Barnett 2011).

7 Human rights were synonymous with citizenship rights in the American Declaration of Independence, the US Bill of Rights, and the French Declaration of the Rights of Man and of the Citizen that first made the regulation of sovereign states by law an ideal to live up to (see Hunt 2008). It was only as a member of a political community within a national territory that a person could have expected to enjoy rights until the Universal Declaration of Human Rights in 1948. For a very interesting account of the refusal to extend rights to people subjected in French colonies after the Revolution, and the Haitian Revolution that resulted, see Césaire 1960.

8 There has been much discussion in recent years of the overlap and the differences between humanitarianism and human rights. Though they do now overlap, humanitarianism and human rights have different histories and they are contested and defined in different fields (Krause 2014). It is in this respect that Michael Barnett – though he outlines the range of humanitarianisms in his global history – sees humanitarianism and human rights as quite distinct in their core elements (Barnett 2011: 16).

9 The most notorious recent example is the attempt of lawyers working for the Bush administration to redefine interrogation techniques that were considered to amount to torture as acceptable in order to fight the 'Global War on Terror' (see Hajjar 2013; Khalili 2012). The fact that the Bush administration adopted a legalistic strategy in public to try to legitimate torture should not, of course, lead us to suppose that the United States is the only state that is guilty of such practices.

10 I have argued elsewhere that establishing a 'human rights culture' should be understood in this way, as a cosmopolitan ethical framework within which questions concerning 'which human rights?', 'for which subjects?' and 'how are they to be decided?' might routinely be raised (Nash 2009a).

Further reading

A useful general introduction for those who know very little about human rights is Michael Freeman, *Human Rights: An Interdisciplinary Approach* (Cambridge: Polity, 2011).

Similarly, in general terms, the various editions of Jack Donnelly's *Universal Human Rights in Theory and Practice* – all of which are quite different – are very well written and cover an immense range of debates. The most recent is Jack Donnelly, *Universal Human Rights in Theory and Practice* (Ithaca: Cornell University Press, 2013). An introduction to the making of international human rights law which is also an invaluable reference to keep by your side is Philip Alston and Ryan Goodman (eds), *International Human Rights* (Oxford: Oxford University Press, 2013). For well-written and engaging essays on almost all the topics of human rights that are covered in this book, see Cindy Holder and David Reidy (eds), *Human Rights: The Hard Questions* (Cambridge: Cambridge University Press, 2013).

For the themes dealt with in Chapter 1, the debate between Turner and Waters on 'the social construction of human rights' has become a classic in sociology and it helps illuminate what is at stake in thinking of human rights in this way: Bryan Turner, 'Outline of a Theory of Human Rights', *Sociology* 27 1993: 489–512; Malcolm Waters, 'Human Rights and the Universalisation of Interests', *Sociology* 30(3) 1996: 593–600; Bryan Turner, 'A Neo-Hobbesian Theory of Human Rights: A Reply to Malcolm Waters', *Sociology* 31(1) 1997: 565–71. Also useful as a way into these questions is Jack Donnelly's 'The Social Construction of Human Rights' in Tim Dunne and Nicholas Wheeler (eds), *Human Rights and Global Politics* (Cambridge: Cambridge University Press, 1999). The model of authority I outline in Chapter 1 comes from Michael Barnett and Martha Finnemore, *Rules for the World: International Organizations in Global Politics* (Ithaca: Cornell University Press, 2004). The best collection of writings on culture and human rights is Jane Cowan, Marie-Bénédicte Dembour and Richard Wilson (eds), *Culture and Rights: Anthropological Perspectives* (Cambridge: Cambridge University Press, 2001). I consider the cultural politics of human rights more fully in Kate Nash, *The Cultural Politics of Human Rights: Comparing the US and UK* (Cambridge: Cambridge University Press, 2009). A classic volume of essays on cultural politics – though it is not explicitly on human rights – is Sonia Alvarez, Evelina Dagnino and Arturo Escobar (eds), *Cultures of Politics, Politics of Cultures* (Colorado: Westview Press, 1998).

On the themes of Chapter 2, Aryeh Neier's *The International Human Rights Movement: A History* (Princeton: Princeton University Press, 2012) is entertaining and informative – though it is also an example of how the fact that Human Rights Watch is an INGO (not a movement) is obscured. Margaret Keck and Kathryn Sikkink, *Activists beyond Borders: Advocacy Networks in International Politics* (Ithaca: Cornell University Press, 1998) is now a classic. For interesting case studies of different forms of organisations that mobilise for human rights the following are excellent: Clifford Bob, *The Marketing of Rebellion: Insurgents, Media and International Activism* (Cambridge: Cambridge University Press, 2005); Clifford Bob, *The International Struggle for New Human Rights* (Philadelphia: University of Pennsylvania, 2009); Boaventura De Sousa Santos and Cesar Rodríguez-Garavito (eds), *Law and Globalization from Below: Towards a Cosmopolitan Legality* (Cambridge: Cambridge University Press, 2005); Sanjeev Khagram, James Riker and Kathryn Sikkink (eds), *Restructuring World Politics: Transnational Social Movements, Networks, and Norms* (Minneapolis: University of Minnesota Press, 2002); Lucy White and Jeremy Perelman (eds), *Stones of Hope: How African Activists Reclaim Human Rights to Challenge Global Poverty* (Stanford: Stanford University Press, 2002). Harri Englund's *Prisoners of Freedom: Human Rights and the African Poor* (Berkeley: University of California Press, 2006) is a salutary warning against over-optimism with respect to human rights 'from below'.

In general there is a need for far more sociological work on states of human rights, so it is difficult to recommend further reading for the ideas outlined in Chapter 3. There has been something of a debate over sovereignty – see Daniel Levy and Natan Sznaider, 'Sovereignty Transformed: A Sociology of Human Rights', *The British Journal of Sociology* 57(4) 2006: 657–76; Kate Nash, *Contemporary Political Sociology: Globalization, Politics, and Power* (Chichester: Wiley-Blackwell 2010). International discourse on states and human rights concern UN attempts to rebuild 'failed states' above all. For a good example of an account by UN 'insiders' see Ashraf Ghani and Clare Lockhart, *Fixing Failed States: A Framework for Rebuilding a Fractured World* (Oxford: Oxford University Press, 2009). From a sociological point of view, Manuel Castells, *End of Millennium* (Oxford: Blackwell, 1998) is exemplary in its attempt to develop different models to understand different types of states – but it is not on human rights. There is now a growing literature on the need to understand state formation as linked to the history of colonialism that offers some interesting leads in this area. Julian Go (ed.), *Postcolonial Sociology (Political Power and Social Theory)* (Bingley: Emerald Publishing, 2013) is an excellent collection of writings to this end.

In contrast, there is a very good literature on the UN to follow up on from Chapter 4. Mark Mazower's enjoyable history of the UN illuminates the structural limits of geo-politics today: Mark Mazower, *Governing the World* (London: Allen Lane, 2012). Similarly engaging is Rosa Freedman, *Failing to Protect: The UN and the Politicisation of Human Rights* (London: Hurst and Company, 2014). Sally Engle Merry gives a very vivid account of bureaucratic processes involved in human rights monitoring in *Human Rights and Gender Violence: Translating International*

Law into Local Justice (Chicago: University of Chicago Press, 2006). Michael Barnett's *Eyewitness to a Genocide: The United Nations and Rwanda* (Ithaca: Cornell University Press, 2003) is a shocking story as well as a forensic analysis of what went wrong. For accessible and interesting accounts of debates over 'humanitarian intervention', US imperialism and 'the Responsibility to Protect', see Anne Orford, *International Authority and the Responsibility to Protect* (Cambridge: Cambridge University Press, 2011) and Alex Bellamy, *Responsibility to Protect: The Global Effort to End Mass Atrocities* (Cambridge: Polity, 2009).

There is also a lack of work on capitalism and human rights that is the theme of Chapter 5 – though many of the case studies in the edited volumes listed as further reading for Chapter 2 are relevant here as they address social and economic rights. The most important books that argue for the compatibility of global capitalism and human rights are Rhona Howard-Hassman, *Can Globalization Promote Human Rights?* (Philadelphia: University of Pennsylvania Press, 2010) and David Kinley, *Civilising Globalisation: Human Rights and the Global Economy* (Cambridge: Cambridge University Press, 2009). Galit Sarfaty has written a book on her ethnographic study of human rights at the World Bank: *Values in Translation: Human Rights and the Culture of the World Bank* (Stanford: Stanford University Press, 2012). Ray Kiely's *Rethinking Imperialism* (Basingstoke: Palgrave Macmillan, 2010) is good on the big picture of global economics over the last few decades – though it is not specifically on human rights. On 'local communitarianism' and human rights, as well as chapters in the collections on movements listed in the paragraph above for Chapter 3, especially interesting is Mark Edelman and Carwil Bjork-James, 'Peasants' Rights and the UN System: Quixotic Struggle? Or Emancipatory Idea whose Time has Come?', *The Journal of Peasant Studies* 38(1) 2011: 81–108.

On gender violence and women's human rights, Sally Engle, *Human Rights and Gender Violence: Translating International Law into Local Justice* (Chicago: University of Chicago Press, 2006) is the most important in-depth study. For criticisms of 'governance feminism', including case studies, it is worth looking at Janet Halley, Prabha Kotiswaran, Hila Shamir and Chantal Thomas, 'From the International to the Local in Feminist Legal Responses to Rape, Prostitution/Sex World, and Sex Trafficking: Four Studies in Contemporary Governance Feminism', *Harvard Journal of Law and Gender* 29 2006: 335–423. On the NGO-isation of the women's movement, it is worth comparing Sonia Alvarez, 'Latin American Feminisms "Go Global": Trends of the 1990s and Challenges for the New Millennium' in Sonia Alvarez, Evelina Dagnino and Arturo Escobar, *Cultures of Politics, Politics of Cultures* (Colorado: Westview Press, 1998) with Maxine Molyneux and Sian Lazar, *Doing the Rights Thing: Rights-based Development and Latin American NGOs* (London: ITDG Publishing, 2003). Despite its rather old-fashioned title, Rajeswari Sunder Rajan's chapter 'Women's Human Rights in the Third World' in N. Bamford (ed.), *Sex Rights* (Oxford: Oxford University Press, 2005) is a good and reasonably up-to-date introduction to human rights and women's mobilisations in India.

Although it is just a few pages of the book, the section on human rights in Hannah Arendt's *Origins of Totalitarianism* (New York: Harcourt Brace, 1979) is so often the starting point of discussions of migrants' rights that it is well worth following up. It is also important to remember the historical context of Arendt's writings, however; she was writing before the legal framework and the mobilisations for migrants' rights that we see today. Marie-Bénédicte Dembour and Tobias Kelly (eds), *Are Human Rights for Migrants: Critical Reflection on the Status of Irregular Migrants in Europe and the United States* (London: Routledge, 2012) is an excellent collection. On post-national citizenship Yasemin Soysal, *Limits of Citizenship: Migrants and Postnational Membership in Europe* (Chicago: University of Chicago, 1994) is a classic. I have written an appreciative but critical appraisal of her argument in Kate Nash, 'Between Citizenship and Human Rights', *Sociology* 43(6) 2009: 1067–83. Guglielmo Verdirame and Barbara Harrell-Bond, *Rights in Exile: Janus-Faced Humanitarianism* (New York: Berghahn Books, 2005) is a detailed account of human rights violations in refugee camps. The essays in Gil Loescher, James Milner, Edward Newman and Gary Troeller (eds), *Protracted Refugee Situations: Political, Human Rights and Security Implications* (Tokyo: United Nations University, 2008) are also critical, but somewhat more sympathetic to the difficulties of working within the structural limitations of the UNHCR.

For more discussion of the measurement of human rights violations, it is worth following up Chapter 8 by reading Sally Engle Merry, 'Measuring the World: Indicators, Human Rights, and Global Governance', *Current Anthropology* 52(3) 2011: 583–95 and Ann Marie Clark and Kathryn Sikkink, 'Information Effects and Human Rights Data', *Human Rights Quarterly* 35(3) 2013: 539–68. I discuss how I understand 'field' more fully in Kate Nash, *The Cultural Politics of Human Rights: Comparing the US and UK* (Cambridge: Cambridge University Press, 2009).

Bibliography

Abbott, K. and Snidal, D. (2001) 'Hard and Soft Law in International Governance' in J. Goldstein, M. Kahler, R. Keohane and A.-M. Slaughter (eds) *Legalization and World Politics*, Cambridge, MA: MIT Press.

Abrams, P. (2006) 'Notes on the Difficulty of Studying the State' in A. Sharma and A. Gupta (eds) *The Anthropology of the State: A Reader*, Oxford: Blackwell.

Abu-Lughod, L. (2013) *Do Muslim Women Need Saving*, Cambridge, MA: Harvard University Press.

Acosta, A. (2013) 'Extractivism and Neoextractivism: Two Sides of the Same Curse' in M. Lang and D. Mokrani (eds) *Beyond Development: Alternative Visions from Latin America*, Quito: Rosa Luxemburg Foundation.

Alexander, J. (2003) *The Meanings of Social Life: A Cultural Sociology*, Oxford: Oxford University Press.

Alston, P. (ed.) (2005) *Non-State Actors and Human Rights*, Oxford: Oxford University Press.

Alston, P. and Crawford, J. (eds) (2000) *The Future of UN Human Rights Treaty Monitoring*, Cambridge: Cambridge University Press.

Alston, P. and Goodman, R. (eds) (2013) *International Human Rights*, 4th edition, Oxford: Oxford University Press.

Alvarez, S. (1998) 'Latin American Feminisms "Go Global": Trends of the 1990s and Challenges for the New Millennium' in S. Alvarez, E. Dagnino and A. Escobar, *Cultures of Politics, Politics of Cultures*, Colorado: Westview Press.

Alvarez, S., Dagnino, E. and Escobar, A. (1998) *Cultures of Politics, Politics of Cultures*, Colorado: Westview Press.

Amnesty International (2009) 'Dodging Responsibility: Corporations, Governments and the Bhopal Disaster', www.amnesty.org.au/images/uploads/aus/Bophal.pdf (last accessed 20 February 2012).

Amnesty International (2011) *Don't Trade Away Women's Human Rights*, London: Amnesty International.

Amnesty International (2012) Press Release: 'Court Decision in Kilwa Massacre Case Denies Right to Remedy for Victims of Corporate Human Rights Abuses', www.amnesty.org/en/library/asset/AMR20/002/2012/en/9b197ecf-c743-4f4a-809f-3f83e9620753/amr200022012en.html (last accessed 17 February 2012).

Amnesty International (2013a) *Iraq: A Decade of Abuses*, London: Amnesty International.

Amnesty International (2013b) 'Major Powers Fuelling Atrocities: Why the World Needs a Robust Arms Trade', www.amnesty.org/en/library/ asset/ACT30/001/2013/en/4f9b654c-47a4-49ae-8cba-c0a02011ade8/ act300012013en.pdf (last accessed 1 December 2014).

Amnesty International USA (2013) 'The Afghan Women and Girls Security Promotion Act Is Now Law', www.amnestyusa.org/our-work/ latest-victories/the-afghan-women-and-girls-security-promotion-act-is-now-law (last accessed 20 August 2014).

Andreas, P. and Greenhill, K. (eds) (2010) *Sex, Drugs and Body Counts: The Politics of Numbers in Global Crime and Conflict*, Ithaca: Cornell University Press.

Araujo, S. (2010) 'The Promise and Challenges of Food Sovereignty in Latin America', *Yale Human Rights and Development Law Journal* 13: 493–506.

Archibold, R. (2010) 'Arizona Enacts Stringent Law on Immigration', *New York Times*, 23 April 2010.

Arendt, H. (1979) *Origins of Totalitarianism*, New York: Harcourt Brace.

Arieff, A., Margesson, R. and Browne, M.A. (2009) 'International Criminal Court Cases in Africa: Status and Policy Issues', Library of Congress, Washington, DC, Congressional Research Service.

Asad, T. (2003) *Formations of the Secular: Christianity, Islam, Modernity*, Stanford: Stanford University Press.

Ayoob, M. and Zierler, M. (2005) 'The Unipolar Concert: The North-South Divide Trumps Transatlantic Difficulties', *World Policy Journal:* 31–42.

Badie, B. (2000) *The Imported State: The Westernization of the Political Order*, Stanford: Stanford University Press.

Barnett, M. (2003) *Eyewitness to a Genocide: The United Nations and Rwanda*, Ithaca: Cornell University Press.

(2011) *Empire of Humanity: A History of Humanitarianism*, Ithaca: Cornell University Press.

Barnett, M. and Finnemore, M. (2004) *Rules for the World: International Organizations in Global Politics*, Ithaca: Cornell University Press.

Basu, A. (1995) *The Challenge of Local Feminisms: Women's Movements in Global Perspective*, Boulder: Westview Press.

Batliwala, S. (2002) 'Grassroots Movements as Transnational Actors: Implications for Global Civil Society', *Voluntas: International Journal of Voluntary and Nonprofit Organizations* 13(4): 393–409.

Baubock, R. (2002) 'Political Community Beyond the Sovereign State, Supranational Federalism, and Transnational Minorities' in S. Vertovec and R. Cohen (eds) *Conceiving Cosmopolitanism: Theory, Context and Practice*, Oxford: Oxford University Press.

Baxi, U. (2008) *The Future of Human Rights*, 3rd edition, Oxford: Oxford University Press.

Bayart, J.-F. (2009) *The State in Africa: The Politics of the Belly*, 2nd edition, Cambridge: Polity.

Bayefsky, A. (2011) *The UN Human Rights Treaty System in the 21st Century*, The Hague: Kluwer Law International.

Beck, U. and Beck-Gernsheim, E. (2001) *Individualization: Institutionalized Individualism and its Social and Political Consequences,* London: Sage.

Beck, U. and Grande, E. (2007) *Cosmopolitan Europe*, Cambridge: Polity.

Belausteguigoitia, M. (2000) 'The Right to Rest: Women's Struggles to be Heard in the Zapatistas' Movement', *Development* 43(3): 81–7.

Bellamy, A. (2009) *Responsibility to Protect: The Global Effort to End Mass Atrocities*, Cambridge: Polity.

Bellamy, A. and Williams, P. (2010) *Understanding Peacekeeping*, Cambridge: Polity.

Bello, W. (2004) *Deglobalization: Ideas for a New World Economy*, London: Zed Books.

Belloni, R. (2008) *State-Building and International Intervention in Bosnia*, London: Routledge.

Benenson, P (1961) 'Forgotten Prisoners', *Observer*, www.theguardian.com/theobserver/2001/may/27/life1.lifemagazine5 (last accessed 9 December 2013).

Benhabib, S. (2004) *The Rights of Others: Aliens, Residents and Citizens*, Cambridge: Cambridge University Press.

(2007) 'Twilight of Sovereignty or the Emergence of Cosmopolitan Norms? Rethinking Citizenship in Volatile Times', *Citizenship Studies* 11(1): 19–36.

Berger, P. and Luckmann, T. (1991) *The Social Construction of Reality: A Treatise in the Sociology of Knowledge*, London: Penguin.

Bhabha, J. (1996) 'Embodied Rights: Gender Persecution, State Sovereignty, and Refugees', *Public Culture* 9: 3–32.

(2002) 'International Gatekeepers? The Tension Between Asylum Advocacy and Human Rights', *Harvard Human Rights Journal* 15: 155–81.

Bhambra, G. (2007) *Rethinking Modernity: Postcolonialism and the Sociological Imagination*, Houndmills: Palgrave Macmillan.

Bhatt, C. (2012) 'Human Rights and the Transformation of War', *Sociology* 46(5): 813–28.

Blau, J. and Moncado, A. (2005) *Human Rights Beyond the Liberal Vision*, Lanham: Rowman & Littlefield.

(2007) *Freedoms and Solidarities: In Pursuit of Human Rights*, Lanham and Boulder: Rowman & Littlefield.

Bloch, A. and Chimienti, M. (2011) 'Irregular Migration in a Globalising World', *Ethnic and Racial Studies* 34(8): 1271–85.

Bob, C. (2005) *The Marketing of Rebellion: Insurgents, Media and International Activism*, Cambridge: Cambridge University Press.

(2009) *The International Struggle for New Human Rights*, Philadelphia: University of Pennsylvania.

Boltanski, L. (2011) *On Critique: A Sociology of Emancipation*, Cambridge: Polity.

Borras, S. and Franco, J. (2010) 'From Threat to Opportunity? Problems with the Idea of a "Code of Conduct" for Land-Grabbing', *Yale Human Rights and Development Law Journal* 13: 507–23.

Bosniak, L. (2006) *The Citizen and the Alien: Dilemmas of Contemporary Membership*, Princeton: Princeton University Press.

—— (2011) 'Human Rights within One State: Dilemmas of Personhood in Liberal Constitutional Thought', in M.-B. Dembour and T. Kelly (eds) *Are Human Rights for Migrants: Critical Reflection on the Status of Irregular Migrants in Europe and the United States*, London: Routledge.

Bourdieu, P. (1979) *Outline of a Theory of Practice*, Cambridge: Cambridge University Press.

Brahimi, L. (2007) 'State-Building in Crisis and Post-Conflict Countries', presented at the 7th Global Forum on Reinventing Government Building Trust in Government, Vienna, Austria, http://unpan1.un.org/intradoc/groups/public/documents/un/unpan026305.pdf (last accessed 2 March 2015).

Branford, S. (2009) 'Brazil: Has the Dream Ended?' in G. Lievesley and S. Ludlam (eds) *Reclaiming Latin America: Experiments in Radical Social Democracy*, London: Zed Books.

Brick, K. (2011) *Regularizations in the European Union: The Contentious Policy Tool*, Washington, DC: Migration Policy Institute.

Brock, L., Holm, H.-H., Sorenson, G. and Stohl, M. (2012) *Fragile States*, Cambridge: Polity.

Brown, W. (1995a) 'Rights and Losses' in *States of Injury: Power and Freedom in Late Modernity*, Princeton: Princeton University Press.

—— (1995b) 'Rights and Identity in Late Modernity: Revisiting the "Jewish Question"' in A. Sarat and T. Kearns (eds) *Identities, Politics, Rights*, Ann Arbor: University of Michigan Press.

—— (2002) 'Suffering Rights as Paradoxes', *Constellations* 7(2): 208–29.

Bruno, K. and Karline, J. (2000) 'Tangled Up In Blue: Corporate Partnerships at the United Nations', www.corpwatch.org/article.php?id=996 (last accessed 7 February 2012).

Butler, J. (2005) 'On Being Beside Oneself: On the Limits of Sexual Autonomy' in N. Bamford (ed.) *Sex Rights*, Oxford: Oxford University Press.

Calhoun, C. (2013) 'The Idea of Emergency: Humanitarian Action and Global (Dis)Order' in D. Fassin and M. Pandolfi (eds) *Contemporary States of Emergency: The Politics of Military and Humanitarian Interventions*, Cambridge, MA: Zone Books.

Calhoun, C. and Derluguian, G. (eds) (2011) *Business as Usual: The Roots of the Global Financial Meltdown*, New York: New York University Press.

Call, C. and Wyeth, V. (eds) (2008) *Building States to Build Peace*, Boulder: Lynne Rienner Publishers.

Campbell, K. (2007) 'The Gender of Transitional Justice: Law, Sexual Violence and the International Criminal Tribunal for the Former Yugoslavia', *The International Journal of Transitional Justice* 1: 411–32.

Cardenas, S. (2010) *Human Rights in Latin America: A Politics of Terror and Hope*, Philadelphia: University of Pennsylvania.

Castells, M. (1997) *The Power of Identity*, Oxford: Blackwell.
(1998) *End of Millennium*, Oxford: Blackwell.
(2001) *Internet Galaxy: Reflections on the Internet, Business and Society*,
Oxford: Oxford University Press.
Castles, S. (2004) 'The Factors That Make and Unmake Migration Policies',
International Migration Review 38(3): 852–84.
Castles, S., De Haas, H. and Miller, M. (2014) *The Age of Migration: International
Population Movements in the Modern World*, Basingstoke: Palgrave
Macmillan.
Césaire, A. (1960) *Toussaint Louverture: la Révolution Française et le problème
colonial*, Paris: le club français du livre.
Chandler, D. (2006) *Empire in Denial: The Politics of State-Building*, London: Pluto.
Chang, H.-J. (2010a) *23 Things They Don't Tell You About Capitalism*,
Harmondsworth: Penguin.
(2010b) 'Hamlet without the Prince of Denmark: How Development has
Disappeared from Today's "Development" Discourse' in S. Khan and J.
Christiansen (eds) *Towards New Developmentalism: Markets as Means
rather than Master*, London: Routledge.
Charlesworth, H. and Chinkin, C. (2006) 'The Gender of *Jus Cogens*' in B.
Lockwood (ed.) *Women's Rights: A Human Rights Quarterly Reader*,
Baltimore: Johns Hopkins University Press.
Chatterjee, P. (2004) *The Politics of the Governed: Reflections on Popular Politics
in Most of the World*, New York: Columbia University Press.
Cherif Bassiouni, M. and Schabas, W. (eds) (2011) *New Challenges for the UN
Human Rights Machinery: What Future for the UN Treaty Body System and
the Human Rights Council Procedures*, Cambridge: Intersentia.
Chesterman, S. (2004) *You, The People: The United Nations, Transitional
Administration, and State-Building*, Oxford: Oxford University Press.
Ching, F. (2008) *China: The Truth about its Human Rights Record*, London: Rider.
Claeys, P. (2012) 'The Creation of New Rights by the Sovereignty Movement: The
Challenge of Institutionalizing Subversion', *Sociology* 46(5): 844–60.
Clapham, A. (2006) *Human Rights Obligations of Non-State Actors*,
Oxford: Oxford University Press.
Clark, A. (2001) *Diplomacy of Conscience: Amnesty International and Changing
Human Rights Norms*, Princeton: Princeton University Press.
Clark, A. and Sikkink, K. (2013) 'Information Effects and Human Rights Data',
Human Rights Quarterly 35(3): 539–68.
Clark, P. (2007) 'In the Shadow of the Volcano: Democracy and Justice in Congo',
Dissent, www.dissentmagazine.org/article/?article=724 (last accessed 30
November 2010).
Cohn, C. (2008) 'Mainstreaming Gender in UN Security Policy' in S. Rai and G.
Waylen, *Global Governance: Feminist Perspectives*, Basingstoke: Palgrave
Macmillan.

Comaroff, J. and Comaroff, J. (2012) *Theory From the South or How Euro-America Is Evolving Toward Africa*, Boulder: Paradigm Publishers.

Committee on Legal Affairs and Human Rights of the Council of Europe (2006) 'Alleged Secret Detentions and Unlawful Inter-State Transfers Involving Council of Europe Member States', 7 June 2006, http://assembly.coe.int/ committeedocs/2006/20060606_ejdoc162006partii-final.pdf (last accessed 1 December 2014).

Conill, J., Castells, M., Cardenas, A. and Servon, L. (2012) *Beyond the Crisis: The Emergence of Alternative Economic Practices*, Oxford: Oxford University Press.

Coomaraswamy, R. (1994) 'To Bellow like a Cow: Women, Ethnicity and the Discourse of Rights' in R. Cook (ed.) *Human Rights of Women: National and International Perspectives*, Philadelphia: University of Pennsylvania Press.

Copelon, R. (1994) 'Intimate Terror: Understanding Domestic Violence as Torture' in R. Cook (ed.) *Human Rights of Women: National and International Perspectives*, Philadelphia: University of Pennsylvania Press.

Cowan, A. (2012) 'A New Watershed? Re-evaluating Bankovic in Light of Al-Skeini', *Cambridge Journal of International and Comparative Law* 1(1): 213–27.

Cowan, J., Dembour, M.-B. and Wilson, R. (2001) *Culture and Rights: Anthropological Perspectives*, Cambridge: Cambridge University Press.

Crisp, J. (2003) 'New Solution in Sight: The Problem of Protracted Refugee Situations in Africa', New Issues in Refugee Research No.75, UNHCR.

Crouch, C. (2011) *The Strange Non-Death of NeoLiberalism*, Cambridge: Polity.

Curtis, B. (1995) 'Taking the State Back Out: Rose and Miller on Political Power', *The British Journal of Sociology* 46(4): 575–89.

Curtis, P. (2011) 'Reality Check: Can Owning a Cat be Grounds for Appeal against Deportation?', *Guardian*, 4 October, www.theguardian.com/politics/reality-c heck-with-polly-curtis/2011/oct/04/reality-check-cat-theresa-may (last accessed 24 March 2014).

Dai, X. (2013) 'The "Compliance Gap" and the Efficacy of International Institutions' in T. Risse, S. Ropp and K. Sikkink (eds) *The Persistent Power of Human Rights: From Commitment to Compliance*, Cambridge: Cambridge University Press.

De Brouwer, A.-M. (2005) *Supranational Criminal Prosecution of Sexual Violence: The ICC and the Practice of the ICTY and the ICTR*, Intersentia nv.

Decoteau, C.L. (2013) 'Hybrid Habitus: Towards a Post-Colonial Theory of Practice' in J. Go (ed.) *Postcolonial Sociology (Political Power and Social Theory)*, Bingley: Emerald Publishing.

Delanty, G. (2000) *Citizenship in a Global Age*, Buckingham: Open University Press.

Della Porta, D. (ed.) (2007) *The Global Justice Movement: Cross-National and Transnational Perspectives*, Colorado: Paradigm Publishers.

Della Porta, D. and Diani, M. (2005) *Social Movements: An Introduction*, Oxford: Wiley-Blackwell.

Dembour, M.-B. (2001) 'Following the Movement of the Pendulum: Between Universalism and Relativism' in J. Cowan, M.-B. Dembour and R. Wilson (eds) *Culture and Rights: Anthropological Perspectives*, Cambridge: Cambridge University Press.

(2006) *Who Believes in Human Rights? Reflections on the European Convention*, Cambridge: Cambridge University Press.

Dembour, M.-B. and Kelly, T. (eds) (2012) *Are Human Rights for Migrants: Critical Reflection on the Status of Irregular Migrants in Europe and the United States*, London: Routledge.

Desmarais, A. (2007) *La Via Campesina*, London: Pluto Press.

Diani, M. (1992) 'The Concept of Social Movement', *Sociological Review* 40: 1–25.

Dieter, H. (2008) 'The Failure of the IMF', *The German Times*, www.german-times.com/index.php?option=com_content&task=view&id=10072&Itemid=112 (last accessed 2 March 2012).

Dodge, T. (2013) *Iraq: From War to a New Authoritarianism*, London: Routledge.

(2014) 'Iraq Doesn't Have to Fall Apart', *Guardian*, 13 June.

Donnelly, J. (1999) 'The Social Construction of Human Rights' in T. Dunne and N. Wheeler (eds) *Human Rights and Global Politics*, Cambridge: Cambridge University Press.

(2006) 'Sovereign Inequalities and Hierarchy in Anarchy: American Power and International Society', *European Journal of International Relations* 12(2): 139–70.

(2013) *Universal Human Rights in Theory and Practice*, 3rd edition, Ithaca: Cornell University Press.

Doogan, K. (2009) *New Capitalism? The Transformation of Work*, Cambridge: Polity.

Douzinas, C. (2000) *The End of Human Rights*, Oxford: Hart Publishing.

(2007) *Human Rights and Empire: The Political Philosophy of Cosmopolitanism*, Abingdon, Oxford and New York: Routledge-Cavendish.

Doyle, M. and Sambanis, N. (2006) *Making War and Building Peace*, Princeton: Princeton University Press.

Dreyer, J. (2010) *China's Political System: Modernization and Tradition*, 7th edition, New York: Longman.

Dreze, J. and Sen, A. (2013) *An Uncertain Glory: India and Its Contradictions*, London: Penguin.

Dudai, R. (2009) '"Can you describe this?" Human Rights Reports and What They Tell Us About the Human Rights Movement' in R. Wilson and R. Brown (eds) *Humanitarianism and Suffering: The Mobilization of Empathy*, Cambridge: Cambridge University Press.

Edelman, M. (2012) 'Rural Social Movements' in E. Amenta, K. Nash and A. Scott (eds) *The Wiley-Blackwell Companion to Political Sociology*, Chichester: Wiley-Blackwell.

Edelman, M. and James, C. (2011) 'Peasants' Rights and the UN System: Quixotic Struggle? Or Emancipatory Idea Whose Time has Come?', *The Journal of Peasant Studies* 38(1): 81–108.

Edwards, A. (2011) *Violence Against Women under International Human Rights Law*, Cambridge: Cambridge University Press.

Engle, K. (2007) '"Calling in the Troops": The Uneasy Relationship Among Women's Rights, Human Rights, and Humanitarian Intervention', *Harvard Journal of International Law* 20: 189–226.

Engle, S. (2006) *Human Rights and Gender Violence: Translating International Law into Local Justice* (Chicago: University of Chicago Press).

Englund, H. (2006) *Prisoners of Freedom: Human Rights and the African Poor*, Berkeley: University of California Press.

Escobar, A. (1995) *Encountering Development: The Making and Unmaking of the Third World*, Princeton: Princeton University Press.

Esping-Andersen, G. (1990) *The Three Worlds of Welfare Capitalism*, Cambridge: Polity.

European Coalition for Economic Justice (2013) 'The decision released by the US Supreme Court in the Kiobel v. Shell case highlights the need for European states to protect human rights against business' www.corporatejustice.org/The-decision-released-by-the-U-S.html (last accessed 22 April 2015).

Ferree, M.M. and Tripp, A.M. (eds) (2006) *Global Feminism: Transnational Women's Activism, Organizing and Human Rights*, New York: New York University Press.

Ferris, E. (2008) 'Protracted Refugee Situations, Human Rights and Civil Society' in G. Loescher, J. Milner, E. Newman and G. Troeller (eds) *Protracted Refugee Situations: Political, Human Rights and Security Implications*, Tokyo: United Nations University.

Flaherty, M. (2002) *Human Rights and the UN: Practice Before the Treaty Bodies*, 2nd edition, The Hague: Kluwer Law International.

Fligstein, N. and McAdam, D. (2012) *A Theory of Fields*, Oxford: Oxford University Press.

Flynn, M. and Cannon, C. (2010) 'Detention at the Borders of Europe: Report on the Joint Global Detention Project', www.globaldetentionproject.org/fileadmin/publications/GDP_Workshop_Report_2010.pdf (last accessed 14 April 2014).

Forbath, W. with Achmat, Z., Budlender, G. and Heywood, M. (2011) 'Cultural Transformation, Deep Institutional Reform and ESR Practice: South Africa's Treatment Action Campaign' in L. White and J. Perelman (eds) *Stones of Hope: How African Activists Reclaim Human Rights to Challenge Global Poverty*, Stanford: Stanford University Press.

Foucault, M., Burchell, G., Gordon, C. and Miller, P. (eds) (1991) *The Foucault Effect: Studies in Governmentality*, Chicago: University of Chicago Press.

Fox, J. and Brown, L. (1998) *The Struggle for Accountability: The World Bank, NGOs and Grassroots Movements*, Cambridge, MA: MIT Press.

Fraser, N. (2008) 'From Discipline to Flexibilisation? Rereading Foucault in the Shadow of Globalization' in *Scales of Justice*, Cambridge: Polity.

Freedman, R. (2014) *Failing to Protect: The UN and the Politicisation of Human Rights*, London: Hurst and Company.

Freeman, M. (2011) *Human Rights: An Interdisciplinary Approach*, Cambridge: Polity.

Friedman, S. and Mottiar, S. (2005) 'A Rewarding Engagement? The Treatment Action Campaign and the Politics of HIV/AIDS', *Politics and Society* 33(4): 511–65.

Fruttero, A. and Gauri, V. (2005) 'The Strategic Choices of NGOs: Location Decisions in Rural Bangladesh', *The Journal of Development Studies* 41(5): 759–87.

Fuller, C.J. and Harriss, J. (eds) (2001) *The Everyday State and Society in Modern India*, New Delhi: Social Science Press.

Gargarella, R. (2013) *Latin American Constitutionalism 1810–2010: The Engine Room of the Constitution*, Oxford: Oxford University Press

Gauri, V. and Brinks, D. (2008) *Courting Social Justice: Judicial Enforcement of Social and Economic Rights in the Developing World*, Cambridge: Cambridge University Press.

Ghani, A. and Lockhart, C. (2009) *Fixing Failed States: A Framework for Rebuilding a Fractured World*, Oxford: Oxford University Press.

Gibney, M. (2005) 'Beyond the Bounds of Responsibility: Western States and Measures to Prevent the Arrival of Refugees', Global Migration Perspectives, No. 22, www.refworld.org/docid/42ce4f304.html (last accessed 14 April 2014).

Gibson-Graham, J.K. (2006) *A Postcapitalist Politics*, Minneapolis: University of Minnesota Press.

Giddens, A. (1984) *The Constitution of Society*, Cambridge: Polity.
    (1985) *The Nation-State and Violence*, Cambridge: Polity.

Go, J. (ed.) (2003) 'A Globalizing Constitutionalism? Views from the Postcolony, 1945–2000', *International Sociology* 18(1): 71–95.
    (2013) *Postcolonial Sociology (Political Power and Social Theory)*, Bingley: Emerald Publishing.

Goffman, E. (1986) *Frame Analysis: An Essay on the Organization of Experience*, Boston: Northeastern University Press.

Golash-Boza, T. and Menjívar, C. (2012) 'Causes and Consequences of International Migration: Sociological Evidence for the Right to Mobility', *The International Journal of Human Rights* 16(8): 1213–27.

Goldfarb, S. (2011) 'A Clash of Cultures: Women, Domestic Violence, and Law in the United States' in D. Hodgson (ed.) *Gender and Culture at the Limit of Rights*, Philadephia: University of Pennsylvania Press.

Goldstein, D. (2007) 'Human Rights as Culprit, Human Rights as Victim: Rights and Security in the State of Exception' in M. Goodale and S. Merry (eds)

The Practice of Human Rights: Tracking Law Between the Global and the Local, Cambridge: Cambridge University Press.

Gond, J.-P., Kabeer, N. and Moon, J. (2011) 'The Government of Self-Regulation: On the Dynamics of Corporate Social Responsibility', *Economy and Society* 40(4): 640–71.

Goodwin-Gill, S. (2007) *The Refugee in International Law*, Oxford: Oxford University Press.

Grant, S. (2011) 'The Recognition of Migrants' Rights within the UN Human Rights System: The First 60 Years' in M.-B. Dembour and T. Kelly (eds) *Are Human Rights for Migrants: Critical Reflection on the Status of Irregular Migrants in Europe and the United States*, London: Routledge.

Gready, P. (2004) *Fighting for Human Rights*, London: Routledge.

Grewal, I. (1999) ' "Women's Rights as Human Rights": Feminist Practices, Global Feminism, and Human Rights Regimes in Transnationality', *Citizenship Studies* 3(3): 337–54.

Guardian (2013) 'Taliban Peace Talks: "Peace and Reconciliation" Negotiations to take Place in Qatar', www.theguardian.com/world/2013/jun/18/us-peace-talks-taliban-afghanistan (last accessed 1 September 2014).

Guardian (2014) 'Snowden Welcomes Obama's Plans for NSA Reform as "Turning Point" ', www.theguardian.com/world/2014/mar/25/edward-snowden-welcomes-obama-nsa-reforms (last accessed 2 July 2014).

Gudynas, E. (2010) 'The New Extractivism of the 21st Century: Ten Urgent Theses about Extractivism in Relation to Current South American Progressivism', *Americas Policy Program*, www10.iadb.org/intal/intalcdi/PE/2010/04716.pdf (last accessed 1 August 2014).

Gunning, I. (2002) 'Global Feminism at the Local Level: The Criminalization of Female Genital Surgeries' in F. Valdes, J. Culp and A. Harris (eds) *Crossroads, Directions and a New Critical Race Theory*, Philadelphia: Temple University Press.

Guttal, S. (2008) 'Client and Competitor: China and International Financial Institutions' in D.-G. Guerrero and F. Manji (eds) *China's New Role in Africa and the South*, Cape Town: Networks for Social Justice.

Hafner-Burton, E. and Tsutsui, K. (2005) 'Human Rights Practices in a Globalizing World: The Paradox of Empty Promises', *American Journal of Sociology* 110(5): 1373–411.

—— (2007) 'Justice Lost! The Failure of International Human Rights Law to Matter Where Needed Most', *Journal of Peace Research* 44(4): 407–25.

Hajjar, L. (2013) *Torture: A Sociology of Violence and Human Rights*, London: Routledge.

Halley, J. (2004) 'Take a Break from Feminism?' in K. Knop (ed.) *Gender and Human Rights*, Oxford: Oxford University Press.

—— (2006) 'Describing Governance Feminism' in J. Halley, P. Kotiswaran, H. Shamir and C. Thomas 'From the International to the Local in Feminist Legal Responses to Rape, Prostitution/Sex World, and Sex Trafficking: Four

Studies in Contemporary Governance Feminism', *Harvard Journal of Law and Gender* 29: 335–423.

Halley, J., Kotiswaran, P., Shamir, H. and Thomas, C. (2006) 'From the International to the Local in Feminist Legal Responses to Rape, Prostitution/Sex World, and Sex Trafficking: Four Studies in Contemporary Governance Feminism', *Harvard Journal of Law and Gender* 29: 335–423.

Hansen, T. and Stepputat, F. (2005) *Sovereign Bodies: Citizens, Migrants and States in the Postcolonial World*, Princeton: Princeton University Press.

Harvey, D. (2003) *The New Imperialism*, Oxford: Oxford University Press.

  (2005) *A Brief History of Neo-Liberalism*, Oxford: Oxford University Press.

Hathaway, O. (2002) 'Do Treaties Make a Difference? Human Rights Treaties and the Problem of Compliance', *Yale Law Journal* 111: 1932–2042.

Held, D. (1995) *Democracy and Global Order: From the Modern State to Cosmopolitan Governance*, Cambridge: Polity Press.

  (2004) *Global Covenant: The Social Democratic Alternative to the Washington Consensus*, Cambridge: Polity.

Heywood, M. (2008) 'Can Campaigns to Prevent and Treat HIV and AIDS Revive and Strengthen Campaigns for the Right to Health, Access to Legal Services and Social Justice?', www.tac.org.za/community/heywood (last accessed 8 August 2013).

  (2009) 'South Africa's Treatment Action Campaign: Combining Law and Social Mobilization to Realize the Right to Health', *Journal of Human Rights Practice* 1: 14–36.

Hilhorst, D. (2003) *The Real World of NGOs: Discourses, Diversity and Development*, London: Zed Books.

Hilhorst, D. and Jansen, B. (2012) 'Constructing Rights and Wrongs in Humanitarian Action', *Sociology* 46(5): 891–905.

Holder, C. and Reidy, D. (eds) (2013) *Human Rights: The Hard Questions*, Cambridge: Cambridge University Press.

Holt-Gimenez, E. and Patel, R. (2009) *Food Rebellions! Crisis and the Hunger for Justice*, Cape Town: Pambazuka Press.

Hoogevelt, A. (2001) *Globalization and the Postcolonial World: The New Political Economy of Development*, 2nd edition, Basingstoke: Palgrave.

Hopgood, S. (2006) *Keepers of the Flame*, Ithaca: Cornell University Press.

  (2011) 'Amnesty International's Growth and Development since 1961' in W. de Jonge, B. McGorrigle Leyh, A. Mihr and L. van Troost (eds) *50 Years of Amnesty International – Reflections and Perspectives*, Utrecht: SIM.

Howard-Hassman, R. (2010) *Can Globalization Promote Human Rights?* Philadelphia: University of Pennsylvania Press.

Howe, A. (2012) 'SB 1070: In Plain English', www.scotusblog.com/2012/06/s-b-1070-in-plain-english/ (last accessed 14 April 2014).

Hsing, Y. (2010) *The Great Urban Transformation: Politics of Land and Property in China*, Oxford: Oxford University Press.

Hsing, Y. and Lee, C. (eds) (2010) *Reclaiming Chinese Society: The New Social Activism*, London: Routledge.

Human Rights Watch (1999) 'Genocide in Rwanda', www.hrw.org/reports/1999/rwanda/Geno1-3-04.htm (last accessed 2 September 2014).

Human Rights Watch (2013a) 'Russia: Harsh Toll of "Foreign Agents" Law', www.hrw.org/news/2013/06/25/russia-harsh-toll-foreign-agents-law (last accessed 8 August 2013).

Human Rights Watch (2013b) 'Unwelcome Guests: Iran's Violation of Afghan Refugee and Migrant Rights', www.hrw.org/reports/2013/11/20/unwelcome-guests-0 (last accessed 28 April 2014).

Hunt, L. (2008) *Inventing Human Rights: A History*, New York: W.W. Norton & Co.

Hynes, P., Lamb, M., Short D. and Waites, M. (2012) 'Editorial Foreword to Special Issue on the Sociology of Human Rights', *Sociology* 46/5: 787–96.

Hyrcak, A. (2002) 'From Mothers' Rights to Equal Rights: Post-Soviet Grassroots Women's Associations' in N. Naples and M. Desai (eds) *Women's Activism and Globalization: Linking Local Struggles and Transnational Politics*, New York: Routledge.

Ignatieff, M. (2003) *Human Rights as Politics and Idolatry*, Princeton: Princeton University Press.

 (ed.) (2005) *American Exceptionalism and Human Rights*, Princeton: Princeton University Press.

Ingham, G. (2008) *Capitalism*, Cambridge: Polity.

International Council on Human Rights Policy (2009) 'When Legal Worlds Overlap: Human Rights, State and Non-State Law', Geneva: International Council on Human Rights Policy.

Jackson, J. (2007) 'Rights to Indigenous Culture in Columbia' in M. Goodale and S. Merry (eds) *The Practice of Human Rights: Tracking Law Between the Global and the Local*, Cambridge: Cambridge University Press.

Jacobson, D. (1997) *Rights Across Borders: Immigration and the Decline of Citizenship*, Baltimore: Johns Hopkins University.

Jenkins, R. and Goetz, A.M. (1999) 'Accounts and Accountability: Theoretical Implications of the Right-to-Information Movement in India', *Third World Quarterly* 20(3): 603–22.

Jessop, B. (1982) *The Capitalist State: Marxist Theories and Methods*, Oxford: Blackwell.

 (1990) *Putting the Capitalist State in its Place*, Cambridge: Polity.

Johnson, J. (2009) *Gender Violence in Russia: The Politics of Feminist Intervention*, Bloomington: University of Indiana Press.

Joppke, C. (2010) *Citizenship and Immigration*, Cambridge: Polity.

Jordan, L. and van Tuijl, P. (2006) *NGO Accountability: Politics, Principles and Innovations*, London: Earthscan.

Judt, T. (2011) *Ill Fares the Land: A Treatise on Our Present Discontents*, London: Penguin.

Kagwanja, P. and Juma, M. (2008) 'Somali Refugees: Protracted Exile and Shifting Security Frontiers' in G. Loescher, J. Milner, E. Newman and G. Troeller (eds) *Protracted Refugee Situations: Political, Human Rights and Security Implications*, Tokyo: United Nations University.

Kaiser, T. (2008) 'Sudanese Refugees in Uganda and Kenya' in G. Loescher, J. Milner, E. Newman and G. Troeller (eds) *Protracted Refugee Situations: Political, Human Rights and Security Implications*, Tokyo: United Nations University.

Kannabiran, K. and Kannabiran, V. (2002) *De-Eroticizing Assault: Essays on Modesty, Honour and Power*, Calcutta: STREE.

Kapur, R. (2005) *Erotic Justice: Law and the New Politics of Postcolonialism*, London: Glasshouse Press.

Keck, M. and Sikkink, K. (1998) *Activists beyond Borders: Advocacy Networks in International Politics*, Ithaca: Cornell University Press.

Keck, M. and Smith, J. (2002) 'Infrastructures for Change: Transnational Organizations 1953–93' in S. Khagram, J. Riker and K. Sikkink (eds) *Restructuring World Politics: Transnational Social Movements, Networks, and Norms*, Minneapolis: University of Minnesota Press.

Keller, H. and Ulfstein, G. (eds) (2012) *UN Human Rights Treaty Bodies: Law and Legitimacy*, Cambridge: Cambridge University Press.

Kelly, T. (2011) 'The Legalization of Human Rights and the Protection of Torture Survivors: Asylum, Evidence and Disbelief' in M.-B. Dembour and T. Kelly (eds) *Are Human Rights for Migrants: Critical Reflection on the Status of Irregular Migrants in Europe and the United States*, London: Routledge.

(2013) *This Side of Silence: Human Rights, Torture, and the Recognition of Cruelty*, Philadelphia: University of Pennsylvania Press.

Kennedy, D. (2002) 'The International Human Rights Movement: Part of the Problem?', *Harvard Human Rights Journal* 15: 101–25.

Khagram, S. (2002) 'Restructuring the Global Politics of Development: The Case of India's Narmada Valley Dams' in S. Khagram, J. Riker and K. Sikkink (eds) *Restructuring World Politics: Transnational Social Movements, Networks, and Norms*, Minneapolis: University of Minnesota Press

Khagram, S., Riker, J. and Sikkink, K. (2002) 'From Santiago to Seattle: Transnational Advocacy Groups Restructuring World Politics' in *Restructuring World Politics: Transnational Social Movements, Networks, and Norms*, Minneapolis: University of Minnesota Press.

(eds) (2002) *Restructuring World Politics: Transnational Social Movements, Networks, and Norms*, Minneapolis: University of Minnesota Press.

Khalili, L. (2012) *Time in the Shadows: Confinement in Counterinsurgencies*, Redwood City: Stanford University Press.

Kiely, R. (2010) *Rethinking Imperialism*, Basingstoke: Palgrave Macmillan.

Kinley, D. (2009) *Civilising Globalisation: Human Rights and the Global Economy*, Cambridge: Cambridge University Press.

Kinzelbach, K. (2013) 'Resisting the Power of Human Rights: The People's Republic of China' in T. Risse, S. Ropp and K. Sikkink (eds) *The Persistent Power of Human Rights: From Commitment to Compliance*, Cambridge: Cambridge University Press.

Kivisto, P. and Faist, T. (2007) *Citizenship: Discourse, Theory, and Transnational Prospects*, Oxford: Blackwell.

Koh, H. (1999) 'How is International Human Rights Law Enforced?', *Indiana Law Journal* 74(4).

Koser, K. (2005) 'Irregular Migration, State Security and Human Security', Geneva: Global Commission on International Migration, http://iom.int/jahia/webdav/site/myjahiasite/shared/shared/mainsite/policy_and_research/gcim/tp/TP5.pdf (last accessed 4 January 2014).

Kothari, S. (2002) 'Globalization, Global Alliances, and the Narmada Movement' in S. Khagram, J. Riker and K. Sikkink (eds) *Restructuring World Politics: Transnational Social Movements, Networks, and Norms*, Minneapolis: University of Minnesota Press.

Kotiswaran, P. (2006) 'Governance Feminism and the Postcolonial Predicament' in J. Halley, P. Kotiswaran, H. Shamir and C. Thomas, 'From the International to the Local in Feminist Legal Responses to Rape, Prostitution/Sex World, and Sex Trafficking: Four Studies in Contemporary Governance Feminism', *Harvard Journal of Law and Gender* 29: 335–423.

Krause, M. (2014) *The Good Project: Humanitarian Relief NGOs and the Fragmentation of Reason*, Chicago: University of Chicago Press.

Kurasawa, F. (2007) *The Work of Global Justice: Human Rights as Practices*, Cambridge: Cambridge University Press.

Landman, T. (2006) *Studying Human Rights*, London: Routledge.

Langlois, A. (2001) *The Politics of Justice and Human Rights: Southeast Asia and Political Theory*, Cambridge: Cambridge University Press.

Latour, B. (2005) *Reassembling the Social: An Introduction to Actor-Network Theory*, Oxford: Oxford University Press.

Lazonick, W. and O'Sullivan, M. (2000) 'Maximising Shareholder Value: A New Ideology for Corporate Governance', *Economy and Society* 29(1): 13–35.

Leatherman, J. (2011) *Sexual Violence and Armed Conflict*, Cambridge: Polity.

Levy, D. and Sznaider, N. (2006) 'Sovereignty Transformed: A Sociology of Human Rights', *The British Journal of Sociology* 57(4): 657–76.

Lischer, S. (2005) *Dangerous Sanctuaries: Refugee Camps, Civil War, and the Dilemmas of Humanitarian Aid*, Ithaca: Cornell University Press.

Loescher, G. (2001) *The UNHCR and World Politics: A Perilous Path*, Oxford: Oxford University Press.

Loescher, G., Milner, J., Newman E. and Troeller, G. (eds) (2008) *Protracted Refugee Situations: Political, Human Rights and Security Implications*, Tokyo: United Nations University.

Lutz, E. and Sikkink, K. (2001) 'International Human Rights Law and Practice in Latin America' in J. Goldstein, M. Kahler, R. Keohane and A.-M. Slaughter (eds) *Legalization and World Politics*, Cambridge, MA: MIT Press.

Macleod, E. (2008) 'Afghan Refugees in Iran and Pakistan' in G. Loescher, J. Milner, E. Newman and G. Troeller (eds) *Protracted Refugee Situations: Political, Human Rights and Security Implications*, Tokyo: United Nations University.

McMahon, R. (2003) *The Cold War: A Very Short Introduction*, Oxford: Oxford University Press.

Madhok, S. and Rai, S. (2012) 'Agency, Injury, and Transgressive Politics in Neoliberal Times', *Signs* 37(3): 645–69.

Madsen, M. (2004) 'France, the UK, and the "Boomerang" of the Internationalisation of Human Rights' in S. Halliday and P. Schmidt (eds) *Human Rights Brought Home: Socio-Legal Perspectives on Human Rights in the National Context*, Oxford: Hart Publishing.

(2011) 'Reflexivity and the Construction of the International Object: The Case of Human Rights', *International Political Sociology* 5: 259–75.

Madsen, M. and Verschraegen, G. (2013) 'Introduction' in M. Madsen and G. Verschraegen (eds) *Making Human Rights Intelligible: Towards a Sociology of Human Rights*, Oxford: Hart Publishing.

Mamdani, M. (2000) *Beyond Rights Talk and Culture Talk: Comparative Essays on the Politics of Rights and Culture*, New York: St Martins Press.

(2009) *Saviors and Survivors*, London: Verso.

Marshall, T.H. (1987) *Citizenship and Social Class*, London: Pluto.

Martinez-Torres, M. and Rosset, P. (2010) 'La Via Campesina: The Birth and Evolution of a Transnational Social Movement', *The Journal of Peasant Studies* 37(1): 149–75.

Matua, M. (2002) *Human Rights: A Political and Cultural Critique*, Philadelphia: University of Pennsylvania Press.

Mazower, M. (2004) 'The Strange Triumph of Human Rights, 1933–1950', *The Historical Journal* 47(2): 379–98.

(2012) *Governing the World*, London: Allen Lane.

Mbembe, A. (2001) *On the Postcolony*, Berkeley: University of California Press.

Mendez, J., O'Donnell, G. and Sergio, P. (eds) (1999) *The Un-Rule of Law and the Underprivileged in Latin America*, Notre Dame, IN: University of Notre Dame Press.

Menon, N. (2004) *Recovering Subversion: Feminist Politics Beyond the Law*, Champaign: Permanent Black.

Merry, S. (1988) 'Legal Pluralism', *Law and Society Review* 22(5): 869–96.

(2006) *Human Rights and Gender Violence: Translating International Law into Local Justice*, Chicago: University of Chicago Press.

(2011) 'Measuring the World: Indicators, Human Rights, and Global Governance', *Current Anthropology* 52(3): 583–95.

Merry, S., Levitt, P., Rosen, M. and Yoon, D. (2010) 'Law From Below: Women's Human Rights and Social Movements in New York City', *Law and Society Review* 44(1): 101–28.

Mertus, J. (2004) *Bait and Switch: Human Rights and US Foreign Policy*, London and New York: Routledge.

(2005) *The United Nations and Human Rights: A Guide for a New Era*, London: Routledge.

(2009) *Human Rights Matters: Local Politics and National Human Rights Institutions*, Stanford: Stanford University Press.

Michaels, R. (2009) 'Global Legal Pluralism', *Annual Review of Law and Social Science* 5: 243–62.

Mitchell, T. (1999) 'Society, Economy, and the State Effect' in G. Steinmetz (ed.) *State/Culture: State Formation after the Cultural Turn*, Ithaca: Cornell University Press.

Moghadam, V. (2005) *Globalizing Women: Transnational Feminist Networks*, Baltimore: Johns Hopkins University Press.

Molyneux, M. and Lazar, S. (2003) *Doing the Rights Thing: Rights-based Development and Latin American NGOs*, London: ITDG Publishing.

Moon, C. (2012) 'What One Sees and How One Files Seeing: Human Rights Reporting, Representation and Action', *Sociology* 46(5): 876–90.

Morehouse, C. and Blomfield, M. (2011) 'Irregular Migration in Europe', Washington DC: Migration Policy Institute.

Morgan, R. (2009) 'Introduction' in R. Morgan and B. Turner (eds) *Interpreting Human Rights: Social Science Perspectives*, London and New York: Routledge.

(2011) *Transforming Law and Institution: Indigenous Peoples, the United Nations, and Human Rights*, Farnham: Ashgate.

Morris, L. (2006) 'A Foundation for Rights or Theories of Practice?' in L. Morris (ed.) *Rights: Sociological Perspectives*, London: Routledge.

(2010) *Asylum Welfare and the Cosmopolitan Ideal*, London: Routledge-Cavendish.

Moyn, S. (2012) 'Do Human Rights Treaties Make Enough of a Difference?' in C. Gearty and C. Douzinas (eds) *The Cambridge Companion to Human Rights Law*, Cambridge: Cambridge University Press.

Muir, J. (2013) 'Syria: Proxy War Heats Up as Endgame Moves Closer', www.bbc.co.uk/news/world-middle-east-22123660 (last accessed 5 September 2013).

Musalo, K., Moore, J. and Boswell, R. (2011) *Refugee Law and Policy: A Comparative and International Approach*, 4th edition, Durham, NC: Carolina Academic Press.

Nair, R. (2013) 'Time to Challenge India for its Stranglehold on Funding for Rights Organisations', *Open Democracy*, www.opendemocracy.net/open-globalrights/ravi-nair/time-to-challenge-india-for-its-stranglehold-on-funding-for-rights-organi (last accessed 9 December 2013).

Nam, C.Y.J. (2006) 'Competing for FDI through the Creation of Export Processing Zones: The Impact on Human Rights' in O. De Schutter (ed.) *Transnational Corporations and Human Rights*, Oxford: Hart.

Nash, K. (2007) 'The Pinochet Case: Cosmopolitanism and Intermestic Human Rights', *The British Journal of Sociology* 58(2): 417–35.

    (2009a) *The Cultural Politics of Human Rights: Comparing the US and UK*, Cambridge: Cambridge University Press.

    (2009b) 'Between Citizenship and Human Rights', *Sociology* 43(6): 1067–83.

    (2010) *Contemporary Political Sociology: Globalization, Politics, and Power*, Chichester: Wiley-Blackwell.

Neier, A. (2012) *The International Human Rights Movement: A History*, Princeton: Princeton University Press.

Nelson, P. (2007) 'Between Heroic Independence and Dependent Subservience' in P. Opoku-Mensah, D. Lewis and T. Tvedt (eds) *Reconceptualising NGOs and their Roles in Development*, Aalborg: Aalborg University Press.

New York Times (2013) 'Obama Calls Surveillance Programmes Legal and Limited', www.nytimes.com/2013/06/08/us/national-security-agency-surveillance. html?pagewanted=all&_r=0 (last accessed 2 July 2014).

Nilsen, A. (2010) *Dispossession and Resistance in India: The River and the Rage*, London: Routledge.

Nyers, P. (2008) 'No One is Illegal between City and Nation' in E. Isin and G. Nielson (eds) *Acts of Citizenship*, London: Zed Books.

Oberleitner, G. (2007) *Global Human Rights Institutions*, Cambridge: Polity.

O'Brien, R., Goetz, A.M., Scholte, J. and Williams, M. (2000) *Contesting Global Governance: Multilateral Economic Institutions and Global Social Movements*, Cambridge: Cambridge University Press.

Orford, A. (2011) *International Authority and the Responsibility to Protect*, Cambridge: Cambridge University Press.

Ortener, S. (2006) *Anthropology and Social Theory: Culture, Power and the Acting Subject*, Durham, NC: Duke University Press.

Otto, D. (2010) 'Power and Danger: Feminist Engagement with International Law Through the UN Security Council', *Australian Feminist Journal* 32: 97–121.

Paarlberg, R. (2010) *Food Politics: What Everyone Needs to Know*, Oxford: Oxford University Press.

Paris, R. and Sisk, T. (eds) (2009) *The Dilemmas of Statebuilding: Confronting the Contradictions of Postwar Peace Operations*, London: Routledge.

Patel, R., Balakrishnan, R. and Narayan, U. (2007) 'Transgressing Rights: La Via Campesina's Call for Food Sovereignty/Exploring Collaborations: Heterodox Economics and an Economic Social Rights Framework/Workers in the Informal Sector: Special Challenges for Human Rights', *Feminist Economics* 13(1): 87–116.

Piccone, T. (2012) *Catalysts for Change: How the U.N.'s Independent Experts Promote Human Rights*, Washington, DC: Brookings Institute.

Poggi, G. (1990) *The State: Its Nature, Development and Prospects*,
     Cambridge: Polity.
Possamai, A., Richardson J. and Turner, B. (2015) *The Sociology of Shari'a: Case
     Studies from around the World*, New York: Springer.
Prieto-Carron, M., Lund-Thomsen, P., Chan, A. and Bhushan, C. (2006) 'Critical
     Perspectives on CSR and Development: What We Know, What We Don't
     Know, and What We Need to Know', *International Affairs* 82(5): 977–87.
Rai, S. and Waylen, G. (2008) *Global Governance: Feminist Perspectives*,
     Basingstoke: Palgrave Macmillan.
Rajagopal, B. (2003) *International Law from Below: Development, Social
     Movements and Third World Resistance*, Cambridge: Cambridge
     University Press.
Rajan, R. (2005) 'Women's Human Rights in the Third World' in N. Bamford (ed.)
     Sex Rights, Oxford: Oxford University Press.
Reilly, N. (2009) *Women's Human Rights: Seeking Gender Justice in a Globalizing
     Age*, Cambridge: Polity.
Reyntjens, F. (2009) *The Great African War: Congo and Regional Geopolitics,
     1996–2006*, Cambridge: Cambridge University Press.
Risse, T., Ropp, S. and Sikkink, K. (1999) *The Power of Human
     Rights: International Norms and Domestic Change*, Cambridge: Cambridge
     University Press.
Rose, N. and Miller, P. (1992) 'Political Power beyond the State: Problematics of
     Government', *The British Journal of Sociology* 43(2): 173–205.
Roseman, M. and Miller, A. (2011) 'Normalizing Sex and Its
     Discontents: Establishing Sexual Rights in International Law', *Harvard
     Journal of Law and Gender* 34: 313–75.
Rotberg, R. (ed.) (2008) *China Into Africa: Trade, Aid and Influence*, Washington,
     DC: Brookings Institute.
Roth, K. (2004) 'Defending Economic, Social and Cultural Rights: Practical Issues
     Faced by an International Human Rights Organization', *Human Rights
     Quarterly* 26: 63–73.
     (2005) 'War in Iraq: Not a Humanitarian Intervention' in R. Wilson (ed.) *Human
     Rights in the 'War on Terror'*, Cambridge: Cambridge University Press.
Ruh, M. (2013) *The Price of Rights: Regulating International Labour Migration*,
     Princeton: Princeton University Press.
Salomon, M. (2007) 'International Economic Governance and Human Rights
     Accountability', LSE Law, Society and Economy Working Papers, www.eldis.
     org/assets/Docs/34932.html (last accessed 9 January 2012).
Sandbrook, R., Edelman, M., Heller, P. and Teichman, J. (eds) (2007) *Social
     Democracy in the Global Periphery: Origins, Challenges and Prospects*,
     Cambridge: Cambridge University Press.
Sands, P. (2005) *Lawless World: America and the Making and Breaking of Global
     Rules*, London: Allen Lane.

Santos, B. De Sousa (2002a) *Towards a New Legal Common Sense*, 2nd edition, London: Butterworths LexisNexis.

(2002b) 'Toward a Multicultural Conception of Human Rights' in B. Hernandez-Truyol (ed.) *Moral Imperialism: A Critical Anthology*, New York: New York University.

(2006) *The Rise of the Global Left: The World Social Forum and Beyond*, London: Zed Books.

Santos, B. De Sousa and Rodríguez-Garavito, C. (eds) (2005) *Law and Globalization from Below: Towards a Cosmopolitan Legality*, Cambridge: Cambridge University Press.

Sarfaty, G. (2009) 'Why Culture Matters in International Institutions: The Marginality of Human Rights at the World Bank', *American Journal of International Law* 103: 647–83.

(2012) *Values in Translation: Human Rights and the Culture of the World Bank*, Stanford: Stanford University Press.

Sassen, S. (2006) *Territory, Authority, Rights: From Medieval to Global Assemblages*, Princeton: Princeton University Press.

Sautman, B. and Hairong, Y. (2008) 'Friend and Interests: China's Distinctive Links with Africa' in D.-G. Guerrero and F. Manji (eds) *China's New Role in Africa and the South*, Cape Town: Networks for Social Justice.

Scheingold, S. (2004) *The Politics of Rights: Lawyers, Public Policy, and Political Change*, 2nd edition, Ann Arbor: University of Michigan Press.

Scholte, J. (2005) *Globalization: A Critical Introduction*, Basingstoke: Palgrave Macmillan.

(2011) *Building Global Democracy: Civil Society and Accountable Global Governance*, Cambridge: Cambridge University Press.

Scott, J. (1997) *Only Paradoxes to Offer: French Feminists and the Rights of Man*, Cambridge, MA: Harvard University Press.

Seitz, J. and Hite, K. (2012) *Global Issues: An Introduction*, Chichester: Wiley-Blackwell.

Sen, A. (1999) *Development as Freedom*, Oxford: Oxford University Press.

(2007) 'Human Rights and the Limits of Law', *Cardozo Law Review* 26(5): 2913–27.

Sewell, W. (2005) *Logics of History: Social Theory and Social Transformation*, Chicago: Chicago University Press.

Shamir, H. (2006) 'The Empirical Problem' in J. Halley, P. Kotiswaran, H. Shamir and C. Thomas, 'From the International to the Local in Feminist Legal Responses to Rape, Prostitution/Sex World, and Sex Trafficking: Four Studies in Contemporary Governance Feminism', *Harvard Journal of Law and Gender* 29: 335–423.

Shirk, S. (ed.) (2011) *Changing Media, Changing China*, Oxford: Oxford University Press.

Short, D. (2008) 'Sociological and Anthropological Approaches' in M. Goodhart
(ed.) *Human Rights: Politics and Practice*, Oxford: Oxford University Press.

Sikkink, K. (2011) *The Justice Cascade: How Human Rights Prosecutions are
Changing World Politics*, New York: W.W. Norton and Co.

Simmons, B. (2009) *Mobilizing for Human Rights: International Law in Domestic
Politics*, Cambridge: Cambridge University Press.

(2013) 'From Ratification to Compliance: Quantitative Evidence on the Spiral
Model' in T. Risse, S. Ropp and K. Sikkink (eds) *The Persistent Power of
Human Rights: From Commitment to Compliance*, Cambridge: Cambridge
University Press.

Sjoberg, G., Gill, E. and Williams, N. (2001) 'A Sociology of Human Rights', *Social
Problems* 48(1): 11–47.

Slaughter, A. and Crisp, J. (2008) 'A Surrogate State? The Role of the UNHCR in
Protracted Refugee Situations' in G. Loescher, J. Milner, E. Newman and G.
Troeller (eds) *Protracted Refugee Situations: Political, Human Rights and
Security Implications*, Tokyo: United Nations University.

Smith, J. (2008) *Social Movements for Global Democracy*, Baltimore: Johns
Hopkins University.

Somers, M. (2008) *Genealogies of Citizenship: Markets, Statelessness, and the
Right to Have Rights*, Cambridge: Cambridge University Press.

Somers, M. and Roberts, C. (2008) 'Toward a New Sociology of
Rights: A Genealogy of "Buried Bodies" of Citizenship and Human Rights',
Annual Review of Law and Social Science 4: 385–425.

Soysal, Y. (1994) *Limits of Citizenship: Migrants and Postnational Membership in
Europe*, Chicago: University of Chicago.

Speed, S. (2008) *Rights in Rebellion: Indigenous Struggle and Human Rights in
Chiapas*, Stanford: Stanford University Press.

Sperling, V., Ferree, M. and Risman, B. (2001) 'Constructing Global
Feminism: Transnational Advocacy Networks and Russian Women's
Activism', *Signs* 26(4): 1156–86.

Spires, A.J. (2011) 'Contingent Symbiosis and Civil Society in an Authoritarian
State: Understanding the Survival of China's Grassroots NGOs', *American
Journal of Sociology* 117(1): 1–45.

Spivak, G. (1999) *A Critique of Postcolonial Reason: Toward a History of the
Vanishing Present*, Cambridge, MA: Harvard University Press.

(2002) 'Righting Wrongs' in N. Owen (ed.) *Human Rights, Human Wrongs*,
Oxford: Oxford University Press

Stammers, N. (1999) 'Social Movements and the Social Construction of Human
Rights', *Human Rights Quarterly* 21: 980–1008.

(2009) *Human Rights and Social Movements*, London: Pluto; Stanford: Stanford
University Press.

Steinmetz, G. (2013) *Sociology and Empire: The Imperial Entanglements of a
Discipline*, Durham, NC: Duke University Press.

Stiglitz, J. (2010) *Freefall: Free Markets and the Sinking of the Global Economy*, London: Allen Lane.

Stroup, S. (2012) *Borders Among Activists: International NGOs in the United States, Britain, and France*, Ithaca: Cornell University Press.

Sunstein, C. (2006) *The Second Bill of Rights: FDR's Unfinished Revolution – and Why We Need It More Than Ever*, New York: Basic Books.

Tamanaha, B. (2008) 'Understanding Legal Pluralism: Past to Present, Local to Global', *Sydney Law Review* 30(3): 374–411.

Therborn, G. (2003) 'Entangled Modernities', *European Journal of Social Theory* 6(3): 293–305.

(2013) *The Killing Fields of Inequality*, Cambridge: Polity.

Thomas, C. (2006) 'Governance Feminism and Sex Trafficking' in J. Halley, P. Kotiswaran, H. Shamir and C. Thomas, 'From the International to the Local in Feminist Legal Responses to Rape, Prostitution/Sex World, and Sex Trafficking: Four Studies in Contemporary Governance Feminism', *Harvard Journal of Law and Gender* 29: 335–423.

Tilly, C. (1985) 'Warmaking and Statemaking as Organized Crime' in D. Rueschemeyer and T. Skocpol (eds) *Bringing the State Back In*, Cambridge: Cambridge University Press.

Tonkiss, F. (2006) *Contemporary Economic Sociology*, London: Routledge.

Tripp, A. (2006) 'Challenges in Transnational Feminist Mobilization' in M.M. Ferree and A. Tripp (eds) *Global Feminism: Transnational Women's Activism, Organizing and Human Rights*, New York: New York University Press.

Troeller, G. (2008) 'Ayslum Trends in Industrialized Countries and their Impact on Protracted Refugee Situations' in G. Loescher, J. Milner, E. Newman and G. Troeller (eds) *Protracted Refugee Situations: Political, Human Rights and Security Implications*, Tokyo: United Nations University.

Turner, B. (1993) 'Outline of a Theory of Human Rights', *Sociology* 27: 489–512.

(1997) 'A Neo-Hobbesian Theory of Human Rights: A Reply to Malcolm Waters', *Sociology* 31(1): 565–71.

Turner, G. (2002) *British Cultural Studies*, London: Routledge.

UN (2000) 'Human Development Report 2000', http://hdr.undp.org/sites/default/files/reports/261/hdr_2000_en.pdf (last accessed 14 August 2014).

UN (2007) 'World Urbanization Prospects', www.un.org/esa/population/meetings/EGM_PopDist/Heilig.pdf (last accessed 22 February 2012).

UN (2009) *State of the World's Indigenous Peoples*, www.un.org/esa/socdev/unpfii/documents/SOWIP_web.pdf (last accessed 22 February 2012).

UN (2013) MONUSCO Mandate, www.un.org/en/peacekeeping/missions/monusco/mandate.shtml (last accessed 6 June 2013).

UNHCR (2013) 'Mid-Year Trends 2013', www.unhcr.org/52af08d26.html (last accessed 28 April 2014).

UNRWA (2014) 'Who We Are', www.unrwa.org/who-we-are (last accessed 28 April 2014).

Verdirame, G. (2013) *The UN and Human Rights: Who Guards the Guardians?* Cambridge: Cambridge University Press.

Verdirame, G. and Harrell-Bond, E. (2005) *Rights in Exile: Janus-Faced Humanitarianism*, New York: Berghahn Books.

Walby, S. (2011) *The Future of Feminism*, Cambridge: Polity.

Waters, M. (1996) 'Human Rights and the Universalisation of Interests', *Sociology* 30(3): 593–600.

Watkins, S. and Swidler, A. (2013) 'Working Misunderstandings: Donors, Brokers, and Villagers in Africa's AIDS Industry', *Population and Development Review 38*: 197–218.

Webber, F. (2012) *Borderline Justice: The Fight for Refugee and Migrant Rights*, London: Pluto.

Weber, M. (1948) 'The Social Psychology of the World Religions' in H.H. Gerth and C. Wright Mills (eds) *From Max Weber: Essays in Sociology*, London: Routledge and Kegan Paul.

Weiss, T. (2007) *Humanitarian Intervention*, Cambridge: Polity.
  (2009) *What's Wrong with the United Nations and How to Fix It*, Cambridge: Polity.
  (2013) *Global Governance: Why? What? Whither?* Cambridge: Polity.

Wells, C. and Elias, J. (2005) 'Catching the Conscience of the King: Corporate Players on the International Stage' in P. Alston (ed.) *Non-State Actors and Human Rights*, Oxford: Oxford University Press.

White, L. and Perelman, J. (eds) (2011) *Stones of Hope: How African Activists Reclaim Human Rights to Challenge Global Poverty*, Stanford: Stanford University Press.

Williams, R. (2010) *The Divided World: Human Rights and Its Violence*, Minneapolis: University of Minnesota.

Wilson, R. (ed.) (1998) *Human Rights, Culture and Context: Anthropological Perspectives*, London: Pluto.

Wood, J. (2007) *The Politics of Water Resource Development in India: The Narmada Dams Controversy*, New Delhi: Sage.

Woods, N. (2003) 'Global Governance and the Role of Institutions' in D. Held and A. McGrew (eds) *Governing Globalization: Power, Authority and Global Governance*, Cambridge: Polity.

Wright, T. (2010) *Accepting Authoritarianism: State-Society Relations in China's Reform Era*, Stanford: Stanford University Press.

Ziammatto, B. (2011) 'The Duty to Protect Against Human Rights Violations Committed Abroad by Transnational Corporations and their Subsidiaries' in D.M. Nault and S. England (eds) *Globalization and Human Rights in the Developing World*, Basingstoke: Palgrave Macmillan.

Zizek, S. (2005) 'Against Human Rights', *New Left Review* 34.

Index

Page numbers with 'n' are notes.